LIBERALISM
AND
EMPIRE

LIBERALISM

AND

EMPIRE

A Study in Nineteenth-Century

British Liberal Thought

UDAY SINGH MEHTA

THE UNIVERSITY OF CHICAGO PRESS

CHICAGO AND LONDON

UDAY SINGH MEHTA teaches political science at the University of Pennsylvania and is the author of *The Anxiety of Freedom: Imagination and Individuality in the Political Thought of John Locke* (1992).

The University of Chicago Press, Chicago 60637
The University of Chicago Press, Ltd., London
© 1999 by The University of Chicago
Printed in the United States of America
All rights reserved. Published 1999

08 07 06 05 04 03 02 01 00 99   1 2 3 4 5
ISBN: 0-226-51881-7 (cloth)
ISBN: 0-226-51882-5 (paper)

Library of Congress Cataloging-in-Publication Data

Mehta, Uday Singh.
    Liberalism and empire : a study in nineteenth-century British liberal thought /
Uday Singh Mehta.
        p.   cm.
    Includes bibliographical references and index.
    ISBN 0-226-51881-7 (alk. paper).—ISBN 0-226-51882-5 (pbk. : alk. paper)
    1. Liberalism—Great Britain—History—19th century.   2. Great Britain—
Colonies—History—19th century.   I. Title.
JC574.2.G7M44   1999
320.5′13′0941—dc21   98-40812
                                                                                CIP

An earlier version of chapter 2 appeared as "Strategies of Exclusion," *Politics & Society*
18, no. 4 (1989): 427–54. Reprinted by permission of Sage Publications.

In memory of my late grandfather Mohan Sinha Mehta
and for my father.

Both consummate citizens, and for me
so much, much more.

◄ C O N T E N T S ►

◄ A C K N O W L E D G M E N T S ►

The writing of this book has been a schooling in the various ways in which the autonomy of one's mind and the singularity of one's effort are, at best, supporting fictions to the process of thinking and writing. It is impossible to retrace the process by which extravagant and undisciplined hunches get chiseled to assume the shape of ideas backed by the requisite evidence. What is clear, however, is that through the course of that meandering journey, which so often returns to the initial hunches at stranger and stranger angles, one is moved along and held together by currents of support in which one's own role is quite limited. My debts at the completion of this book are so numerous, multifaceted, and deep that it is only by relying on a long-standing convention that I can claim it as fully mine. Three institutions and numerous individuals have made this book possible.

The initial encouragement to think about the philosophic link between liberalism and the British empire came in the form of a fellowship from the Society for the Humanities at Cornell University. The staff, the other associates, and especially its then director, Jonathan Culler, made the Society a place of luxurious intellectual seriousness. The fact that this book had its origins within the fold of the Society's interdisciplinary vitality has, I am sure, contributed enormously to it. It is a pleasure to thank the Society and Jonathan Culler for that wonderful year.

While at MIT I was the beneficiary of several grants from the office of the Dean of Social Sciences and the Provost that allowed me to take time off from teaching, hire research help, and travel to libraries in Britain and India. MIT is a remarkably self-confident institution. One of the many ways in which that is expressed is in the priority it gives to supporting research. I am deeply indebted to it for that emphasis.

Various friends and colleagues in Cambridge read substantial portions of this book. I am grateful for the help and critical promptings of Hayward Alker, Suzanne Berger, Archon Fung, Maria Clelia Guinazu, Ellen Immergut, Annabelle Lever, Steven Macedo, Pratap Mehta, Martha Minow, Barry Posen, and Myron Weiner. I thank Fareed Zakaria for an extended loan of his copy of the collected works of Edmund Burke. Eva Nagy and Maria Clelia Guinazu tried to compensate for my disorganized and delinquent ways by their generous and meticulous efficiency. I thank them for their unstinting help and concern.

There is, I am sure, a large group of academics who have come to rely on Joshua Cohen's fierce intelligence and intellectual generosity as a way to encourage and guide them in their work. I belong to that group. His meticulous care as a reader, his ability to discern a coherence of purpose despite the cracks and crevices in a draft, and his openness to styles of thought and writing other than his own, make him an exemplary interlocutor. He has read this manuscript in many forms and at every juncture given me supportive and valued advice. And this despite what I think is a disagreement, or at least disquiet, with significant parts of the argument I offer.

Much of this book was written and rewritten while I was teaching at the University of Chicago. Anyone familiar with its intellectual culture in the humanities and social sciences would testify to its remarkable vibrancy. This book has benefited enormously from that culture and numerous individuals who contribute to it. Lloyd and Suzanne Rudolph read the manuscript and were generous in their comments, consistently insightful in their suggestions, and extremely kind in their warmth and concern. I thank them with gratitude and enormous admiration for their spirited curiosity and intellectual conviviality. Deborah Boucoyannis, Jim Chandler, Michael Dawson, Faisal Devji, Mahnaz Fancy, Joseph Cropsey, Carol Horton, Leslie Keros, Bernard Manin, William Sewell, Frank Sposito, Nathan Tarcov, John Tryneski, and Lisa Wedeen all read and commented on portions of the manuscript. I thank each of them for their effort and suggestions. David Laitin read most of the manuscript and commented on it with engaged acuity. While at Chicago I received from Akeel Bilgrami and Timothy Mitchell detailed and extremely helpful comments on the entire manuscript. I am very thankful for their effort and suggestions. Rebecca Bryant read the manuscript with a care that included attending to the peculiar vagaries of my punctuation and grammatical skills. I and in turn the reader are deeply in her debt. Fiona Maharg-Bravo and Mithi Mukerjee helped with library research and in doing so saved me considerable time and effort.

While living in Chicago I often attended the Lawndale Community Church in a neighborhood blighted by poverty, unemployment, drugs, and crime, though not by the destitution of hope. On numerous Sundays various members of the congregation, mindful of my struggle with this book, publicly and privately prayed for me. Their heartfelt concern and the sincerity of their conviction in the power of prayer touched me deeply. Moreover, it created a common ground for mutual respect and possible understanding despite the contrasting conditions of our daily lives. I have often thought that what I saw and learned at Lawndale Community Church vindicates the central message of this book: the salutary possibility of relating to what is different not by denying one's deepest convictions but by encasing them in a prior commitment to a humility that trumps the certainties of reason or revelation and in doing so denies space to power.

In this context I thank Dawn Neukirchner, who introduced me to Lawndale Community Church. As a member of several communities, a neighbor, and a teacher she exemplifies that striving of which 1 Corinthians 13:13 speaks, "And now these three remain: faith, hope and love. But the greatest of these is love." As a deeply cherished friend Dawn gave me the benefit of care and advice while constantly challenging me to integrate into my work a kind of honesty which can so easily be lost sight of amid the thicket of academic considerations. I know that this book is better on account of that challenge, even if only because its inadequacies and its achievements are more deeply mine.

The writing of a book, like any challenging endeavor, draws on the broader conditions of one's well-being. Missy Allen, Abhijit Banerjee, Arundhati Banerjee, Jackie Bhabha, Paul Horwich, Peter Katzenstein, Suzanne Katzenstein, Tai Katzenstein, Ira Katznelson, Mona Khalidi, Rashid Khalidi, Sarah McConaghie, Anne Norton, Shankar Ramaswami, E. Somnathan, Rohini Somnathan, Mallory Stark, Tej Thapa, Dale Torrengo, Carole Travis, Jeffery Tulis, and Stephen Van Evera have in their own ways supplied the tactile conditions of care, encouragement, warmth, and sheer decency without which it is hard to imagine this book in its present form.

Homi Bhabha, Dipesh Chakrabarty, and Gary Herrigel were at times daily interlocutors who shared in this project. There is very little in this book that is not marked by the diverse ways in which they engage with the predicaments of the modern world. But what makes that influence so especially pleasurable to acknowledge, and moreover a model of the possible joys of academic and conversational life, is that it occurred within the embrace of recognizing profound differences of experience, styles of thought, trajectories of arrival and viewpoint; and a yet deeper commitment to the imperatives of affection, loyalty, and friendship. Each of them knows the enormous extent of my debt to them. It is a pleasure to acknowledge and thank them publicly.

For many years now I have come to presume on Mary Katzenstein's intelligence, insight, and compassion as a support of first, and certainly of last, resort. During the writing of this book, there was not a single mental predicament—be it intellectual confusion, self-doubt, or exhilaration—in which I did not lean on her with assurance. Absent her encouragement, sustained support, and guidance I know this book would not have been written. But even beyond that my greatest debt to her is simply on account of who she is, a deeply caring person whose intelligence is always tethered to her compassion and understanding.

Finally, I wish to thank my family. Over the years the constancy of their support, care, and love has anchored and guided me. They have with unqualified generosity supplied the emotional integuments of having a home, and thus made it possible for me to be physically separated from it. Under conditions of extended and vast geographical separation any notion of home is bound to be lifted from its traditional fixity and rendered strangely mobile. It becomes something that is necessarily infused by the uncertain vagaries of the imagination that refract such forms of emotional longing. And yet over the years the assurances of my family have been so engaged, supportive, and unfailing that they are the most tactile of blessings for me. To my father in particular I owe, among other things, a special intellectual debt. Chapter 4 of this book, which deals with the liberal inability to comprehend the imperatives of territory and locational attachments, received its original impetus from hearing him reflect on the geographical unity of India and the enduring costs of its hasty partition in 1947. To me it seems entirely fitting that many of his thoughts should have Burke as their precursor. This book is partially dedicated to my father—with gratitude and admiration.

Uday Singh Mehta
Chicago and Philadelphia

Introduction

Philosophers . . . have wanted to furnish the *rational ground* of morality—and every philosopher hitherto has believed he has furnished this rational ground; morality itself, however, was taken as "given". . . . It was precisely because moral philosophers knew the facts of morality only somewhat vaguely in an arbitrary extract or as a chance abridgement, as morality of their environments, their class, their church, the spirit of their times, their climate and zone of the earth,—it is precisely because they were ill informed and not even very inquisitive about other peoples, ages and former times, that they did not so much as catch sight of the real problems of morality—for these come into view only if we compare *many* moralities.

FRIEDRICH NIETZSCHE, *Beyond Good and Evil*

This book studies British liberal thought in the late eighteenth and nineteenth centuries by viewing it through the mirror that reflects its association with the British Empire. Liberalism in those centuries was self-consciously universal as a political, ethical and epistemological creed. Yet, it had fashioned this creed from an intellectual tradition and experiences that were substantially European, if not almost exclusively national. In the empire it found a challenge to this creed, even before nationalism along with other responses expressed that challenge, because there was no avoiding the strange and unfamiliar. This book considers the various responses of liberal thinkers when faced with the unfamiliarity to which their association with the British Empire exposed them.

The empire was a complex phenomenon informed by the multiple purposes of power, commerce, cultural and religious influence, and the imperatives of progress, along with the myriad subsidiary motives of pride, jealousy, compassion, curiosity, adventure, and resistance. These purposes and motives bear on this book only to the extent that they are relevant, as indeed they often are, to understanding how liberal theorists responded to parts of the world with which they were largely unfamiliar but which also intensely preoccupied them. Unfamiliarity is not ignorance. In fact, all the thinkers considered in this work were knowledge-

able about the parts of the empire on which they wrote; indeed, many
of them met the most fastidious standards of that knowledge. Of course,
some of what they took to be knowledge is today viewed as incorrect or
jaundiced by some prior perspective to which they held. Still, it was not
ignorance, and the charge of having prior perspectives is both a condition of knowledge and one that no doubt awaits our own contemporaneous claims regarding it. By unfamiliarity, I mean not sharing in the
various ways of being and feeling that shape experience and give meaning to the communities and the individuals who constitute them—in a
word, not being familiar with what was experientially familiar to others
in the empire. Understood as such, unfamiliarity is obviously a relative
and shifting condition. But the mere fact that the boundaries between
the familiar and unfamiliar are fuzzy is no reason to deny that there is,
and in the case of the liberal preoccupation with the empire was, a vast
arena where the distinction is quite clear.

This concern with unfamiliarity leads to a secondary and derivative
query that also informs this book. That query might broadly be classi-
fied under the heading: the liberal justification of the empire. As a general matter, it is liberal and progressive thinkers such as Bentham, both
the Mills, and Macaulay, who, notwithstanding—indeed, on account
of—their reforming schemes, endorse the empire as a legitimate form
of political and commercial governance; who justify and accept its
largely undemocratic and nonrepresentative structure; who invoke as
politically relevant categories such as history, ethnicity, civilizational hierarchies, and occasionally race and blood ties; and who fashion arguments for the empire's at least temporary necessity and foreseeable pro-
longation.

In contrast, Edmund Burke—who is commonly designated as a
leading modern conservative—expresses a sustained and deep reluc-
tance toward the empire whether it be in India, in Ireland, or in America. He did not demand, as did none of his major contemporaries and
few in the century that followed, that the British dismantle the empire
altogether. Nevertheless there is, I think, no question that of all the British thinkers and politicians who wrote and spoke on imperial and colonial issues in this period, it is Burke who is most sensitive to the complexities of imperial links and to the strengths and vulnerabilities upon
which they draw at both ends.[1] Similarly, no thinker or statesman of the

1. Throughout this book I use the terms *empire* and *colony* and their philological
cognates interchangeably. In this I am following Burke's usage and the accepted no-
menclature of the times. Michael Doyle defines empire as "a relationship, formal or
informal, in which one state controls the effective political sovereignty of another

eighteenth or nineteenth century expresses anything like the moral and political indignation that Burke voiced against the injustices, cruelty, caprice, and exploitation of the empire. And finally, no other thinker, not even John Stuart Mill in the mid–nineteenth century, reflected with such depth and moral seriousness on the issues raised by the composition of the constituency over which British power and dominion were being exercised. The left-wing critic Harold Laski rightly commented that "[on] Ireland, America, and India, he [Burke] was at every point upon the side of the future" and that "he was the first English statesman to fully understand the moral import of the problem of subject races."[2]

In terms of the contemporary associations of the categories liberal and conservative, there is therefore a striking irony in the writings by British political thinkers from the late eighteenth to the late nineteenth century that deal with the British Empire. We rightly think of liberalism as committed to securing individual liberty and human dignity through a political cast that typically involves democratic and representative institutions, the guaranty of individual rights of property, and freedom of expression, association, and conscience, all of which are taken to limit the legitimate use of the authority of the state. Moreover, at least since the mid–nineteenth century, liberal theorists have tended, though by no means universally, to champion the claims of minority groups, and have respected religious bodies as entitled to the same toleration as

political society. It can be achieved by force, by political collaboration, by economic, social, or cultural dependence. Imperialism is simply the process or policy of establishing or maintaining an empire." Michael Doyle, *Empires* (Ithaca: Cornell University Press, 1986), 45.

By the mid–nineteenth century the term *colonialism* was used to designate the implanting of metropolitan settlements in distant lands. J. S. Mill in *Considerations on Representative Government* uses the term in this sense. But even then it was often used as synonymous with the term *imperialism*, in part because it was often a consequence of the latter. See Sir Ernest Barker, *The Ideas and Ideals of the British Empire* (Cambridge: Cambridge University Press, 1951).

There is, however, one important sense in which the two terms refer to very different conceptual and concrete realities. In European settler "colonies" there was often an ideology and practice of exterminating aboriginal populations. In view of such ideas and practice the distinction between empire and colony is very significant. The liberal endorsement of the "empire" is, as I argue in this book, crucially predicated on notions of tutelage and kinship. It is therefore not consistent with the notion of "colony" where this refers to the idea of exterminating aboriginals. Liberals did not advocate or countenance this practice.

2. Harold Laski, *Political Thought in England from Locke to Bentham* (Oxford: Oxford University Press, 1950), 149, 153.

other groups, so long as they did not threaten social peace and order. In general, liberals have looked with favor on the idea of national self-determinism—though often they have done so without reflecting deeply on the wellsprings of nationalism and the imperatives of nationhood under conditions of modernity. In terms of its mood or culture, as distinct from its doctrine, liberalism has often had a flavor of romanticism that allows the subjective to tilt in an anarchist breeze by insisting that the seeds of social good stem from individual and even eccentric initiative. These claims are of course not the exclusive reserve of liberals, and conservatives can rightly argue that they share in the defense and promotion of many of these accolades. Nevertheless, the irony of the liberal defense of the empire stands, because in some at least intuitively obvious sense, that defense vitiates what we take liberalism to represent and historically stand for.

LIBERALISM AND EMPIRE: A DENIED LINK

The liberal association with the British Empire was extended and deep. Indeed, if one considers Locke's significant, even if only occasional, remarks on America and the constitution he wrote for the state of Carolina, the liberal involvement with the British Empire is broadly coeval with liberalism itself. With scarcely any exceptions, every British political thinker of note wrote on the empire and most of them wrote on the British Empire in India. More often than not, these writings were copious, as in the cases of Edmund Burke, Jeremy Bentham, James Mill, Lord Macaulay, Sir Henry Maine, and John Stuart Mill; and when they were of a more occasional nature, as with Adam Smith, David Ricardo, and David Hume, they are nevertheless marked by a seriousness of purpose.

This fact should not be surprising. After all, following the British conquest of Ireland during the Tudor period the idea of the British as an "imperial" people was an ascending one all the way into the twentieth century. From 1 January 1600, when fifty-eight merchants incorporated themselves to form the East India Company and received a royal charter from Queen Elizabeth to have a monopoly on trade with the East, the idea of an empire in the East was already a prospective hope and a faint image. By 1606, when the first charter was given to Virginia and shortly thereafter others along the North American eastern seaboard, the empire there was an incipient reality. By the eighteenth century, when British settlements on the eastern coast of North America had been consolidated and the East India Company had assumed political and revenue-collecting authority in eastern and parts of southern India, the empire had clearly grown in extent and political significance. Following the Seven Years' War (1756–63), the establishment of Fort York in the East Indies, Saint Louis, Fort James, and Cape Coast Castle in west Africa, Manila in the Far East, and the transferring to the crown of much of the Caribbean, the British Empire now included French Catholics in Quebec and millions who were neither Christians nor white. Referring to this period the avowedly nationalist and imperialist historian J. R. Seeley said, "[T]he history of England [was] not in England but in America and Asia."[3] By 1920, the British Empire included much of eastern Canada in the northwest of the globe, the Falkland Islands, the South Orkneys and Graham Land in the southwest, Australia and New Zealand in the southeast, Hong Kong in east Asia, India, Afghanistan, Burma, and Ceylon in south Asia, much of Africa and the Middle East, and small islands sprinkled across all the oceans. Of this vast collection of places and peoples, it was true to say that the "sun never set on it." It is hard to imagine any feature of British political, social, economic, and cultural life, except perhaps the purely municipal, not being somehow affected by this grand predicament. This was no doubt in part what Lord Curzon, the governor general and viceroy of India, meant, when he said in 1898, "Imperialism is becoming everyday less and less the creed of a party and more and more the faith of a nation."[4]

It is therefore only to be expected that British political thinkers, especially those of a cosmopolitan cast of mind, should have found their thoughts almost ineluctably engaging with this vast scene of British action. And yet, this fact belongs to that peculiar set of facts that are strangely hidden from a canon that presumes on obviousness as its basis. Despite the chronological correspondence in the development of liberal thought and the empire, the unmistakable political gravity of the latter, and, most importantly, the clear, if complex, link between the ideas that were central to the former and those that undergirded practices of the latter, the relationship between liberalism and the empire has scarcely been considered in recent times by political theorists.

This neglect is evident in both historical political theory and contemporary normative scholarship. Historically, the fact that most Brit-

3. J. R. Seeley, *The Expansion of England* (Chicago: University of Chicago Press, 1971; originally published in 1883), 13. Seeley was the most influential and widely read historian of the empire. See also Charles Dilke, *Greater Britain* (New York: 1869).

4. Quoted in Harold Nicolson, *Curzon: The Last Phase 1919–1925* (New York: Harcourt, Brace and Company, 1939), 13.

ish political theorists of the eighteenth and nineteenth centuries were deeply involved with the empire in their writings and often in its administration is seldom given any significance or even mentioned in the framing of this intellectual tradition. As a consequence of this neglect, it is often overlooked that, for instance, the overwhelming majority of Edmund Burke's published writings deal with the British Empire, be it in India, America, or Ireland; that for the last twenty years of his life Bentham was preoccupied with issues of constitutional and legislative design for India (a fact that perhaps explains a comment he made toward the end of his life: "I shall be the dead legislative of British India");[5] that the major work of James Mill's career was the monumental six-volume *History of British India;* that John Stuart Mill—the author of over a dozen parliamentary and other reports on matters of imperial policy in India and Jamaica—did not just work at the East India Company, he worked there for thirty-five years (indeed, it was the only full-time job he ever held), and that apart from discussing the empire in all his major works, two of his best known writings, *On Liberty* and *Considerations on Representative Government,* were originally conceived as responses to Lord Macaulay's "Minute on Indian Education"; and that finally, a similar concern with the empire is evident in the work of Thomas Carlyle, Lord Macaulay, Sir Henry Maine, John Bright, T. H. Green, Walter Bagehot, John Morley, and James Fitzjames Stephen. In terms of contemporary scholarship in the post–World War II era, that is, in the period of decolonization, with the exception of John Plamenatz's *On Alien Rule and Self-Government* published in 1960 and the second part of Hannah Arendt's *The Origins of Totalitarianism,* there is no book by a political theorist writing in English that deals with sustained focus on the empire.

All this is not to suggest that the terrain of modern political thought and the empire has not been studied—that is anything but the case. But the considerable and often theoretically subtle and powerful efforts that characterize research in this province have come primarily from the fields of history, including art history, anthropology, and more recently, literary criticism and cultural studies. It is obvious why an era marked by an extended and multifarious contact among people of often sharply contrasting perspectives, backgrounds, customs, traditions, and imaginations, and where that contact has had and continues to have enduring

5. *The Works of Jeremy Bentham,* ed. J. Bowring (London: Simpkin, Marshall, 1843), 10:490, quoted in Eric Stokes, *English Utilitarians in India* (Oxford: Clarendon Press, 1959), 68.

effects, should have elicited the attention of these disciplines and often led to the hybridization of their insights.[6]

But this very obviousness makes the indifference of political theory all the more marked. After all, already by the eighteenth and certainly following the Reform Bills of the nineteenth century, Britain, in its self-image, was a democracy, yet it held a vast empire that was, at least ostensibly, undemocratic in its acquisition and governance; following Locke, there was a broad consensus that linked the exercise of political power with the rights of citizens, and yet the existence of the empire meant that British power was overwhelmingly exercised over subjects rather than citizens; again following Locke, and in the aftermath of the Glorious Revolution (1688), the idea of the power of the state being limited and checked by the separation of the branches of government had taken hold, and yet imperial power, as George III and his ministers emphasized and as later liberals such as both the Mills concurred (at least with respect to India), had no such constraints placed on its exercise; similarly, by the mid–nineteenth century among radicals and liberals, the conditions for good government had been recognized as intimately linked with the conditions of self-government, and yet in someone like John Stuart Mill, who most forcefully articulated this argument, it applied only to the Anglo-Saxon parts of the empire.[7] At a more general level, from the seventeenth century onward, the British, the Dutch, and the French rightly conceived of themselves as having elaborated and integrated into their societies an understanding of political freedom, and yet during this very period they pursued and held vast empires where such freedoms were either absent or severely attenuated for the majority of the native inhabitants.

My point is not that the existence of the empire and the political thought or even more specifically the liberal thought that emerged concurrently with it were obviously in contradiction. That claim is neither obvious, nor, I believe, ultimately true. In any case the language of contradictions is too precise an instrument to say anything of interest about generalities that range across centuries and involve the complicated intersection of ideas and practices, not to mention the differing logics of

6. An important and helpful bibliography of the scholarship on imperialism that draws on all these fields can be found in *Tensions of Empire*, ed. Frederick Cooper and Ann Laura Stoler (Berkeley and Los Angeles: University of California Press, 1997), 40–56.

7. John Stuart Mill, *Considerations on Representative Government*, in *Three Essays* (Oxford: Oxford University Press, 1985), esp. chaps. 2, 18.

domestic and international imperatives. Moreover, contradictions, if they do exist, do not close the space on the complexities that emerge from the extended link between liberalism and the empire. They should be taken as an invitation to that space. Instead, my point is simply that there are prima facie factors that give the existence of the British Empire, especially in view of the extended and close link it had with leading political thinkers, a potential theoretical significance that has been largely overlooked. As Eric Stokes pointed out in a book that dealt with the Utilitarian connection to India, "it is remarkable how many of the movements of English life tested their strength upon the Indian question."[8] Moreover, from the standpoint of liberalism, the "Indian question" was paradigmatically the issue of how a body of ideas that professed a universal reach responded to the encounter with the unfamiliar. There are, as I argue, reasons internal to liberalism why this question is not articulated with such starkness within this body of ideas. This denial is both a clue to the problem and a provisional indicator of its unsatisfactory resolution within liberal thought.

THE CIRCUMSTANCES OF THOUGHT IN AN UNFAMILIAR CONTEXT

At the broadest level this book attempts to redress the indifference of modern and historical scholarship to the extended link between liberalism and the empire by taking seriously the writings of a small though significant group of political thinkers as they reflected on British rule in India. The conditions of that rule, and hence of those reflections, are one in which imperial power was exercised over people separated from Britain by thousands of miles and numerous other distances—as James Mill put it, the government was conducted "by correspondence" from London;[9] where the historical connection between these two peoples was limited, or rather almost wholly internal to the framework established by the empire, and where moreover there were contrasting traditions, self-understandings, extant political and social practices, belief

8. Eric Stokes, *English Utilitarians in India* (Oxford: Clarendon Press, 1959), xii. Stokes goes on to mention the movements for the cause of free trade, evangelicalism, utilitarianism, and liberalism. See also George D. Bearce, *British Attitudes toward India 1784–1858* (Oxford: Oxford University Press, 1961), and Thomas R. Metcalf, *The New Cambridge History of India: Ideologies of the Raj* (Cambridge: Cambridge University Press, 1994), chaps. 1, 2.

9. Letter from James Mill to Dumont, in *The Works and Correspondence of David Ricardo*, ed. Piero Sraffa in collaboration with M. Dobb (Cambridge: Cambridge University Press, 1951), 7:40 n.

systems: in a word, diversities of experience and life forms across virtually every relevant register of reckoning. In these conditions resides the
unfamiliarity that this book explores. All this at a time when European
thought, certainly liberal thought, had a growing confidence in its universality and cosmopolitanism. These were some of the conditions under which the leading liberal theorists of the late eighteenth and nineteenth centuries came to view India as the promised land of liberal
ideas—a kind of test case laboratory. This was before they could take
heed of E. M. Forster's tantalizing epigram, "She [India] is not a promise, only an appeal."[10]

In this work, I reverse the position of the viewing eye to look at
British liberalism, not so much *from* India, but rather, by focusing on
the particular amplifications and inflections in liberalism that get revealed in the writings by liberals on India and the empire. This perspective on late eighteenth- and nineteenth-century liberal thought relates
to a matter of scale and of substance. The claims I make about liberalism are, I believe, integral to its political vision and not peculiar amend-
ments or modifications imposed on it by the attention to India. Given
liberalism's universalism, this is definitionally the case. At one level,
what the attention to India adds is simply a magnification onto a larger
canvas of certain ideas and ways of thinking that structure the theories
in any case. It brings out what is implicit or in other contexts deeply
recessed. It examines theorists making choices that otherwise and in
more familiar situations they simply took for granted, thus often overlooking the element of choice and the conditions that made possible its
apparent denial. It is not that the engagement with India somehow exposes all the synaptic links in liberal thinking. But it does, as it were,
often strain the conscious to the point where liberals are forced to bring
to mind what otherwise remained unconscious. Here India does to liberalism what the unfamiliar more generally does to the instincts of
thought and practice—it induces reflection. Of course sometimes that
reflection simply denies the strangeness of the encounter it is confronted with and asserts the familiar or "natural" with added vigor. But
that addition itself leaves a trace in the thought.

But the focus on liberal thought in the context of the empire also
relates to a matter of substance, namely what comes to be understood
as liberalism. Political ideas, even theoretically self-conscious ones, do
not just have implications that flow from them with the frictionless ease
of a mathematical deduction, assuming that to be the case. Their mean-

10. E. M. Forster, *A Passage to India* (Harmondsworth: Penguin, 1979), 135.

ing, as ideas, has everything to do with the context of their provenance and reception, and the friction they encounter in their engagement with reality. If this is a concession to a relativist theory of meaning it is also simply a statement of the fact that ideas and words need to be interpreted to have meaning. And here the various presuppositions that inform the context of interpretation plainly affect the ideas being interpreted. History does not sustain the choice—really the fantasy—of not being in medias res; neither for theorists nor their ideas. This claim is especially important with respect to liberal ideas. Precisely because of their typically abstract and decontextual presentation the modifications affected on them by specific contexts can be particularly telling. They are telling of the interaction of ideas and context and not merely of the ideas themselves. For example, in his book on *The Liberal Tradition in America* which is also exemplary as a study in comparative European and American liberalism, Louis Hartz argued that the liberalism associated with Locke in seventeenth-century England was implicitly reliant on the surrounding intellectual context of Filmer's and Hobbes's absolutism and the political and social structures of English feudalism. It was this buttress that animated the radical and progressive implications associated with Locke's political thought in England. In contrast, in the absence of this surrounding context in America, the radical edge to Locke's thought got severely eviscerated, and it became the voice of a matter-of-fact conservatism. His ideas were no longer the vehicle for making people equal, because here they were assumed to have been born equal.[11]

The circumstances that structure liberal ideas in the late eighteenth and nineteenth centuries are of course numerous, and they operate at both ends of the imperial connection, Britain and India, and in the perceptions of each other. Regarding the perception of liberalism in India or by Indians of that time this work is largely silent.[12] Moreover that

11. Louis Hartz, *The Liberal Tradition in America* (New York: Harcourt, Brace & World, 1955). Hartz and his collaborators expanded on the comparative dimensions of his work through the category of the "fragment" in *The Founding of New Societies* (New York: Harcourt, Brace & World, 1964).

12. The study of the reception and modification of British liberal ideas in India is still in its early stages. It is simply not enough, and is in any case partial and misleading, to repeat the perennial claims that Indian nationalists such as Mahatma Gandhi and Nehru were liberals who successfully turned the intellectual armaments of the British against themselves. If they were liberals on some issues, there was, nevertheless, a very distinctive hue to that creed in their appropriation of it. And if there was mimicry in these efforts there was also camouflage and subterfuge. The recent writings by Ashis Nandy, S. Kaviraj, Bipan Chandra, and Partha Chatterjee

perspective is only distantly related to my primary motivation, which is with how liberal theorists responded to the challenge of a world marked by unmistakably different ways of organizing social and political life, molding and expressing individuality and freedom: in a word, an unfamiliar world marked by different ways of being in it.

A number of factors condition the liberal response to this predicament. At the most general and background level—and because it is that, it is often the most implicit, though always tangible—is the fact and the awareness of the inequality of power. After 1818, when coincidentally the term *liberalism* comes into popular usage, and the British succeed in quelling the Marathas—the last serious internal threat they faced in India—Britain, in effect, rules India.[13] Her task now is mainly political governance, and only secondarily and very occasionally, military conquest.[14] When liberals and others in Britain reflect on India or other posts of the empire, they do so with a knowledge of this inequality. In their most reforming, compassionate, or anxious moments—and these were numerous—their thought has the quality of confidence, inner certainty, and the perspective from which unhindered judgments can be issued. This is of course primarily a comfort experienced in thought and not in the reality of imperial practice, where all sorts of "inconveniences" refract intended outcomes. Nevertheless, even before liberalism becomes explicitly paternalistic, following the Napoleonic Wars and the ascendancy of the Whigs in the 1830s, it assumes a paternal posture—an odd mix of maturity, familial concern, and an underlying awareness of the capacity to direct, and if need be, coerce. One gets a sense of these varied sentiments in the frequently used expressions "*our* Indian subjects," "*our* Empire," "*our* dependents." The possessive pronoun simultaneously conveys familiarity and distance, warmth and sternness, responsibility and raw power.

The effect of this background condition, of having power and ruling, is striking on the thought that is produced from within its fold. On the one hand, it gives to this thought vis-à-vis India an assertive expansiveness, a confidence of judgment, an unqualified energy, and often an acute sense of urgency and mission. The image one gets of India

---

have gone some distance to offer important correctives to this unitary caricature and bring out the enormous subtleties in the process of appropriating ideas.

13. On the issue of the dating of the empire see also Metcalf, *The New Cambridge History of India: Ideologies of the Raj*, for a rich overview of the British Empire in India.

14. The mutiny of 1857 is of course a watershed in imperial relations. It did involve the use of military force but did not result in conquest in the ordinary sense.

is of a vacant field, already weeded, where history has been brought to
a nullity and where extant social and political practices are narrowly
contained, or altogether absent, primed for reform and constructive efforts.[15] Even when these stark conditions of *terra nullius* are acknowledged not to exist—a concession to reality—from the perspective of
thought, they could easily be made to exist. From the writings on India
and the empire more generally, one gets the vivid sense of thought that
has found a *project*, with all the grandeur of scale, implicit permanence,
purposefulness, and the absence of a need to negotiate with what is extant that the Enlightenment associated with the prerogatives of that
term.[16] Even politicians and administrators who faced the turgid realities of the empire paid obeisance to this vision of a clear philosophic
horizon. In December 1827, Lord William Bentinck, at a farewell din-
ner in London before he sailed to India to assume the post of governor

15. One gets a vivid pictorial sense of this vacancy in the enormously influential and popular early nineteenth-century etchings of the painter William Daniells.
The central motive of Daniells's paintings is typically a monument such as a temple,
a mosque, or a marketplace. This is always in the foreground of the canvas. But the
marked absence or the miniaturization of human beings in his paintings has the effect of imbuing the monument with a ghostly ahistorical and unlived vacancy.

In a different register of perception one sees the same effect being reproduced
in the intense preoccupation that the British had from as early as 1765 through the
next century with the surveying of India. The climax of this concern was the Great
Trigonometrical Survey of India conducted by the East India Company. Its purpose
was to define in precise scientific terms using the latest scientific techniques the
exact image of the Indian empire. As Matthew Edney argues in *Mapping and Empire:
The Geographical Construction of British India, 1765–1843* (Chicago: University of Chicago Press, 1997), the purpose of this enterprise was to vindicate liberalism, the rationality of science, and its link with "Civilization" in contrast with the irrational
and the mystical.

16. See David Lachterman, *The Ethics of Geometry* (New York: Routledge,
1989), esp. chap. 1.

Adam Smith, an early critic and insightful student of the empire, understood
the extent to which the empire was a project that relied on its own implicit incomple-
tion to sustain itself. Apart from the long chapter "On Colonies," the significance
that he gives to this is also evident in the passage with which he chose to end the
Wealth of Nations:

> This empire [i.e., in America], however, has hitherto been, not an empire,
> but the project of an empire . . . It is surely now time that our rulers should
> either realize this golden dream, in which they have been indulging them-
> selves, perhaps as well as the people; or that they should awaken from it
> themselves, and endeavor to awaken the people. . . . If the project cannot
> be completed, it ought to be given up.

Adam Smith, *Wealth of Nations* (Chicago: University of Chicago Press, 1976), 486.

general, made this point with blunt precision to James Mill: "I am going to British India, but I shall not be Governor General. It is *you* that will be Governor General."[17] This investiture and offer of impersonation by power to philosophy captures a broader sense of mission that pervades nineteenth-century liberalism and imperialism. This liberalism is nothing if not reformist and activist. It has none of the benign indifference that is often associated with a liberal attitude toward the private and collective identities of peoples. Philosophy has perhaps never had greater political latitude. After all, even Cleon demanded Plato's presence in Syracuse when he requested the latter's political counsel.

On the other hand, the same predicament of ruling India lends to the disagreements within British thoughts on India a tone of doubt, dilemmatic discomfort, and heightened and contentious acrimony. There is a revealing irony here. For it is in these struggles, exacerbated by their very internecine character, that one gets the clearest view of British thought (and practice) straining to come to terms with an unfamiliar world. It is the Orientalist Sir William Jones and others like him who are the object of sustained rebuke through the volumes of James Mill's *History of British India;* the evangelicals of the Clapham Sect who provoke and return the ire of the utilitarians and the liberals on the issue of Christian missions in India; James Mill who is the object of Macaulay's caricatures regarding the government of India; John Stuart Mill who is the defendant in James Fitzjames Stephen's accusations of bad faith regarding consent, equality, and fraternity. The strangeness of India, the various ways in which it confounds familiar categories, which nevertheless remain buried and largely concealed in the writings on India, is obvious and on the surface in this discussion. Here new issues emerge. We see, for example, John Stuart Mill and Tocqueville, in their letters, discussing the need for European states to have empires, but not in terms of the imperatives of the civilizing process or the most efficient modalities of administration or commerce, but rather, in terms of the importance of power and the possibility of resuscitating Roman conceptions of virtue and freedom and medieval notions of honor on a grand scale. We see Sir Henry Maine acknowledging and then, as it were, instantaneously denying the paradox of ruling people on the other side of the globe:

> As has been truly said, the British rulers of India are like men bound to keep time in two longitudes at once. Nevertheless, the paradoxical position must be accepted in the extraordinary

17. Bentham to Col. Young, 28 December 1828, in *Works,* 10:576–78.

experiment, the British Government of India, the virtually despotic government of a dependency by a free people.[18]

We see Rev. Alexander Duff admitting a dilemma whose grip extended
far beyond the evangelicals on whose behalf it is here expressed: "Do
not send men of compassion here for you will soon break their hearts;
do send men of compassion here, where millions perish for lack of their
knowledge."[19] We see him again nervously rely on the fragile prospect
of evangelical Christianity issuing in a thoroughly pacific world in
which the modalities of ruling and being ruled are in perfect synchrony:
"[As] Christianity has never taught rulers to oppress, so it will never
teach subjects to rebel."[20] Or consider the remarkable statement by Macaulay that brings together the themes of writing, distance, compassion,
and kinship, around the ambivalence of which colonial discourse develops its special affectivity.

> It is probable that writing 15,000 miles from the place where
> their orders were to be carried into effect [the directors of the
> East India Company] never perceived the gross inconsistency
> of which they were guilty. . . . Whoever examines their letters
> written at that time, will find there many just and humane sen-
> timents . . . an admirable code of political ethics . . . Now these
> instructions, being interpreted, mean simply, "Be the father
> and the oppressor of the people; be just and unjust, moderate
> and rapacious."[21]

What Macaulay recognizes is that strange, contradictory mutation that
occurs in the effect of words when the distance between the places of
their "humane" enunciation and the places to which they are addressed
is not simply one of miles but of a power whose truth can be spoken
of only with liberal ambivalence, or what Homi Bhabha has called "sly
civility." The gulf between fathers who must also be oppressors—just
and unjust, moderate and rapacious—and their people is not filled by
the probity of intentions but by a language and way of thinking in which
the stranger has from the very outset been coded as a child.

Similarly, the issue of race has a different valence in this intra-

18. Sir Henry Maine, "The Effects of Observation of India on Modern European Thought" (Cambridge: The Rede Lecture, 1875).
19. Rev. Alexander Duff, *India and India Missions: Sketches of the Gigantic System
of Hinduism Etc.* (Edinburgh: John Johnstone, 1839), 211.
20. Ibid., 587.
21. T. B. Macaulay, "Warren Hastings," in *Critical and Historical Essays* (London: Methuen, 1903), 3:85–86.

European discussion. The matter is of course complicated by the fact that British political ideologies did not know race until they encountered its plurality, largely through the empire. In fact, race is seldom deployed as an explicit political category in the writings by British liberals in their works on India.[22] There are, of course, well-known reasons on account of which liberals typically view race as morally and politically irrelevant, or at any rate a "suspect" category. Yet the mention of race is conspicuous in its absence. Maybe, one might think, this absence is explained by a deeper denial: that of not wishing to engage with, or fully acknowledge, the unfamiliar. Perhaps, in the liberal imagination, race is a visible mark of the unfamiliar, so that to allow it to stand for that alterity and the plethora of differences that lie behind it might limit the very constructive enterprise through which it can be molded to become, or at least appear, familiar. This is precisely how Lord Macaulay imagines the role of imperial pedagogy: it operates in the malleable and concealed space behind the starkness of blood and color to reproduce the familiar, even if somatically refracted, category of being English. "We must at present do our best to form a . . . class of persons, Indians in blood and color, but English in taste, in opinions, in morals, and in intellect."[23] Macaulay's strategy recalls and repeats the arduous processes through which the effortless, the rational, the gentlemanly, and the civi-

22. Here John Stuart Mill is a surprising exception. He invests race with far greater seriousness than most of his liberal contemporaries, who generally view it as a catchall term that loosely designates what might be called cultural difference. Instead Mill elaborates the term through the biological notion of "blood." Hence for example in the *Considerations on Representative Government* (chaps. 16, 18) he draws what he takes to be the crucial distinction in terms of readiness for representative institutions by reference to "those of our blood" and those not of our blood.

23. Thomas B. Macaulay, "Minute on Indian Education" (1835), in *Thomas Babington Macaulay: Selected Writings*, ed. John Clive (Chicago: University of Chicago Press, 1972), 249.

The specific context in which Macaulay wrote his minute was a dispute regarding a small subvention given by the British to schools that taught Sanskrit and Arabic along with English. The "Anglicists," whose cause Macaulay championed, in contrast with the "Orientalists," wished this subsidy to go more or less exclusively toward the study of English. Written in his capacity as the legal member of council, Macaulay not only won the day for the Anglicists, but his minute significantly influenced the subsequent direction of British education in India. See Kenneth Ballhatchet, "The Home Government and Bentinck's Educational Policy," *Cambridge Historical Journal* 10 (1951); Gerald and Natalie Sirkin, "The Battle of Indian Education: Macaulay's Opening Salvo," *Victorian Studies* 14 (1971): 42–61; John Clive, *Macaulay: The Shaping of a Historian* (Cambridge: Harvard University Press, 1973), chaps. 12, 13; and Gauri Viswanathan, *Masks of Conquest* (New York: Columbia University Press, 1989), chap. 6.

lized are made to appear natural, via the complex interdictions of liberal
education, and all of them by working behind the scene. They are bor-
rowed, consciously or otherwise, from Locke's *Thoughts Concerning Education*, that remarkable work that approaches a manual and that stands
partially obscured behind the *Second Treatise*, monitoring entry into the
consensual politics of this latter work. Louis Hartz is, I think, quite
right in his statement, "If we go beneath the surface of the racial attitudes, we will soon encounter the familiar figures of Suarez and Locke
and Cobbett, each struggling in his own terms to deal with an unfamiliar world."[24] In terms of the focus of this work, it is the intra-British
conversation that clouds the clear horizon.

There is another issue that relates to the matter of having power
and ruling. To what extent and in what manner is having power a condition of the liberal political and ethical imagination? The question obviously has various aspects to it. At the broadest level, with respect to the
empire, there is the dilemma that Arnaldo Momigliano claimed was at
the root of the ancient Greek and Persian empires: "[F]reedom required
power, because power is a condition of freedom, but power proved in
fact unobtainable without ruling others."[25] Momigliano's claim relates
to the complex issue of the extent to which freedom, as the basis of a
society, is a stable notion, in the sense of being able to limit the impulse
for its reactive amplification and expansion. Nations, including those
whose identity was self-consciously forged with an eye to liberal conceptions of freedom, equality, and human dignity, typically retain the
resources of reactive and expansive nationalism. The program of making people even formally equal, is always (i.e., historically) implicitly
bounded and has the potential to rebound on those outside the national
community.[26] In the context of the empire in the late eighteenth century,

24. Hartz, *The Founding of New Societies*, 16.
25. Arnaldo Momigliano, "Persian Empire and Greek Freedom," in *The Idea of
Freedom*, ed. Alan Ryan (Oxford. Oxford University Press, 1979), 139–51, quoting
p. 149. See also Peter Brown, *Power and Persuasion in Late Antiquity: Towards a Christian Empire* (Madison: University of Wisconsin Press, 1992).
David Ricardo appreciated the dilemma Momigliano articulates. This is evident
in his extended correspondence with James Mill regarding the empire. In one such
letter he states, "The people of England, who are governors, have an interest opposed to that of the people of India, who are the governed, in the same manner
as the interests of a despotic sovereign is opposed to that of his people. In both
cases there are no limits to the abuse of power but those which the Governors
themselves choose to impose." *The Works and Correspondence of David Ricardo*,
7:239.
26. This point is richly developed in Roger Brubaker, *Citizenship and Nationhood in France and Germany* (Cambridge: Harvard University Press, 1992). Again
with respect to Germany, Leah Greenfeld makes the claim, which I believe is inade-

most conspicuously with Burke though also with Adam Smith and Hume, there is a persistent theme that calls for a vigilance against freedom becoming a stratagem for power and even tyranny. As Hume wrote, "[F]ree governments have been commonly the most happy for those who partake of their freedom; yet are they the most ruinous and oppressive to their provinces."[27] For Burke, as I argue in the fourth and fifth chapters, this vigilance issues in a broader and profound critique of the British Empire. That critique is itself informed by an alternative view, in contrast for example to that of both the Mills, regarding the very possibility of reason and freedom, as distinct from spatially located sentiments and entrenched feelings, being the basis for the boundaries of a nation. As part of that critique, Burke offers an argument as to how power can be denied space or contained within narrow bounds in the understanding of the strange and unfamiliar. The relevance of the epistemology and psychology of what Hume and Smith called *sympathy*, which clearly influenced Burke's thought, informs all these essays because it relates directly to the issue of understanding experience and power, especially in the unfamiliar context of the empire.

THE COSMOPOLITANISM OF REASON AND THE COSMOPOLITANISM OF SENTIMENTS

Finally and most centrally for this book, the issue of power is pertinent to the very relationship that a body of ideas imagines between itself and the world. Here the issue is less the actual reliance on having the power to coerce or effect change at will, but rather the very stance and the point of view that particular ideas assume with respect to other ideas and forms of life. For example, James Mill's *History* is explicitly presented as judgmental, not simply because Mill chooses to be judg-

---

quately defended in her work, that "[a] direct line connected Hitler to the idealistic Romantic patriots of the Wars of Liberation" (384), in *Nationalism: Five Roads to Modernity* (Cambridge: Harvard University Press, 1992). Linda Colley in her study of the formation of Britain similarly points to the extended *ressentiment* against the French and the Catholicism, among other things, that they represented; see *Britons: Forging the Nation 1707–1837* (New Haven: Yale University Press, 1992). Julia Kristeva emphasizes the same point in her books *Nations without Nationalism*, trans. Leon S. Roudiez (New York: Columbia University Press, 1993), and *Strangers to Ourselves*, trans. Leon S. Roudiez (New York: Columbia University Press, 1991). With respect to the United States, Louis Hartz pointed to how American conceptions of liberty and equality were suspicious of both internal and external outsiders. See *The Liberal Tradition in America* and "The European Fragment, Africa, and the Indian Tribes," in *The Founding of New Societies*.

27. David Hume, "Politics a Science," in *Essays: Moral, Political and Literary* (Indianapolis: Liberty Classics, 1985), 18–19.

mental, but rather on account of what he considers far more important, namely that the reason, the very rationality, upon which the writing of history depends is itself judgmental.[28] That rationality specifies in advance of the encounter with the "facts" of history the general structure of what it would mean for facts to hang together "rationally", and only thus could they have meaning. Absent that general structure, or absent from that general structure, which reason supplies, a specific event would be an orphaned mass with no identifying genealogical markings and hence no meaning.

In Mill's *History* the specific, but, more relevantly, the strange and the unfamiliar, are at the epistemological mercy of a rationality that is vouched for in advance of "viewing" and certainly experiencing the strange and the unfamiliar. The project of the empire is inscribed in the judgments of that way of "doing" history, which relentlessly attempts to align or educate the regnant forms of the unfamiliar with its own expectations. Liberal imperialism is impossible without this epistemological commitment—which by the nineteenth century supports both the paternalism and progressivism—that is, the main theoretical justifications—of the empire. As I argue in the second chapter, when the strategy of education or realignment through political change is unserviceable, Mill's *History* and numerous others that share its convictions impute to the unfamiliar an impenetrable inscrutability that eviscerates their potential as forms of life and terminates the quest for understanding them.

The general structure that rationality presents as the condition for

---

28. The general structure of rationality that in Mill's view authorizes history also allows, indeed obligates, the historian to pass judgment on the widest domain of that history:

> It is the business of the historian not merely to display the obvious outside of things—the qualities which strike the most ignorant observer, in the acts, the institutions and the ordinances, which form the subject of his statements. . . . To qualify a man for this great duty hardly any kind or degree of knowledge is not demanded. . . . It is plain, for example, that he needs the most profound knowledge of the laws of human nature, which is the end, as well as instrument, of everything. . . . The historian requires a clear comprehension of the practical play of the machinery of government—for, in like manner as the general laws of motion are counteracted and modified by friction, the power of which may yet be accurately ascertained and provided for. In short, the whole field of human nature, the whole field of legislation, the whole field of judicature, the whole field of administration, down to war, commerce, and diplomacy, ought to be familiar to his mind. (James Mill, *History of British India* [New York: Chelsea House, 1968], 1:xvii)

the intelligibility of the specific is of course neither arbitrary nor a simple ruse of power. In the Western philosophic tradition it originates in the question of the correctness of the name to the object, in the correspondence and hiatus between the "nature of language" and the "nature of things." In its Cartesian expression this structure takes as its ideal mathematical knowledge.[29] But that ideal has served for Descartes's successors, as it certainly was intended by him, as an ideal for knowing and understanding not just geometrical entities but rather the realm of "extension," or what might simply be called the objective world, including its historical dimensions.[30] History as a discipline retains in many ways the traces of this Cartesian genealogy in which the singular can be understood only by reference to the general of which it is an instance. Paul Veyne makes the point as follows:

> History is interested in individualized events . . . but it is not interested in their individuality; it seeks to understand them—that is, to find among them a kind of generality or, more precisely specificity. It is the same with natural history; its curiosity is inexhaustible, all species matter to it and none is superfluous, but it does not propose the enjoyment of their singularity in the manner of beastiary of the Middle Ages, in which one could read descriptions of noble, beautiful, strange or cruel animals.[31]

But the singularity of the strange is not limited to animals, or to the Middle Ages, or to the possessed sorcerer speaking in tongues, or to puzzling the question that hangs over *A Passage to India*: What happened in the echoes of the Marabar Caves? These are only dramatic and not unique instances of what Homi Bhabha has called "the repeated threat of the *loss* of a 'teleologically significant world.'"[32] This threat and the

---

29. Hans-Georg Gadamer, *Truth and Method* (New York: Seabury Press, 1975), 153–204, and Gadamer, "The Science of the Life-World," in *Philosophic Hermeneutics*, trans. David E. Linge (Berkeley and Los Angeles: University of California Press, 1976), 182–97. See also Lachterman, *The Ethics of Geometry*, 188–205; and Charles Taylor, "Overcoming Epistemology," in *Philosophic Arguments* (Cambridge: Harvard University Press, 1977), 1–19.

30. David Lachterman, "Descartes and the Philosophy of History," *Independent Journal of Philosophy*, no. 4 (1983): 31–46.

31. Paul Veyne, *Writing History: Essay on Epistemology*, trans. Mina Moore Rinvoluri (Middletown, Conn.: 1984), 56. See also Michel De Certeau, *The Writing of History* (New York: Columbia University Press, 1988): "Making History," 19–55, "Discourse Disturbed: The Sorcerer's Speech," 244–68.

32. Homi Bhabha, "Articulating the Archaic," in *The Location of Culture* (London: Routledge, 1994), 125; see also in the same volume "How Newness Enters the World," 212–35.

problem that underlies it are in fact much broader. The problem quite simply is this: How does one understand, articulate (or rather understand what others articulate and experience), and—perhaps based on that knowledge or what might turn out to be that shared experience—accept what is strange and unfamiliar?

Such a statement of the problem resonates with what we think liberalism has all along aspired to, and what in its self-conception is its claim to distinction, namely articulating political and social norms of toleration and comity. But there is, I think, a danger in the comfort of this resonance, because it is often predicated on the assumption that the strange is just a variation on what is already familiar, because both the familiar and the strange are deemed to be merely specific instances of a familiar structure of generality. The epistemological perspective that articulates that structure also undergirds an elaborate vision of how politically to assimilate things, even when those things are thoroughly unfamiliar. This is what I refer to as the cosmopolitanism of reason.

The historian in James Mill, the legislator in Bentham, the educator in Macaulay, and the apostle of progress and individuality in J. S. Mill, all, I believe, fail in the challenge posed by the unfamiliar; because when faced with it they do no more than "repeat," presume on, and assert (this where power becomes relevant) the familiar structures of the generalities that inform the reasonable, the useful, the knowledgeable, and the progressive. These generalities constitute the ground of a cosmopolitanism because in a single glance and without having *experienced* any of it, they make it possible to compare and classify the world. But that glance is braided with the urge to dominate the world, because the language of those comparisons is not neutral and cannot avoid notions of superiority and inferiority, backward and progressive, and higher and lower. Urges can of course be resisted, and liberals offer ample evidence of this ability, which is why I do not claim that liberalism *must be* imperialistic, only that the urge is *internal* to it.

In the repetition, presumption, and assertion of the familiar, what is denied is precisely the archaic, the premodern, the religious, the Indian[33]—in a word, the unfamiliar, along with the sentiments, feelings,

---

33. These terms are themselves what Dipesh Chakrabarty rightly calls "rough translations," because in pointing to something outside the structures of generalities, they nevertheless do so from within those structures. The terms, as it were, "point" to something that cannot, and at any rate is not, itself articulated within that language. See Dipesh Chakrabarty, "Realist Prose and the Problem of Difference: The Rational and the Magical in Subaltern History," in *The Unworking of History* (forthcoming).

sense of location, and forms of life of which they are a part. These are the places that Franz Fanon with evocative simplicity called "the zone of occult instability where people dwell"[34]—places that when identified by the grid of Enlightenment rationality were only spots on a map or past points on the scale of civilizational progress, but not *dwellings* in which peoples lived and had deeply invested identities. And all this is by reference to other singular grids of emotive significance. In their denial lie their incorporation into the teleologies of imperial and liberal imperatives.

Here again, as I elaborate in the fourth and fifth chapters, Burke parts company with his nineteenth-century successors. But not because he can fuse the hiatus between the "nature of language" and the "nature of things" or because he has a more "realist" epistemology and prose that "correspond" to or better describe the nature of Indians, but rather because his thought is pitched at a level that takes seriously the sentiments, feelings, and attachments through which peoples are, and aspire to be, "at home." This posture of thought acknowledges that the integrity of experience is tied to its locality and finitude, what Gadamer calls "prejudice." By doing so it is congruent with the psychological aspects of experience, which always derive their meaning, their passionate and pained intensity, from within the bounded, even if porous, spheres of familial, national, or other narratives.[35] For Burke, in contrast with both the Mills, the significance of experience and the forms of life of which they are a part is not provisional on their incorporation in a rationalist teleology. Reason, freedom, and individuality, as nineteenth-century liberals understood them, are not, for Burke, the arbiters of the significance of these forms of life; when they are assumed to be such arbiters, he is aware that it was usually by relying on an implicit alliance with political and other forms of power.

Burke anticipates Richard Rorty's claim that "solidarity has to be constructed out of little pieces, rather than found already waiting, in the form of an *ur*language which all of us recognize when we hear it."[36] Burke's pragmatism, if it is that, is an expression of his profound humility in the face of a world that he did not presume to understand simply on account of his being rational, modern, or British, and hence a mem-

34. Franz Fanon, *The Wretched of the Earth* (Harmondsworth: Penguin, 1967), 182–83.

35. See David Bromwich, *A Choice of Inheritance* (Cambridge: Harvard University Press, 1989), 43–78, for a wonderfully insightful and original interpretation of Burke's thought that is especially attentive to its psychological dimensions.

36. Richard Rorty, *Contingency, Irony, and Solidarity* (Cambridge: Cambridge University Press, 1989), 190–91.

ber of the most powerful nation on Earth.[37] Burke appreciates with respect to India what Wittgenstein, referring to the religious believer, recognizes as the strangeness and viability of his way of life: "[He] is like a tightrope walker. He almost looks as though he were walking on nothing but thin air. His support is the slenderest imaginable. *And yet it really is possible to walk on it.*"[38] By his openness, which is undergirded by humility and a concern with the sentiments that give meaning to people's lives, Burke exposes himself and enters a dialogue with the unfamiliar and accepts the possible risks of that encounter. Those risks include the possibility of being confronted with utter opacity—an intransigent strangeness, an unfamiliarity that remains so, an experience that cannot be shared, prejudices that do not readily fuse with a cosmopolitan horizon, a difference that cannot be assimilated. In accepting these risks and not settling them in advance of the encounter, Burke, I believe, shatters the philosophic underpinnings of the project of the empire by making it no more than a conversation between *two* strangers. There is, I believe, a cosmopolitanism in this perspective too. It is what I refer to as the cosmopolitanism of sentiments. It is cosmopolitan because it holds out the possibility, and even the hope, that through the conversation, which has as its purpose the understanding of the sentiments that give meaning to people's lives, wider bonds of sympathy can be forged. In those bonds the singular and not just the specific are acknowledged. But if that contingent conversation leads nowhere, since Burke is himself exposed and has nothing that gives him cover, no authorizing "reason" that is "founded" on the certainty of perception or anything else, no prior teleology, no language that trumps the babble of the other's "superstitions," he can, as he does, countenance the very possibility of a history and way of life of which he and his people have no part—"[I]f we are not able to contrive some method of governing India well which will not of necessity become the means of governing Great Britain ill, a ground is laid for their eternal separation, but none for sacrificing the people of that country to our constitution."[39]

37. "Faults this nation [i.e., India] may have, but God forbid we should pass judgment upon people who framed their laws and institutions prior to our insect origins of yesterday." Burke, "Impeachment of Warren Hastings," in *The Writings and Speeches of Edmund Burke* (New York: J.F. Taylor and Co., 1901), 7:46. This edition is cited hereafter as *Writings and Speeches* (Taylor).

38. Ludwig Wittgenstein, *Culture and Value*, trans. Peter Winch, ed. G. H. von Wright (Chicago: University of Chicago Press, 1980), 73e (emphasis added).

39. Burke, "Fox's India Bill Speech," in *Writings and Speeches of Edmund Burke*, vol. 5, ed. P. J. Marshall (Oxford: Clarendon Press, 1981), 383. This edition is cited hereafter as *Writings and Speeches* (Oxford).

In the acknowledgment of this possible estrangement, this "eternal separation," lies the possibility of *mutual* understanding, *mutual* influence, and *mutual* recognition. Of course none of this is guarantied; but that is just a tragic fact about the world whose effects are often only exacerbated by the attempt to *foreclose* on the differences that separate and potentially unite us. To contain those differences or to mediate them through a prior settlement that fixes on reason, freedom, ethics, internationalism, multiculturalism, the universality of rights, or even democracy, is to deny "the occult," "the parochial," "the traditional," in short the unfamiliar, the very possibility of articulating the meaning and agentiality of its own experiences. The encounter with those experiences is always potentially risky and, as with Hume and in contrast with Descartes, it has uncertainty as a constant, and not just an initial, condition. The etymology of the word *experience* itself bears witness to this. Jean-Luc Nancy while drawing on the work of Philippe Lacoue-Labarthe, explicates it as follows: "[A]ccording to the origin of the word 'experience' in *peira* and in *ex-periri*, an experience is an attempt executed without reserve, given over to the *peril* of its own lack of foundation and security in this 'object' of which it is not the subject but instead the passion, exposed like the pirate *(peirates)* who freely tries his luck on the high seas."[40] On this view, liberalism has had a singularly impoverished understanding of experience because it has sought in an abstract reason a short cut to a perilous journey with its unavoidable surprises.

The Fact of Strangeness and the Norms of Liberalism

As has been suggested, in the eighteenth and nineteenth centuries, liberal thought and India encounter each other as strangers. They literally

40. Jean-Luc Nancy, *The Experience of Freedom*, trans. Bridget McDonald (Stanford: Stanford University Press, 1993), 20. See also Philippe Lacoue-Labarthe, *La poesie comme experience* (Paris: Bourgois, 1986), 30–31.

Similarly, the German word *erfahren* (to experience) also derives from *fahren* (to travel) and is linked with *die Gefahr* (danger).

Hume's description of the experience of philosophizing, as he at least experienced it, suggests the image of a perilous sea voyage. At the conclusion of book 1 of his *Treatise of Human Nature* he states:

Methinks I am like a man, who having struck on many shoals, and having narrowly escaped ship-wreck in passing a small firth, has yet the temerity to put out to sea, in the same leaky weather beaten vessel, and even carries his ambition so far as to think of encompassing the globe under these disadvantageous circumstances. (David Hume, *A Treatise of Human Nature*, ed. L. A. Selby-Bigge [Oxford: Clarendon Press, 1978], 263–64)

do not know each other, do not speak each other's language (in the various senses of the term), and do not share values, cosmologies, or the quotidian norms and rituals of everyday life. The modalities of their experiences are very different. From the perspective of the former, which is what concerns me, India is an abstraction, variously represented through social structure, religion, mythology, and the pervasive influence of unreason, all embodied and represented in its history.

What allows these abstractions to serve as meeting points is something that characterizes the encounter with strangeness more generally. We relate to the strange through the qualities that are most general and are therefore deemed to be common to both sides of the encounter. On the other hand, relations among members of a group are typically conducted through associated and nested links that are singular and that differentiate them from the universal. The paradoxical effect of this has, I think, been best elaborated by Georg Simmel:

> [T]he consciousness of having only the absolutely general in common has exactly the effect of putting a special emphasis on that which is not common. For a stranger to a country, the city, the race, and so on, what is stressed is again nothing individual, but alien origin, a quality which he has, or could have, in common with many other strangers. For this reason strangers are not really perceived as individuals, but strangers of a *certain type*. Their remoteness is no less general than their nearness.[41]

This is the predicament of liberalism (and much else) in the context of the empire. The unity based on what is common does not dissolve the barrier of strangeness but merely articulates a starting position in which each views the other as embodying the abstraction of a *certain type*.[42] Familiarity and understanding, and toleration—to the extent that

41. Georg Simmel, "The Stranger," in *On Individuality and Social Forms*, ed. by Donald Levine (Chicago: University of Chicago Press, 1971), 148, emphasis added. See also the chapter in the same volume on "Prostitution," where Simmel comments, "In prostitution, the relations of the sexes is reduced to its generic content because it is perfectly unambiguous and limited to the sensual act. It consists of that which any member of the species can perform and experience. The most diverse personalities can engage in it and all individual difference appear to be of no importance" (121–22). The theme of impersonality and money is a major one in Simmel's *Philosophie des Geldes*.

42. Ironically, as I suggest in the discussion of childhood, liberals did not even treat what was general with adequate seriousness. Even in a thinker of J. S. Mill's depth there is a singular absence of any understanding of the modes of human experience such as fear, desire, a sense of continuity, memory, and spatiality. The result

it turns on familiarity and understanding—result from the consequences of such unavoidable starting positions.[43] And here there are a
number of choices.

One can—as I believe that liberals, such as both the Mills and Macaulay in the nineteenth century typically did—view the stranger
merely as the embodiment of an abstract type that is then judged, re-
formed, and often assessed as moribund in his extant situation; all this,
by reference to another set of abstract ideals of rationality, individuality,
the morally sanguine, the imperatives of politics, and most generally, to
the requirements of progress. Here liberals both drew on and anticipated various archetypical moments of Western thought: the Socratic
injunctions against the unexamined life, the humanism and rationalism
of the Stoic cosmopolitan, the bounded amplitude of Saint Augustine's
caritas, the confident presumptuousness of Descartes's *mathesis univer-
salis*, the artifice that is the basis of political construction in Hobbes, the
jus cosmopoliticum of Kant, the triumphant Reason of Hegel's universal
history, the reasonableness that helps navigate the thicket of Rawls's universe of moral pluralism, the liberation and transparency that follow
from undistorted communications and the triumph of "better arguments" in Habermas. What were however denied or overlooked were
the very things through which the strangers' singularity, individuality,
social and political identity—in a word, their very "modes of experience"—rendered their lives meaningful to themselves.[44]

As I have suggested, for liberals these judgments represented broad
epistemological and normative commitments. With respect to the former, they stemmed from a view regarding what is deemed relevant to
understanding human existence and flourishing. Normatively, they

---

is that the general gets assimilated through the notions of kinship and childhood,
but this in ways that do not allow for the emergence of the integrity of experience,
either broadly human or within life forms.

43. See Tzvetan Todorov, *The Conquest of America* (New York: Colophon–
Harper & Row, 1984), and Anthony Pagden, *European Encounters with the New World*
(New Haven: Yale University Press, 1993), esp. chap. 3.89–115.

44. Here, though more obviously in much of what follows, my views are plainly
influenced by Michael Oakeshott's understanding of experience and the claim that it
is always "arrested" thinking that gives experience its meaning and coherence. See
Michael Oakeshott, *Experience and Its Modes* (London: Cambridge University Press,
1933) and *Rationalism and Politics* (London: Methuen, 1962). See also the extremely
insightful elaboration of Oakeshott's and others' thinking by Richard Flathman. See
Richard E. Flathman, *Willful Liberalism: Voluntarism and Individuality in Political Theory and Practice* (Ithaca, N.Y.: Cornell University Press, 1992), esp. chap. 3; and
Charles Taylor, "The Politics of Recognition," in *Philosophical Arguments*, 225–56.

were anchored in a particular view of political reason, which is shared
by the Enlightenment and whose disposition and self-assurance is antecedent to the encounter with the strange or the stranger. This view of
political reason originates in a deep suspicion of power, taking despotism as its model of such power. Ironically, it concludes in an affirmation
of political power, which on account of the ubiquity of its suspicion
must leave room for itself being at least potentially equal to what it most
suspects. Hence for nineteenth-century liberals such as John Stuart
Mill, the sociological starting position (i.e., relations based on the universal or common) is never left, because that position supports, by being
congruent with, an epistemological and normative point of view, to
which there is a prior commitment, underwritten by the ideal of individual eccentricity and choice, standards of informational relevance specific to the normative perspective, and, for Mill most importantly, by a
specific ideal of human progress.[45]

I do not start from the view that the singularity of experience must
be appreciated and approved in all the richness of its phenomenological
or nested details. Nor do I assert that one must aspire to overcome the
distance that separates us from the unfamiliar in the specific sense of
wanting to establish an identity with it. Such a starting position would
plainly prejudice the case against liberals by not taking seriously, from
the very outset, the cosmopolitanism and distance that they valorize.
There is a distinguished tradition of thinking, of which modern liberalism is only the most recent exemplar, that takes the common, the general, the universal as the very basis of the ethical and political point of
view.[46] I do not dismiss the perspective sub specie aeternitatis on
grounds of the abstraction of its starting position. That would require
relying on no less an abstraction.

Nor, on the other hand, do I dismiss the singularity—that is, the
conditions through which one may understand and experience life—of
the stranger, or the Indian, and demand, or at any rate hope, that it be
understood (or left alone) because of the coherence and meaning it has
on his or her own terms. If this is a naive expectation, that judgment
may itself represent privileging a realism and an account of progress that
the empire, among other aspects of modernity, did so much to bring
about. In any case, if such a demand is made, it may stem from a com-

45. See chapter 5. See also Thomas Nagel, *The View from Nowhere* (New York:
Oxford University Press, 1986); Bernard Williams, *Ethics and the Limits of Philosophy*
(London: Fontana, 1985).
46. See Julia Kristeva, *Strangers to Ourselves*, which discusses Western traditions
of cosmopolitan thinking from their ancient Greek origins to Kant and the Enlightenment.

mitment to, and awareness of, what the stranger is deeply and hence not provisionally *invested* in. This may include religious piety; the parochial insularity of a city-state that is home, without being Periclean or republican; accepting a position (perhaps fatalistically) in an imperfectly mobile and traditional hierarchy; the pains, pleasures, and injustices of a sociability that is perhaps not wholly voluntary and may be substantially prescribed; the possibilities of individuality that may exist only within the bounded spaces of a densely mannered social world; or what Hegel says about finding in the duties of conventional morality the realm of freedom and liberation,[47] without it being underwritten by an abstract amplitude of individual choice, political equality, or democratic rights. The word *parochialism*, like *prejudice*, is just a way to characterize what for other peoples are the conditions of a meaningful life—the modes of experience by which things hang together. This does not inoculate the parochial from the judgments and even intervention of the outside, but it does give the parochial at least a presumptive defense against those judgments and interventions if they claim the authority of some kind of humanism. Here again one encounters humility as a condition of understanding if not of knowledge. In any case, it is through the parochial that most of us experience and live life, and this can be true even if, as self-conscious cosmopolitans, we are increasingly aware of the global influences that enter on our little platoons. If this is true today, it was so much the more true in the nineteenth century, when neither the self-consciousness of being cosmopolitans nor the effects of global influences were as widespread. Our differences are no less real on account of our essences perhaps being the same. And the claim, which today is really a cant, that both differences and essences are "constructed" is not the final word on whether they can in any concrete situation be reconstructed. That issue turns on the available alternatives and on how thick and settled the perhaps once malleable clay has now become.

What Wittgenstein says about the passionate commitment and acceptance that gives coherence to religious life applies more broadly to many forms of life:

> It strikes me that a religious belief could only be something like a passionate commitment to a system of reference. Hence, although it's *belief*, it's really a way of living, or a way of assessing life. It's passionately seizing hold of *this* interpretation. Instruction in religious faith, therefore, would have to take the form of a portrayal, a description of that system of reference,

47. G. W. F. Hegel, *Philosophy of Right*, trans. T. M. Knox (Oxford: Clarendon Press, 1952), sec. 149, p. 107.

while at the same time being an appeal to conscience. And this combination would have to result in the pupil himself, on his own accord, passionately taking hold of the system of reference.[48]

What holds the system of reference together—what makes it an experience—is a *passionate commitment* that cannot be gleaned from the reason or the truth of the beliefs that are a part of it; still less can that commitment be derived from the reason and truth claims that are not part it but are decided in advance of it. If this is the case, and notwithstanding all the ambivalence that it carries for "us"—since now it is passion that becomes a central feature of experience—nevertheless, it may constitute a form of life; in Wittgenstein's sense, it may constitute a different language game. Perhaps that language game, that form of life, is so different that the invocation of *reason* or *progress* as an arbiter between these games can amount to no more than putting a name to our ignorance and relying on the inequality of power, or an established and favorable consensus, to make that name stick.[49]

LIBERAL JUDGMENTS

Ultimately it is the judgments that follow from the understanding of the stranger and the unfamiliar that matter. I have suggested that it is substantially from within the intra-British and occasionally intra-European conversation that the unfamiliarity of India becomes evident and is taken seriously as a normative concern. Macaulay's comment that the British Empire in India was "the strangest of all political anomalies" has its fullest elaboration in London and in the pages of the *Edinburgh*

48. Ludwig Wittgenstein, *Culture and Value*, 64e.

49. "All testing, all confirmation and disconfirmation of a hypothesis takes place already within a system. And this system is not a more or less arbitrary and doubtful point of departure for all our arguments . . . [It is] *the element in which the arguments have their life* [emphasis added]. . . . My *life* consists in my being content to accept many things." Ludwig Wittgenstein, *On Certainty*, ed. G. E. M. Anscombe and G. H. von Wright, trans. Denis Paul and G. E. M. Anscombe (Oxford: Basil Blackwell, 1969), 105, 344.

"What has to be accepted, the given, is—so one could say—forms of life." Wittgenstein, *Philosophical Investigations*, trans. G. E. M. Anscombe (New York: Macmillan, 1953), II, xi, 226.

Obviously in these views Wittgenstein is less an originator and more a brilliant heir to ideas that are present in Edmund Burke, Nietzsche, Freud, and Heidegger, among others.

Review and *Westminster Review*. It is in these discussions that the judgments of liberalism on the unfamiliar are most starkly evident. It is here
that one sees India amplify—though only amplify—the ambiguity of a
dualism that is there in liberalism in any case. Consider the following
words of James Fitzjames Stephen's—that liberal iconoclast who made
a career of bringing out the implicit and uneasy assumptions of his
brethren:

> The first steps in the political education essential to a change
> in the foundations of the British Government cannot be taken
> without incurring the risk of furious civil war. A barrel of gun-
> powder may be harmless or may explode, but you cannot edu-
> cate it into household fuel by exploding little bits of it. How
> can you possibly teach great masses of people that they ought
> to be rather dissatisfied with a foreign ruler, but not much; that
> they should express their discontent in words and in votes, but
> not in acts; that they should ask from him this and that reform
> (which they neither understand nor care for), but should on no
> account rise in insurrection against him.[50]

Stephen's own response to this predicament is to throw up the liberal
game altogether and affirm that the empire is a brute fact whose existence makes it real and that it can survive without the additional warrant
of also being rational, just, or progressive. There is no dilemma for him
in the empire, no challenge of understanding the strange, just the risk
that attends all adventures along with the prescient awareness that adventures come to an end. Stephen's liberalism, such as it is, in fact expresses itself only domestically within Britain. In the context of the empire, it lacks—or rather denies—the crucial element of *patience* that
supports the judgments of liberals in their justification of the empire. It
is not that he is unwilling to wait and "teach great masses of people" but
that he sees that process as a futile journey in which "they" will ultimately ask for more than he is willing to give and then rise in insurrec-
tion. For Stephen the empire originates in the power of conquest, and
it endures on the same grounds, with no additional justification or basis.
One can imagine Stephen—though in fairness to him it should be said
that he does not draw out this implication in his thought—when faced
with an inconveniently strange obstacle to the power that the empire

50. James Fitzjames Stephen, "The Foundations of the Government of India,"
Nineteenth Century 14 (1883): 562–63. Homi Bhabha discusses this and similar pas-
sages in his extremely thoughtful article "Articulating the Archaic," in *The Location of
Culture*, 123–38.

aspires to, calling for the obliteration of that obstacle. Neither assimilation nor understanding are countenanced if they do not fit into the ontology of the requirements of imperial power. Stephen's antiliberalism
in this sense is on a par with the apocryphal story told about the philosopher F. H. Bradley, who upon discovering that cats did not fit into his
ontology went about shooting the ontologically obstreperous felines.

But the more common liberal response, most searchingly elaborated by Stephen's friendly nemesis John Stuart Mill, is to articulate the
modalities of governance that exist *in between* the explosions of gunpow-
der and the rational use of household fuel, in the temporizing between
educating Indians but *not yet* deeming them worthy of autonomy, in the
penumbra between crafting responsible government but *not yet* giving
Indians self-government—in the morally, politically, and rationally justified ambivalence of liberalism for the *time being* remaining imperial.
This project is infinitely patient, perhaps even secretly counting on its
own extended incompetence, of not getting *there* and hence permanently remaining in between.[51] By the nineteenth century virtually every liberal justification of the empire is anchored in the patience needed
to serve and realize a future. And that future is invariably expressed
through the notion of progress. Here proponents of liberalism are
strangely indistinguishable from their evangelical brethren whose *mission* is braced by an eschatological purposefulness that allows it indefi-
nitely to defer the realization of its purpose.[52] Imperial power is simply

51. It is interesting that the idea of the permanence of the British Empire in
India assumes greater tenacity just when the impetus for liberal reforms also takes
hold. This is especially the case after the mutiny of 1857. Of course in that context
the idea of the permanence of the empire was directly linked to the notion that India
did not constitute a nation but rather a "subcontinent." Therefore it could not have
national aspirations and, more importantly, was not destined for the teleology of
self-determined governance. The most perverse extension of this idea was in J. R.
Seeley's *The Expansion of England*, where the permanence of the empire was vouched
for on the grounds that since India did not exist nor did the correlative notion of a
foreigner, "[t]he fundamental fact is that India has no jealousy of the foreigner because India had no sense whatever of national unity, because there *was* no India and
therefore, properly speaking, no foreigner" (164). See also Francis Hutchins, *The
Illusion of Permanence: British Imperialism in India* (Princeton: Princeton University
Press, 1967).

52. Sir Charles Grant wrote:

It is not . . . the introduction of a new set of ceremonies, nor even a new
creed, that is the ultimate object here. Those who conceive religion to be
conversant merely about forms and speculative notions, may well think
that the world need not be much troubled concerning it. No, the ultimate
object is moral improvement. The preeminent excellence of the morality

the instrument required to align a deviant and recalcitrant history with the appropriate future.[53] The empire as liberals imagine it mirrors the archetypical "stranger," as Georg Simmel describes him, who comes from "elsewhere" bearing new knowledge and the instruments of progress, and who, as Simmel says, "comes today and stays tomorrow" but always remains from "elsewhere."[54] It is in these sandwiched spaces, extended over long periods of time, that one sees assumptions, again often otherwise unstated, about individual and collective identity, religion and superstition, territoriality and cosmopolitanism, and, most broadly, civilizational progress and its stasis, being brought to the foreground of thought to understand, educate, represent, and rule people on a "rational," even if provisional, basis.

Two other thematic examples give a vivid sense of liberal judgments. They are the pervasive deployment of the metaphor of childhood and the view of Indian religiosity in terms of the category of superstition.

Childhood is a theme that runs through the writings of British liberals on India with unerring constancy. It is the fixed point underlying the various imperial imperatives of education, forms of governance, and the alignment with progress. James Mill's characterization of India as being in the infancy of the "progress of civilization,"[55] Macaulay's characterization of the British, who in the context of the empire must be like fathers who are "just and unjust, moderate and rapacious,"[56] Trevelyan's comment that Indians would "grow to man's estate,"[57] J. S. Mill's view

---

which the Gospels teach, and the superior efficacy of this divine system, taken in all its parts, meliorating the condition of human society, cannot be denied by those who are unwilling to admit its higher claims; and on this ground only, the dissemination of it must be beneficial to mankind. ("Observations on the State of Society among the Asiatic Subjects of Britain, Particularly with Respect to Moral: and on the Means of Improving It," in *Parliamentary Papers*, August 1832, 99)

Charles Grant was arguably the most important and influential evangelical in British India. He was a member of the Clapham Sect and rose to be a member of the board of the East India Company. See Ainslie Embree, *Charles Grant and British Rule in India* (New York: Columbia University Press, 1962).

53. See the thoughtful and provocative essay by Bhikhu Parekh, "Superior People: The Narrowness of Liberalism from Mill to Rawls," *Times Literary Supplement*, 25 February 1994, 11–13.

54. Georg Simmel, *On Individuality and Social Forms*, 147.

55. Mill, *History of British India*, 2:107.

56. T. B. Macaulay, "Warren Hastings," 3:86.

57. C. E. Trevelyan, *On the Education of the People of India* (London, 1838), 187.

of the British as forming a "government of leading strings" that would
help "as a means of gradually training the people to walk alone"[58]: all
are claims that constitute a virtual genre in imperial discourse. They all
coalesce around the same general point: India is a child for which the
empire offers the prospect of legitimate and progressive parentage and
toward which Britain, as a parent, is similarly obligated and competent.
For both the Mills as for Macaulay this point is the basis for the justification of denying democratic rights and representative institutions to
Indians, along with various other imperial interdictions. The idea has a
distinguished pedigree and in the liberal tradition originates in Locke's
characterization of tutelage as a necessary stage through which children
must be trained before they acquire the reason requisite for expressing
contractual consent.[59]

Burke too invokes the metaphor of childhood, but the polarities of
its reference are reversed with him. In Burke's understanding it is the
British emissaries in the empire who are children:

> There is nothing in the boys we send to India worse than in the
> boys who are whipping at school, or that we see trailing a pike
> or bending over a desk at home. But as English youth in India
> drink the intoxicating draught of authority and dominion be-
> fore their heads are able to bear it, and as they are full grown in
> fortune long before they are ripe in principle, neither Nature
> nor reason have any opportunity to exert themselves for rem-
> edy of the excesses of their premature power.[60]

Elsewhere in the same speech Burke characterizes the British as "school
boys without tutors, minors without guardians, the world is let loose
upon them, with all its temptations, and they are let loose upon the
world with all the power that despotism involves."[61] And again, in what
is a brilliant and horrifying image, Burke speaks of the British as "animated with all the avarice of age and all the impetuosity of youth, roll-
[ing] in one after another, wave after wave—and there is nothing before

58. J. S. Mill, *Considerations on Representative Government*, 175–76.
59. See Ashis Nandy's very insightful discussion of various aspects of childhood
in the colonial context. Ashis Nandy, "Reconstructing Childhood: A Critique of the
Ideology of Adulthood," in *Traditions, Tyranny, and Utopias: Essays in the Politics of
Awareness* (Delhi: Oxford University Press, 1987), 56–76. See also Shankar Ramaswami, "Childhood and the Anxiety of Empire" (University of Chicago, unpublished
paper, 1996).
60. Burke, "Fox's India Bill Speech," 5:402–3.
61. Ibid.

the eyes of the natives but an endless, hopeless prospect of new flights of birds of prey and passage, with appetites continually renewing for a food that is continually wasting."[62]

For the Mills and the others I cite, the political and imperial gaze is never really surprised by the stranger, for he or she is always recognized as that familiar, though deformed, double of which liberalism has spoken in the cold and corseted language of kinship, having substantially eviscerated that language from one of sentiments.[63] The child/deviant, whose difference threatens the legitimacy of the father by placing a limit on the reach of his authority by straining his understanding, must therefore be assimilated in a power that "knows" or offers a progressive future in which the ambivalence of "not-being-one-of-us" and being "one-of-us" will assuredly get resolved. And because this resolution occurs in the domain of the family, adjacent to the political sphere, but still free from many of the constraints that internally limit the use of power in that sphere, the instruments that can be used for the reform of the deviant are often harsher and more unrestricted. But if this liberal tradition always recognizes the stranger, through its particular conception of the family—and in doing so formally complies with its commitment to tolerance—it nevertheless never acknowledges the problem of recognition as a problem of understanding per se. The family, or rather the naturalized version of a particular view of the family, as something starkly hierarchical and governed by a paterfamilias whose authority is not quite political but who has the *"power of commanding and chastising"* his children[64] is that essential penumbra on which the pure political thought of liberalism relies. In the empire it becomes the dominant metaphor through which liberals conceive of the imperatives of politics; ironically this reveals the incomplete nature of liberalism's self-definition, in which it had hoped to articulate a conception of the political by sharply distancing it from the familial and patriarchal politics of Sir Robert Filmer.

62. Ibid.

63. A clear example of this evisceration is Locke's cold and instrumental characterization of the "conjugal society" as one that "is made by voluntary compact between Man and Woman: and tho' it consist chiefly in such a Communion and Right in one another's Bodies, as is necessary to its chief End, Procreation; yet it draws with it mutual support, and assistance, and Communion of Interest too, as necessary not only to unite their Care, and affection, but also necessary to their Common Off-spring, who have a Right to be nourished and maintained by them, till they are able to provide for themselves." *Two Treatises of Government*, ed. Peter Laslett (New York: Mentor Books, 1960), sec. 78, p. 362.

64. Ibid., sec. 67, p. 355.

In Burke the stranger in never a stranger *simpliciter*. But neither is he assimilated as a familiar deviant through a prior commitment to the enunciative space of kinship. What allows Burke provisionally to recognize the stranger is an ontology in which life, at least human life, occurs within the fold of an arch of certain characteristic modes of human experience that involve fear, pain, interiority, desire, and a sense of continuity linking past and future.[65] But this ontology does not settle the issue of recognition; rather it opens it up as a question for the understanding, and one to which Burke's writings on the empire offer a probing, and again provisional, answer. Ultimately for Burke the empire is horrifyingly superficial precisely because it does not take the task of understanding and recognition seriously. It pertains only to the surface of things, much as the acquiring of fortune, and the exercise of raw power, can grip the fantasy of a reckless adolescent. The reference in the above quotation to birds that fly with a frictionless ease has its contrast for Burke with the "ship of state," constrained by the responsibility imposed by a vast and perilous ocean. But beyond that, Burke's point is to make clear that the task of understanding and of exercising power responsibly cannot be based on the presumption of either group's immaturity. In this acknowledgment is the recognition that both groups have systems of reference through which experiences come to have the valency that they do. For Burke "premature power" is a distorting intoxicant because it is based on a prior denial of the real challenges that attend the task of exercising power and of understanding those over whom it is exercised. Power freed from the constraints of understanding is indeed nothing other than unlimited power, and hence leads to tyrannical and exploitative abuse. For Burke, the challenge of the British and the Indians understanding each other is the ongoing work of an adult conversation in which neither is assured of the outcome. In that conversation the role of power must be denied.

As regards superstition, when both the Mills, among many others, consider the problem of crafting political institutions for millions of Indians who in their view were bound to irrational and diverse systems of "superstition," they revealingly analogize the issue again with children in need of parental tutelage and authority and not with the familiar

65. In his ontology Burke both draws on an ancient tradition in which the metaphysics of Christian natural law have a special poignancy and anticipates Heidegger's understanding of the "aroundness of the surrounding world and the spatiality of Da-sein," "Being-With and Being a Self," and "Fear as a Mode of Attunement." See Martin Heidegger, *Being and Time*, trans. Joan Stambaugh (Albany: SUNY Press, 1996).

problem of accommodation to religious diversity through norms of toleration. By the nineteenth century in Britain, liberalism had plainly
worked out a modus vivendi, if not an alliance, with religion, in part
because religion had been obliged to do the same with liberalism, and
because both serviced the ends of patriotic nationalism.[66] The alleged
antagonism of principle of the British monarch being both the head of
the Anglican church and the prime bearer of secular political sovereignty has after all caused no serious discomfort to either church or
state since the late seventeenth century.

In contrast, irrationality, of which Eastern "superstition" was taken
as paradigmatic, still provoked the threatening horror that Locke associated with the madman's ability to be in the world through a completely
alternative set of conventions and cognitive supports.[67] People who literally claimed to "see" and "touch" multiheaded or winged gods single-
handedly moving mountains, by simply casting those conceptions in
clay or bronze and imbuing those "idols" with the status of divinity, had
more than just deformed imaginations or strange beliefs.[68] In fact they
instantiated in concrete and tactile forms an "irrational" worldview and
lived amid its directives and comforts. In the face of this alterity, as in
the case of the defiantly deviant child, who Locke believed could be
dealt with only by the harsh sting of the parental cane, nineteenth-
century liberals advocated rationalizing India, even if that required en-
dorsing an imperial despotism.[69] In this, as in other instances, the argument had an older source, even though it would have been hard to imagine in Locke's friendly letters to Sir Edward Clarke on the education
of his son, which later became *The Thoughts Concerning Education*, or
in Locke's anxious reflections on madness, the kernel of an imperial
agenda—an agenda that spanned over a century and to which virtually
every liberal and evangelical theorist contributed. This agenda—
namely, the proper education of Indians—became almost the central

66. See Linda Colley, *Britons*, 11–54, and Harold Laski, *The Rise of European Liberalism* (London: Unwin Books, 1936).
67. Uday S. Mehta, *The Anxiety of Freedom: Imagination and Individuality in Locke's Political Thought* (Ithaca: Cornell University Press, 1992), chap. 3.
68. Dipesh Chakrabarty, "Radical Histories and the Question of Enlightenment Rationalism: Some Recent Critiques of *Subaltern Studies*," *Economic and Political Weekly* 30, no. 14 (April 1995): 751–59.
69. This thesis is best elaborated by Bhikhu Parekh, "Superior People: The Narrowness of Liberalism from Mill to Rawls," *Times Literary Supplement*, 25 February 1994, 11–13. See also Eric Stokes, *English Utilitarians in India*; Thomas Metcalf, *The New Cambridge History of India*, chap. 2; and Bernard Cohn, *Colonialism and Its Forms of Knowledge* (Princeton: Princeton University Press, 1996), chap. 3.

preoccupation of imperial reform in the nineteenth century.[70] In the empire, the epistemological commitments of liberalism to rationality and the progress that it was deemed to imply constantly trumped its commitments to democracy, consensual government, limitations on the legitimate power of the state, and even toleration. Moreover, it is the epistemological commitments that are symptomatic of a narrowness in which the challenge of understanding an unfamiliar world, with multiple singularities, forms of living and experiencing life, is most starkly betrayed by liberals.

THE SENTIMENTS OF UNDERSTANDING

Liberalism has come to represent, even in its original motivation, political thought that was cosmopolitan in its imagination and potential reach. Whether the phrases that implied this lofty vision, such as "human nature," "natural rights," "*the* state of nature," "*the* foundation of political society," "*the* laws of nature," "*the* body politic," were merely strategic terms of art designed to support a noble patron or humble a monarch or two in a local conflict, in a context where the protocols of political pamphlets and theoretical texts were much the same, is now a mute point.[71] If these were mere local metaphors they are by now literally inscribed with a universalistic referent. The reason for this, in part, is that successive generations of liberal thinkers have endeavored to give more global and concrete expression to this original imaginary, while simultaneously their compatriots—adventurers, traders, evangelicals,

70. There is a vast secondary literature on imperial educational policy and its motives. It is commensurate with the primary attention that this issue received. James Mill, J. S. Mill, Lord Macaulay, Charles E. Trevelyan, and John Strachey all wrote on educational policy in India and for a while in the 1830s Parliament viewed the matter with utmost urgency. Among the more recent secondary works on this issue, Gauri Viswanathan's *Masks of Conquest* details with great subtlety the imperatives underlying the introduction of English literature into the Indian curriculum and persuasively challenges the assumptions and conclusions of Bruce McCully's *English Education and the Origins of Indian Nationalism* (New York: Columbia University Press, 1942), and David Kopf's *British Orientalism and the Origins of the Bengal Renaissance* (Berkeley and Los Angeles: University of California Press, 1969). See also Peter Robb, "British Rule and Indian 'Improvement,'" *Economic Historical Review* 34, no. 4 (1981): 507–23. For a good general overview see Syed Nurullah and J. P. Naik, *A History of Education in India during the British Period*, rev. 2d ed. (Bombay: Macmillan, 1951).

71. Richard Ashcraft, "Locke's State of Nature: Historical Fact or Moral Fiction," *American Political Science Review* 68, no. 3 (1968): 898–914.

generals, and even occasionally the professed liberal theorist himself—
succeeded in marking more and more of the globe in the color associated with the Union Jack. In the empire, one might say, liberalism had
found the concrete place of its dreams. When Locke, in language that
resonated with the Bible and was no doubt intended to carry some of
its fervor, announced "in the beginning all the World was *America*"[72] we
take him to have meant this as an injunction to make the world a more
useful, free, and productive place—presumably both safe for liberalism
and saved by it.

But these universal and cosmopolitan dreams themselves drew, especially in the late eighteenth century, on the experience of a waking
reality that had been parochial and, for the men of letters and ideas,
secure in a broad conformity to accepted and familiar social standards.
In the political realm this meant that, following the union with Scotland
in 1707, issues of boundaries and membership were substantially settled. Notwithstanding the vulnerabilities and exclusion of Jews and
Catholics, even the problem of Dissenters could be addressed by the
manipulation of familiar categories. Adam Smith and David Hume
could presume on *sympathy* as a natural tendency of the human heart
through which we could share in the joys and sorrows of others and
thereby settle moral conflicts—the same faculty that allowed us, in the
aesthetic context of a theater, to rejoice in the success of a hero and
weep with him in his adversity. Through the empire, perhaps more than
through anything else, the settled assurances that braced parochial sensibilities with a cosmopolitan worldview, got loosened and over time
charged with the threatening realization that perhaps their alloy was just
a happenstance of history, which subsequent history might unsettle.
The prosaic, unthreatening, and purely aesthetic associations that, for
example, David Hume, in the mid–eighteenth century, links with the
imagination, the sublime, and the judgments that follow from them, are
about to assume a more dire valency.

> The *imagination* of man is naturally sublime, delighted with
> whatever is remote and extraordinary, running, without con-
> trol, into the most distant parts of space and time in order to
> avoid the object, which custom has rendered too familiar to it.
> A correct *Judgement* observes a contrary method, and avoiding
> all distant and high inquiries, confines itself to common life,

72. Locke, *Two Treatises of Government*, ed. Peter Laslett (New York: Mentor
Books, 1960), sec. 49, p. 343.

and to such subjects as fall under a daily practice and experience; leaving the more sublime topics to the embellishment of
poets and orators, or to the arts of priests and politicians.[73]

Once the empire is no longer merely imagined, and "the most distant parts of space and time" get weighed down with the responsibility,
and through that the proximity, of political governance, conflict, and
disordered resistance, the delightful sublimity of the imagination loses
the assurance of simply being able to withdraw to safer ground. It is
now mixed with a potential horror of the monstrously unfamiliar that
might lurk within the domain of the familiar. And now of course there
is less refuge in "confining" oneself to the "common life" of "daily practices and experiences"—even though Hume and his friend Burke might
still have preferred that—because there was no avoiding "inquiries"
about distant and strange places, fraught as they were with the vexations
of the empire. Under these conditions "correct judgment," because it
turns on a correspondence between the imagination and the sentiments,
must indeed get mediated by an ever growing array of poets, orators,
priests, politicians, and philosophers. Similarly, in the philosophic and
psychological realm, the principles of *Constant Conjunction, Customary
Connexion*, relations of *Resemblance, Contiguity in Time and Place* and a
resulting order in *Cause and Effect* now get associated with an altogether
new and less familiar and secure potential. When contiguity in time and
place are plainly absent—as in the case of India, "premodern" and far
away—and resemblance is confounded, at minimum on grounds of race
and unusual social practices, the result is an uncertainty regarding cause
and effect.

The empire—for the most part, quietly—unsettles the equanimity
of late eighteenth-century Britain. Aesthetic judgments lose the security
of the familiar on account of which they had simultaneously anchored
aesthetic and moral sentiments. Philosophic and psychological doctrines are freighted with the more radical implications of their own
ideas. In the moral and political sphere, "a Polite and Commercial
People" could no longer simply lean on well-mannered *sentiments* to the
disparagement of rational *understanding*, especially now that the latter
took its province to be universal.

The year 1776 embodies, in its several icons, the tensions of the
cusp that Britain was crossing. It is the year in which Adam Smith's
Wealth of Nations is published—that classic text on the efficiency of the

73. Hume, *Essay Concerning Human Understanding*, pt. 3, sec. 12, p. 268.

division of labor and a free market, with an optimistic faith in a secular providence that *invisibly* guides both, if overseen by the benevolent negligence of the state. Here again there is a reliance on the aesthetic category of *sympathy* that, literally by allowing us to perceive and hence *feel*, makes it possible to enter other worlds and by virtue of their neighborly familiarity to negotiate and ameliorate possible conflicts.[74] But that year is also associated with the first major fissure in the empire through the independence of America, and with the invention of James Watt's steam engine. Following nationalism and the emergence of the working class, *sympathy*, as a shared moral ground, anchored as I am suggesting in a shared visual field, can no longer be presumed on, because under these novel conditions it cannot, by itself, do the task on which the presumption of its efficacy all but explicitly rested. The sentiments of the Americans, despite all that they shared with Britain, have become truly independent, and it is difficult to negotiate with independence, however sympathetically understood, once it has taken hold. Another people's independence, as Burke prophetically foresaw, is always the limiting point of our vision—the darkness that reason does not illuminate. Similarly the emerging proletariat would not long allow its fate to rest in the alleged beneficent understanding or views of its employers.

It has been said of Hume's skepticism that it can be thought but not

74. The most common interpretation of Smith's idea of a "free market" contends that it was obviously meant as a model for a global market. Yet there are passages in *The Wealth of Nations* and elsewhere that at least suggest that Smith understood the term *free* as constrained, if not circumscribed, by the realm of the proximate and familiar. On this view, *free* might mean not just free from mercantile barriers but also free from the sort of power that is required to establish links that are not within the realm of the familiar. This is suggested in the following two passages, both of which emphasize the deleterious effects of distance:

I have little anxiety about the [*sic*] what becomes of the American commerce. By an equality of treatment of all nations we must soon open a commerce with the neighbouring nations of Europe, infinitely more advantageous than that so distant country as America. (Letter from Adam Smith to William Eden, 15 December 1783, in *Journal and Correspondence of William, Lord Auckland* [London, 1861])

The real futility of all distant dominions, of which the defence is necessarily most expensive, and which contribute nothing, either by revenue or military forces, to the general defence of the empire, and very little even to their own defence, is, I think, the subject of which the public prejudices of Europe require to be set right." (Adam Smith to Sir John Sinclair, 14 October 1782, published in J. Rae, *Life of Adam Smith* [London, 1895], 382–83)

lived. Hume asserted that reason, though wonderful, is no more than an unintelligible instinct and that, but for the effect of habit, it would lead to perpetual and paralyzing astonishment.[75] By the late eighteenth century it is not clear that skepticism can even be thought precisely because the lived experience of astonishment is increasingly closer at hand.

It is easy to dismiss the professed cosmopolitanism of the tradition that includes Hume, Adam Smith, and Burke as no more than the mask that late eighteenth-century parochial gentility wears and as an imminent set of developments exposed as being historically moribund. It is certainly true that both Hume's and Smith's thought bear the imprint of a security that stems from the knowledge that the religious and political convulsions of the seventeenth century are behind them, along with a blissful ignorance of the industrial and French revolutions that are still just beyond the horizon. Perhaps only in such times of stability can aesthetic categories serve as an anchor for moral, political, and in Smith's case economic judgments.

All this may be true as a statement of the conditions that made this thought possible, without exhausting its enduring and contemporary significance. In fact, it is precisely in this largely eclipsed, non-English liberal tradition that the conceptual bases of appreciating the strange and the unfamiliar are, I think, to be found. Because this tradition has a conception of the parochial and the singular that, on account of being so, are not deemed to be moribund, even though the specific world of eighteenth-century Britain was historically at a point of being overtaken, it has the resources from which to understand other life forms in terms of their singularity. It is in the emphasis that these thinkers placed on sentiments, ways of viewing and feeling, that the potentiality—and in Burke's case, the actuality—of unfamiliar experiences gets recognized as constituting extant forms of life. When Burke, while addressing the House of Commons in the Fox India Bill speech, compares India with the various kingdoms of Europe, he does so because he wants to elicit from his brethren a reaction that "India might be approximated to our understandings, and if possible to our *feelings;* in order to awaken something of sympathy for the unfortunate natives."[76] In the same speech he refers to "the proper language of our sentiments"[77] so that men familiar

75. Elie Halevy, *The Growth of Philosophic Radicalism,* trans. Mary Morris (Boston: Beacon Press, 1960), 10.
76. Burke, "Fox's India Bill Speech," 5:390.
77. Ibid., 404.

only with the committee rooms of the British government might understand the plight of those they govern in the East.

The emphasis Burke places on sentiments and feelings and via them on experience is of course of a piece with his well-known suspicion of abstract forms of reasoning. Indeed his objection to such forms of reasoning is that by diminishing the significance of "circumstances" they glide over the very things that give texture and meaning to human experiences. The weight that Burke places on traditions, habits, and dwellings are all ways of animating what for him are the constituent forms of experience—what Gadamer calls prejudices.

In other words, Burke gives his attention to local conditions—local because they are always bounded and because they supply the conditions for the possibility of experience. Through his attention to the local, Burke is in a position to see the integrity—literally that which holds things together—of lives that perhaps share nothing more than the fact that they are all constituted by the unavoidable engagement with the local. Moreover, he is in a position to see that these conditions do not of necessity stand in need of the mediation that the empire offers and imposes. Nor does the absence of such mediation mire these societies in a parochial intransigence. There are, as Mahatma Gandhi in a different context emphasized, all sorts of links that can be built across prejudices, links for instance of friendship, that do not require that the two sets of prejudices get mediated through a common register that renders those prejudices negotiable interests.[78] Moreover, Burke's cosmopolitanism does not rely on the strategy of aligning societies that are in fact contemporaneous in their affective attachments, along a temporal grid that moves them "backward" on account of their difference, so as to give a linear coherence to the idea of progress. Once one recognizes, as Burke does, that human experience derives its density from the passionate commitment that a life form produces, then the challenge of cosmopolitanism is to understand these forms as contemporaneous ways of being

78. This in brief is Mahatma Gandhi's prescription for the relations between Hindus and Muslims. He emphasizes the link of friendship because it does not require rendering the conditions internal to the lives of these two communities as mere fungible interests that can divided through contractual conditions. See M. K. Gandhi, *Hind Swaraj and Other Writings*, ed. A. Parel (Cambridge: Cambridge University Press, 1997), and Gandhi's essays on the Khilafat movement in *Young India*. In the former work Gandhi makes repeated denunciations of the legal and imperial attempt to negotiate Hindu and Muslim prejudices through "third parties." In the latter writings he speaks of friendship that can "unconditionally" link these two communities in a way that contractual relations could not.

in the world. This is what Richard Rorty eloquently suggests when he writes, "[Our] identification with our community—our society, our political tradition, our intellectual heritage—is heightened when we see this community as *ours* rather than *nature's*, *shaped* rather than *found*, one among many which men have made."[79] If we see in Burke's emphasis on feelings, viewing, and sentiments simply a rejection of reason, we will have missed his point, because he is not wedded to the binary of reason versus something else. His purpose, like that of Hume, is not to abandon reason but to enlarge its ambit, to make it social and more passionate, and more informed by the uncertain vagaries that attend and form experience.[80] Burke's emphasis stems from an attempt to facilitate an openness to the world, to its unavoidable contingencies, surprises, and ambivalences. It also stems from a belief that the world is not patterned in such a way that its emotional resonances, its passionate attachments, can be read off simply by placing a rational and temporally progressive grid on it.

Of course talk of feelings, viewing, and sentiments has its credence ultimately in the narrative that serves as its surrogate. When Burke, with a plaintive insistence, tries to "approximate" for his fellow parliamentarians the "feelings" of the "unfortunate natives," he is left with nothing more than the power of his narrative—a narrative that can never be unequivocal in its meaning and certainly not in its emotive impact. But Burke is not burdened by the priority of logic over rhetoric. He knows that in the challenge of facilitating what amounts to a conversation across boundaries of strangeness there is no short cut around the messiness of communication, no immanent truth on which words can fix, no easy glossaries of translation; instead, there is only the richness or paucity of the vocabularies we use to describe ourselves and those we are trying to understand. The space defined by Burke's voluminous narratives on the empire is therefore never precise in the sense of being tethered to a reality whose contours and destiny are understood as already programmed, decoded and known in advance. Despite the eloquence and rhetorical force of his words and the stakes he attaches to the debates in which he is involved, there is always something provisional in his narratives. He expects to be surprised and to be puzzled. But precisely because of the provisional nature of this conversation he is more

79. Richard Rorty, *Consequences of Pragmatism* (Minneapolis: University of Minnesota Press, 1982), 166.
80. Regarding Hume see the superb account by Annette C. Baier in *A Progress of Sentiments* (Cambridge: Harvard University Press, 1991).

deeply committed to the ethical and political choices that arise from such a contingent encounter.

For the same reason, it is important to recognize that Burke's reliance and emphasis on the visual is starkly at odds with the Platonic and epistemological tradition that has sought in that capacity, or metaphor, a privileged and direct access in terms of representing the world. When Burke speaks of the visual it is not as a procedure that helps us to tick things off on account of a prior link that associates perception with mapping or correspondence or the picturing of reality. Burke's use and understanding of the visual comes from eighteenth-century poetics and not from the more familiar epistemological tradition. In that aesthetic tradition the visual belongs to the art of conversation, to a form of deliberation in which the boundaries of what can be articulated are never firmly established prior to the conversation and in which the conversation continually modifies those boundaries. The conversation is indeed a medium of communication in which new and unfamiliar information gets transmitted. But beyond that, and more importantly, it is a space in which there is a constant and unsuppressible negotiation of the boundaries of the selves who are party to, and literally participate in, the conversation. In this medium there can be no prior assimilation of the participants into the language of membership or kinship, and hence no prior designation of subordinates or children. Burke prefigures what Richard Rorty associates with his capacious version of the pragmatist tradition: "[I]t is the doctrine that there are no constraints on inquiry save conversational ones—no wholesale constraints derived from the nature of the objects, or of the mind, or of language, but only those retail constraints provided by the remarks of our fellow inquirers."[81] In this tradition sight and the visual hark back to a conception of *phronesis* and not *theoria*.

There is, as I have suggested, a cosmopolitanism in this other liberal tradition because it holds out the possibility, and only the possibility, that through the understanding of what gives experiences their meaning *two* strangers may come to converse with each other, perhaps befriend each other, perhaps disagree with each other, along with the myriad other eventualities that structure where a conversation may lead and end up. The task of understanding through conversation is—to borrow a term Charles Sabel uses in a different context but that captures many of the intonations of a hermeneutic aesthetics—really a *craft* for which no

81. Rorty, *Consequences of Pragmatism*, 165.

algorithm can be offered in advance of the activity.[82] In that conversation, that encounter, it is Burke's purpose that power would be denied space—in particular, the space to infantilize an interlocutor even before knowing him or her, simply on account of the confidence one has in the claims of one's own knowledge. Nowhere, perhaps, is this possibility more evocatively suggested than in Hume's famous description of the philosopher, himself, at the conclusion of book 1 of the *Treatise:*

> I am first affrighted and confounded with that forlorn solitude, in which I am plac'd in my philosophy, and fancy myself some strange uncouth monster, who not being able to mingle and unite in society, has been expell'd all human commerce, and left utterly abandon'd and disconsolate. . . . When I look abroad, I foresee on every side, dispute, contradiction, anger, calumny and detraction. When I turn my eye inward, I find nothing but doubt and ignorance. . . . Every step I take is with hesitation, and every new reflection makes me dread an error and absurdity in my reasoning.[83]

Hume's solitude is not like Descartes's, that fleeting instance before all the metaphysical certainties come flooding back in with added fervor. Instead Hume's philosophic journey, full of trepidation and an awareness of uncertain shoals, always occurs in a vessel of questionable seaworthiness. When the self-image of the philosopher is that of a strange uncouth monster, the philosopher's reasons can assure nothing in advance of the encounter with the opinions and feelings of other strangers. Whatever common ground emerges from such encounters is the contingent product of the play and stretch of sentiments and the imagination. The protagonist of the journey Hume is on acknowledges that what he has in common with those he meets is a background of shared infirmities—"those numberless infirmities peculiar to myself."[84] Under these conditions, and with Hume's skeptical humility in mind, reason alone cannot determine the outcome of such encounters because it cannot, will not, offer progress, or civilization, or even democracy, as necessary benefits of that engagement with the stranger. Hume's liberalism, like that of Burke, remains wedded to the contingency, the experimentalism, the hermeneutics, of a moral aesthetic, and through it, to sentiments and feelings and a more real conception of human experience.

82. Charles Sabel, *Work and Politics* (Cambridge: Cambridge University Press, 1982), 78–126.
83. Hume, *A Treatise of Human Nature*, 264–65.
84. Ibid., 265.

This point is especially significant today because the world we live in is substantially molded by the triumph of a liberalism with its rationalistic certainties. Moreover, that liberalism remains the dominant framework from within which we imagine modifications on this world. Francis Fukuyama's prophecy regarding the "end of history" and the triumph and "universalization of Western liberal democracy as the final form of human government" may be unhelpful and complacent exaggerations that neither give us a rich picture of what is to come nor gainfully enhance understanding to guide us to that future.[85] But at one level they are simply exaggerations and not errors because they merely, and not very helpfully, describe a world that already exists and whose foreseeable transformations can only be variations on what exists. It is true that everyone, including those who perpetrate mass murders in the Balkans and central Africa, speaks of rights and pays a callow obeisance to democratic talk and the laws of international justice. In this not altogether insignificant or especially interesting sense, liberalism rules the roost. On the other hand, perhaps we are at the end of an idea and cannot see beyond the corner where a new road begins. If this is the case, our abiding commitment to liberalism may just be the particular form that our lack of imagination takes—and for which self-congratulation seems like an inappropriate reaction. Nevertheless, in most respects and for the time being at least, political creativity comes from within the broad constellation of liberal thought; but precisely for that reason liberal judgment and its mode of understanding the unfamiliar matter— and now perhaps with even greater urgency than before its putative triumph.

85. Francis Fukuyama, "The End of History?" *National Interest*, summer 1989, 3–18.

————◄ T W O ►————

Strategies: Liberal Conventions and Imperial Exclusions

Pure insight, however, is in the first instance without any content; it is the
sheer disappearance of content; but by its negative attitude towards what
it excludes it will make itself real and give itself a content.

HEGEL, *Phenomenology of Mind*

In its theoretical vision, liberalism, from the seventeenth century to the
present, has prided itself on its universality and politically inclusionary
character. And yet, when viewed as a historical phenomenon, the period
of liberal history is unmistakably marked by the systematic and sustained political exclusion of various groups and "types" of people. The
universality of freedom and derivative political institutions identified
with the provenance of liberalism is denied in the protracted history
with which liberalism is similarly linked. Perhaps liberal theory and liberal history are ships passing in the night, spurred on by unrelated
imperatives and destinations. Perhaps reality—and, as such, history—
always betrays the pristine motives of theory. Putting aside such
possibilities, something about the inclusionary pretensions of liberal
theory and the exclusionary effects of liberal practices needs to be explained.

One needs to account for how a set of ideas that professed, at a
fundamental level, to include as its political referent a universal constituency nevertheless spawned practices that were either predicated on or
directed at the political marginalization of various people. More specifically, one must consider whether the exclusionary thrust of liberal
history stems from the misapprehension of the generative basis of liberal universalism or whether, in contrast, liberal history projects with
greater focus and onto a larger canvas the theoretically veiled and qualified truth of liberal universalism. Despite the enormous contrariety between the profession of political universality and the history of political

46

exclusion, the latter may in fact elaborate the truth and ambivalence of the former.

In considering these issues, I am responding to two distinct, though closely related, questions. First, can one, within the universalistic theoretical framework of liberalism, identify a politically exclusionary impulse,[1] and if so, by what means is this effected? Second, does the work of theorists such as both the Mills evince a similar exlusionary impulse with specific reference to the articulation of colonial exclusions? It is by virtue of this latter question that I hope to suggest a way of linking the reading of liberal texts and the interpretation of liberal practices.

The argument of this chapter involves three related claims. The first concerns the articulation of liberal foundational and institutional principles to make clear the basis of liberal universalism. My purpose here is obviously not to present liberal foundations in all their complexity but rather to suggest the anthropological capacities that are allegedly the basis of liberal universalism. This first claim is substantiated by reference to Locke's *Second Treatise of Government*. The second claim is motivated by the concern with exclusion—that is to say, with how liberal principles, with their attending universal constituency, get undermined in such a manner so as politically to disenfranchise various people. The strategies involved in effecting this closure are crucial to the general argument being made. With Locke this involves the subtle invoking of politically exclusionary social conventions and manners. This is the first strategy I consider. It is the political role played by these exclusionary conventions that is ultimately most crucial in understanding the strategies by which universalistic theories such as Locke's issue in or at least allow for exclusionary practices. My point here, and throughout this chapter, is to underscore the exclusionary effect of the distinction between anthropological capacities and the necessary conditions for their political actualization. Third and finally, I shift my attention to nineteenth-century India to consider once again the strategies through which utilitarianism effected and sustained politically exclusionary practices. Here, in contrast to Locke, exclusion assumes a defiantly self-confident and explicit form. It is defended by reference to the "mani-

1. The use of attitudinal terms such as *impulse* with reference to liberalism is not meant to imply an exclusionary *intention* on the part of the theorists I discuss. Since this chapter considers exclusion from the vantage point of the foundational commitments of liberalism, I do not deny that such intentions may in fact have existed. The argument I am making is simply indifferent to the issue of authorial intent.

fest" political incompetence of those to be excluded and justified by a plethora of anthropological descriptions that serve to buttress the claim of incompetence. With reference to this latter focus on the nineteenth century, I consider exclusionary strategies that involve (1) inscrutability and (2) civilizational infantilism.[2]

Because this chapter claims that liberalism has been exclusionary, and that in this it manifests an aspect of its theoretical underpinnings and not merely an episodic compromise with the practical constraints of implementation, it is important to dispel some possible misapprehensions. I am not suggesting that liberalism's doctrinal commitment to freedom is merely a ruse. Nor am I denying that, from its inception, it has sought to limit the ambit of political authority by anchoring it in constitutional principles, in the process articulating a framework of rights that the state is not entitled to invade. My argument does not rest on the assumption of or encourage the denial of the liberal commitment to respect the claims of conscience and tolerate the voices of dissension. Similarly, in emphasizing its exclusionary character, I am not muffling its favorable disposition to representation, universal suffrage, or claims of self-determination, including those of minority groups. To deny these credentials as fundamental to liberalism, one would have to take a stand that is markedly at odds with common usage.[3]

And yet the exclusionary basis of liberalism does, I believe, derive from its theoretical core, and the litany of exclusionary historical instances is an elaboration of this core. It is so not because the ideals are theoretically disingenuous or concretely impractical,[4] but rather be-

2. In the course of moving from Locke to the nineteenth century, my focus shifts to theorists who are commonly identified as utilitarians. It may therefore be objected that the comparative argument I am making is vitiated by the obvious and important theoretical contrasts between Lockean liberalism and nineteenth-century utilitarianism. The force of this objection is considerable; indeed, it cannot be fully answered within the constraints of this chapter. Nevertheless, with respect to the issues being addressed here—namely the anthropological basis of universalistic claims—it will, I hope become evident that the two theoretical visions share important and relevant similarities.

3. To my knowledge, the best overview of the historical associations of liberalism is still Harold Laski's brief but remarkable *The Rise of European Liberalism*.

4. My point is not to deny the significance of practicality. Indeed, a strong claim can probably be made for the "practical obstacles" that would have attended extending the franchise to women and the propertyless in the seventeenth century or to colonial subjects in the eighteenth and nineteenth centuries. My point, in contrast (although not in necessary contradiction), is to suggest how, irrespective of such constraints, one can identify political exclusion by focusing exclusively on the relevant theoretical imperatives.

cause behind the capacities ascribed to all human beings exists a thicker set of social credentials that constitute the real bases of political inclusion. The universalistic reach of liberalism derives from the capacities that it identifies with human nature and from the presumption, which it encourages, that these capacities are sufficient and not merely necessary for an individual's political inclusion. It encourages this presumption by giving a specifically political significance to human *nature*. With all people being born equal, free, and rational, birth—notwithstanding its various uncertain potentialities—becomes the moment of an assured political identity. That long tutelage through which Plato's guardians acquired their political spurs, and the revolutions through which, in Tocqueville's words, nations and individuals "became equal" is, in Locke's ostensible vision, compressed into the moment of our birth. However, concealed behind the endorsement of these universal capacities are the specific cultural and psychological conditions that are woven in as preconditions for the actualization of these capacities. Liberal exclusion works by modulating the distance between the interstices of human capacities and the conditions for their political effectivity. It is the content between these interstices that settles boundaries between who is included and who is not. Ironically, culture, in the broadest sense, gets mobilized to compensate for the deficiencies of birth—deficiencies whose very existence allows for the qualification of the inclusionary vision associated with the naturalistic assumptions.

This formulation is meant, in part, to explain the use of the term *strategies* in the title of this chapter. Liberal exclusion is neither a theoretically dictated necessity nor a mere occasional happenstance of purely contingent significance. The distinction between universal capacities and the conditions for their actualization points to a space in which the liberal theorist can, as it were, raise the ante for political inclusion.[5] To the extent that such a distinction can be identified within the work of a particular theorist or, more broadly, within liberalism, it points to a theoretical space from within which liberal exclusion can be viewed as intrinsic to liberalism and in which exclusionary strategies become endemic. The distinction becomes, in effect, a gatekeeper to

5. This is not a claim regarding the range of motives that could be at work here. They could, as in the case of Locke, include a commitment to a class-based view of the optimal social order, or, as in the case of a host of colonial administrators, to the view that the exigencies of governing large and distant colonies did not permit of broad representative institutions. On this latter point, see W. H. Morley, *The Administration of Justice in British India* (London, 1858); George Otto Trevelyan, *The Competition Wallah* (London, 1864).

the particular form that liberal society takes, and as such, allows for the incorporation of a variety of strategic considerations. The considerations may amount to no more than having "a sense of justice" or being "reasonable," as with Rawls.[6] In contrast, they may require the significantly more exclusive benefits of a nineteenth-century middle-class European mindset, as with John Stuart Mill. The details structure the outcome without of necessity violating the presumed inclusionary vision.[7]

The significance of strategies can be further elaborated by contrasting it with the common exclusionary bases of eighteenth-and nineteenth-century conservative thought. For Edmund Burke, the most influential critic of liberal universalism or "abstract principles," exclusion is registered in the necessary partiality of inheritance—"it has been the uniform policy of our constitution to claim and assert our liberties, as an *entailed inheritance* derived to us from our forefathers, and to be transmitted to our posterity."[8] The idea of a shared and exclusive inheritance, which in the hands of a Disraeli becomes the grounds of an explicit preference for the "Rights of Englishmen" over the "rights of man" and through various interpretive perversions comes to support nineteenth- and twentieth-century polygenics, circumvents the need for strategic exclusion.[9] For both Locke and Burke, birth has a special political significance. For the former, birth signals the universal potentialities requisite for consensual political society; for the latter, it designates the unique and specific tracks of a historical alignment. For Burke, exclusions define the norm; for Locke, a limiting point whose status

6. John Rawls, "Kantian Constructivism in Moral Theory," *Journal of Philosophy* 77 (1980): 525–28.

7. The distinction between universal capacities and the restrictive conditions for their actualization broadly corresponds to the distinction Robert Dahl makes between *categorical* and *contingent* principles in his very clear and thoughtful "Procedural Democracy" in *Democracy, Liberty, and Equality* (Denmark: Norwegian University Press, 1986), 210.

8. Edmund Burke, *Reflections on the French Revolution* (New York: Dutton, 1971), 3. For a characteristically insightful reflection on the political significance of birth, see Sheldon Wolin's "Contract and Birthright," *Political Theory* 14, no. 2 (1986): 179–95; also Anne Norton's *Reflections on Political Identity* (Baltimore: Johns Hopkins University Press, 1988), pt. 1.

9. Benjamin Disraeli, *Lord George Bentinck: A Political Biography* (London, 1852), 184; A. Carthill, *The Last Dominion* (London, 1924). With particular reference to the significance of polygenics in America, see R. Horsman's *Race and Manifest Destiny* (Cambridge: Harvard University Press, 1981), 132–60. See also Hannah Arendt, *The Origins of Totalitarianism* (New York: Meridian, 1966), 58–222.

requires special, even if veiled, theoretical intensity.[10] By way of contrast with both Locke and Burke, for Filmer birth designates a literal, precise and inescapable source of all obligations, including political obligations.[11]

LIBERAL UNIVERSALISM

Liberal theoretical claims typically tend to be transhistorical, transcultural, and most certainly transracial. The declared and ostensible referent of liberal principles is quite literally a constituency with no delimiting boundary: that of all humankind. The political rights that it articulates and defends, the institutions such as laws, representation, contract all have their justification in a characterization of human beings that eschews names, social status, ethnic background, gender, and race.

In the mere fact of its universality, liberalism is not unique. Indeed, the quest for universal principles and cognate institutions attends political philosophy from its Greek inception.[12] But whereas Plato grounds

10. Burke's deep doubts regarding the effect on Britain of including India within Britain's colonial domain remained acute even after he was reconciled to this fact. It is this concern that resurfaced with unmistakable sincerity and regularity in his long dispute with Warren Hastings. See Edmund Burke, *Works* (London, 1877), vol. 7.

11. The idea of birth as a significant political marker is an ancient one and has a rich lineage. Among the ancient Greeks, the Visigoths, and the Romans, birth, along with place of birth, was a precise political credential. Similarly, in the Islamic tradition, it designated a specific political status. For instance, within some classificatory systems, slaves were defined as those not born of Muslim parentage and/or within a Muslim community. Regarding the Hindu classificatory system of caste, Louis Dumont makes the claim that caste "hierarchy in India certainly involves gradation, but is neither power nor authority" (p. 65). This would suggest that the caste system, while being replete with social gradations, is indifferent to the relative political standing of different castes. Nevertheless, Dumont acknowledges that the caste system specifies precise privileges, many of which must be taken as politically significant. Thus, for instance, Dumont makes clear that "the learned Brahman (*srotriya*) is in theory exempt from taxes, and the Brahman is especially favored by the law about lost objects." Louis Dumont, *Homo Hierarchicus*, trans. Mark Sainsbury (Chicago: University of Chicago Press, 1970), 69–70. I am grateful to Jane Mansbridge and Joshua Cohen for drawing my attention to some of these additional examples regarding the political significance of birth.

12. See, among others, Charles Taylor's *Sources of the Self* (Cambridge: Harvard University Press, 1989), chaps. 1, 5, 6. See also A. H. Adkins, *From the Many to the One* (Ithaca: Cornell University Press, 1970).

universal claims in a transcendent ontology, liberal universalism stems from almost the opposite, what one might call a philosophical anthropology.[13] What I mean by this is that the universal claims can be made because they derive from certain characteristics that are common to all human beings. Central among these anthropological characteristics or foundations for liberal theory are the claims that everyone is naturally free, that they are, in the relevant moral respects, equal, and finally that they are rational. One might therefore say that the starting point for the political and institutional prescriptions of liberal theory is an anthropological minimum, or an anthropological common denominator. Precisely because it is a minimum, and therefore common to all, the normative claims that derive from this minimum are common to all and therefore universally applicable.[14] It is to these common anthropological characteristics that Locke draws our attention at the outset of the state of nature chapter in the *Second Treatise:*

> To understand political power right, and derive it from its Original, we must consider what State *all* Men are naturally in, and that is, a *State of perfect Freedom* to order their Actions, and dispose of their Possessions, and Persons as they think fit, within the bounds of the Law of Nature, without asking leave, or depending upon the Will of any other Man.[15]

13. Throughout this chapter, I use the term *anthropology* in its almost literal sense of referring to the study of human beings. This does not of necessity mean that my usage is in contrast with the more common disciplinary designation, although the associations triggered by the term *anthropology* as a discipline may be quite different.

14. Here it is worth pointing out that the liberal theorist in the broad structure of his or her theoretical enterprise works in a way quite akin to the modern doctor. Presumably, it is by virtue of an understanding of the minimally constitutive features of the human body that the doctor can make prescriptions for people of widely differing social, racial, economic, etc., backgrounds. The image of the political theorist as the medic of the polity was one that Descartes, Hobbes, and Locke quite self-consciously endorsed. See Owsei Temkin's *The Double Face of Janus and Other Essays in the History of Medicine* (Baltimore: Johns Hopkins University Press, 1977); Kenneth Dewhurst's *John Locke (1632–1704) Physician and Philosopher* (London: Wellcome Historical Medical Library, 1963); Patrick Romanell's *John Locke and Medicine: A New Key to Locke* (Buffalo: Prometheus Books, 1984); and more recently, Richard Nelson's "Liberalism, Republicanism and the Politics of Therapy: John Locke's Legacy of Medicine and Reform," *Review of Politics* 51, no. 1 (winter 1989): 68–89.

15. John Locke, *Two Treatises of Government*, 2d ed., ed. P. Laslett (Cambridge: Cambridge University Press, 1967), 2:4.

In this and in the following paragraph, Locke articulates the view that human beings are by their nature free, equal, and rational. It is this view of the individual that becomes the basis of Locke's justly famous opposition to political absolutism and the basis for his endorsement of the sovereignty of the people and limitations on the authority of government. Freedom, equality, and rationality evince what I earlier called an anthropological minimum. As natural attributes, they attend human beings irrespective of conventional norms. As Locke puts it further along in the same paragraph:

> [T]here being nothing more evident, than that Creatures of the same species and rank promiscuously born to all the same advantages of Nature, and the use of the same faculties, should also be equal one amongst another without Subordination or Subjection."[16]

Locke's point, here and elsewhere, is not that human beings are devoid of all natural obligations but rather that these obligations do not include natural *political* obligations. Similarly, the view of natural equality is meant only to establish our moral equality with respect to natural rights and not to deny various social and economic inequalities whose existence he explicitly acknowledges.[17] With respect to political authority, the mere fact of our birth gives to all of us equally the natural right to freedom. The political centrality of birth—and with it the attending identity of our faculties—underscores the informational paucity of Lockean foundations. It eschews, at this foundational level, any reference to a sociological description of individuals. And similarly, in contrast to Filmer, it does not privilege any spatial or temporal context.

Locke's characterization of natural freedom is remarkable not merely for the universal constituency that it champions but also for the explicitly dramatic and expansive elaboration that he gives to it. Not only are we told that *all* men are, by their natures, *perfectly free;* this condition itself allows us to give to our *persons,* our *possessions,* and even to our *actions* strikingly extreme expressions. It is this individual who becomes the subject of the contractual agreement from which liberal institutions derive. Locke's elaboration of the natural condition provokes an obvious question: what ensures that this condition of perfect freedom will not issue in a state of license and anarchical libertinage?

16. Ibid.
17. Ibid., 54.

Put differently, and only for illustrative purposes, How do the *Two Treatises*, with such unrestrained foundations, fortify themselves from being usurped by a variety of theorists who are commonly considered as anathemas to liberalism, including not merely anarchists but also, for instance, the infamous French profligate the Marquis de Sade?

To this query, the obvious and immediate answer would be that the interpretation of the passage I have offered overlooks a crucial, even if textually brief, qualification.[18] That is, I have overlooked the point where Locke, having opened up the expansive possibilities that issue from *perfect freedom*, immediately restricts them with the claim that they must remain "within the bounds of the Law of Nature." The qualification is indeed crucial, not merely because its exclusion is likely from an anarchist's perspective but also because natural laws play an ostensibly critical role in Locke's political thought. As fundamental moral principles, legislated for individuals and societies by God, natural laws are meant as preconventional limits on human actions. For Locke, they designate the plethora of obligations to which we are committed despite the fact of our natural freedom.

Natural laws may sufficiently distinguish the foundational claims Locke is making from those of an anarchist. Nevertheless, since access to these laws is, by Locke, emphasized as being through natural human reason, they do not severely qualify the image of the individual I have presented. That is to say, the moral boundaries that natural laws set upon the potential liberality of human action are themselves presented as part of the natural endowments of human beings.[19] Further along in this chapter, I will suggest how the access to natural law, which Locke in the *Two Treatises* presents as stemming from reason, in fact requires a highly conventionalistic regime of instruction and social manipulations. Such a conventionalistic molding vitiates the naturalistic and universalistic moral limits that natural law is meant to designate. Aside from natural law, the anarchist challenge would most commonly be rebutted by pointing to the distinctly liberal institutions such as contract, rule of law, and representation that Locke endorses. Since all of these institutions are grounded in consent, it might furthermore be argued that they, no less than the expansive possibilities of freedom, are the distinctive features of liberalism. This claim is, I think, true, but only as true as any

18. In ibid., 6, Locke entertains precisely this question by considering the distinction between the state of freedom and that of license. The distinction for him turns on the limits in the former set by natural law, also identified as "the Law of Reason."

19. Ibid., 16, 57.

claim that treats what is really only a hope as a given fact. For although liberal institutions no doubt limit and give to the expressions of human freedom a measure of order, they are themselves never secure from the threat posed by the possibility that their authorizing consent will be withdrawn by anyone who thinks that the order is no longer just and therefore no longer binding. Given that it is natural for the Lockean individual to externalize his or her desires without depending on the will of any other person and, furthermore, given that we know from the *Essay Concerning Human Understanding* that this individual has no innate moral principles impressed upon his or her nature, and finally, again from the *Essay*, given that this individual, at a cognitive level, freely associates and these associations can and do display a striking inconstancy, it can only be hoped that the particular manifestation that individuals give to their freedom will find in contract, representation, etc., an efficacious and adequately disciplined self-expression.[20]

My point is that Locke's minimalist anthropology, which serves as the foundation for his institutional claims, is indeed universalistic, but in this it also exposes the vulnerability of the institutions it is meant to support. The potentialities of the Lockean individual reside as a constant internal threat to the regularities requisite for Lockean institutions. John Dunn has rightly emphasized that the principal problem of Locke's politics was that of creating and ensuring a constancy and moderation in the expressions of desire of the citizens of his commonwealth.[21] It is in recognizing this and the centrality of its significance that one begins to appreciate the way in which Locke's texts, despite their foundational universality, have an effectively exclusionary thrust. It must be emphasized that this problem cannot be sufficiently assuaged at the foundational or anthropological level precisely because it is from this level that the inconstancy and extremity of desire derive their disturbing legitimacy.

Before considering the way in which Locke addresses this issue, it is worth distinguishing my own approach and emphasis to it from two

20. John Locke, *Essay Concerning Human Understanding*, ed. P. H. Nidditch (Oxford: Clarendon Press, 1975), bk. 1, chaps. 2–4: "Principles of action indeed there are lodged in men's appetite, but these are so far from being innate moral principles, that if they were left to their full swing, they would carry Men to the overturning of all Morality": bk. 2, chap. 23, p. 75.

21. John Dunn, "The Concept of 'Trust' in the Politics of John Locke," in *Philosophy in History*, ed. R. Rorty, J. B. Schneewind, and Q. Skinner (Cambridge: Cambridge University Press, 1984), 279–301; see also Dunn, "Trust and Political Agency," in the very thoughtful volume *Trust: Making and Breaking Cooperative Relations*, ed. Diego Gambetta (Oxford: Basil Blackwell, 1990), 73–94.

interpretations that arrive at similar conclusions. C. B. Macpherson in
his justly famous *The Political Theory of Possessive Individualism* articulates
what remains a provocative interpretation of Locke, among other theorists. Macpherson, in considering the issue of political exclusion, claims
that Locke "justifies, as natural, a class differential in rights and in rationality, and by doing so provides a moral basis for capitalist society."[22]
In Macpherson's view, Locke's political and economic partiality plainly
commits him to a theoretical inconsistency. On the one hand, according
to Macpherson, Locke appears to endorse universal rationality and,
with it, supports a crucial condition for the possibility of universal political rights. On the other hand, Macpherson alleges that Locke in fact
associates the difference between the propertyless and the propertied
with a natural difference in their rationalities, and thus justifies the political exclusion of the former. Locke's exclusions stem from this inconsistent commitment. While the broad strokes of this interpretation and
the ingenuity with which it is presented are striking, the claim of differential rationality is, at best, weakly defended and its textual support un-
persuasive.[23]

More recently, Carol Pateman has argued that Locke's naturalistic
and uncritical conception of the "conjugal bond" serves effectively to
eliminate women from Locke's understanding of the term "individual."[24] Despite this, she acknowledges that Locke, both in his polemic
against Filmer and at various points in the *Second Treatise*, sharply distinguishes the power of a husband from that of a political ruler. It remains

22. C. B. Macpherson, *The Political Theory of Possessive Individualism: Hobbes to
Locke* (Oxford: Oxford University Press, 1962), 221.

23. See Joshua Cohen, "Structure, Choice and Legitimacy: Locke's Theory of
the State," *Philosophy and Public Affairs* 15 (1986): 301–24.

24. Carol Pateman, *The Sexual Contract* (Stanford: Stanford University Press,
1988), 52–55.

During the past two decades at least, a number of feminist scholars, including
Pateman, have addressed the problem of political exclusion by critically unpacking
the exclusionary implications underlying the liberal distinction between the public
sphere of political and commercial concerns and the private sphere of domestic life.
Clearly, judging from the range of methodological and normative positions from
which this distinction has been interrogated, it is a rich nexus for considering the
question of political exclusion. See, for example, Susan M. Okin, *Justice, Gender and
the Family* (New York: Basic Books, 1989), chap. 6; Pateman, *The Sexual Contract*,
chap. 4; Martha Minow, "We the Family: Constitutional Rights and American Families," *American Journal of History* 74, no. 3 (1987): 175–210. My own somewhat or-
thogonal though by no means contradictory approach is partially motivated by a
primary concern with colonial exclusions that do not usually turn on the public/
private distinction.

somewhat unclear in Pateman's analysis if the alleged exclusion from the category of "individual" trumps the possibility of being a citizen and, as such, excludes women through a disingenuous textual feint.[25] This possibility is made less likely by the fact that conjugal relationships are never presented as necessary to the designation of citizenship.

For both Macpherson and Pateman, the clue to understanding political exclusion in Locke, indeed the keystone that gives his argument a dubious coherence, is an implicit historical assumption—an assumption to which Locke's texts point through a revealing silence.[26] This is not to suggest that either one of these authors is methodologically committed to a notion in which, at some fundamental level, the boundaries between texts and contexts are irrepressibly porous. That is to say, their conclusions are not driven by methodological presumptions regarding the status of texts. Clearly, the understanding of texts may, on occasion, require them to be supplemented by historical considerations. My own divergence from Macpherson and Pateman on this general point is that, with regard to the issue of exclusion in Locke, one needs no such extra-textual supplementing.

In contrast, my focus draws on some familiar insights from the sociological tradition to elaborate how Locke presumes on a complex constellation of social structures and social conventions to delimit, stabilize, and legitimize, without explicitly restricting, the universal referent of his foundational commitments. The exclusionary transformation of Locke's universalistic anthropology is effected by the implicit divisions and exclusions of the social world that Locke imagines. Sociologists since Durkheim have pointed to how the differentiations of a given society condition both its own reproduction and its various internal

25. Pateman, *The Sexual Contract*. Compare the remark "Women are excluded from the status of 'individual' in the natural condition" (p. 52) with "The subjection of women (wives) to men (husbands) is not an example of political domination and subordination" (p. 53).

Mary Katzenstein has rightly pointed out to me that the argument being made in this chapter is, in a general sense, akin to Pateman's historically anchored position. Both Pateman and I are pointing to the undermining of the presumed universality of Lockean principles (Pateman's argument, of course, extends beyond Locke). Her argument focuses on Locke's implicit reliance on the historical inequality between men and women, an inequality that is embodied in the traditional understanding of the conjugal bond. My own approach is, in this sense, more textual because it locates the undermining of principles in the textually evident reliance on social credentials.

26. Macpherson is, of course, explicit in his reference to the centrality of hidden historical premises for understanding the tradition of possessive individualism. See Macpherson, *The Political Theory of Possessive Individualism*, chap. 1.

boundaries. The reliance on the semicodified social, linguistic, spatial, etc., oppositions of a society decisively reinforce what Durkheim called "logical conformity" by organizing the perception of the social world.[27] Classificatory schemes based on these implicit markings suggest, without explicitly stating, a sense of limits. These limits are inscribed in the dense minutiae of social and cultural descriptions. Their elucidation turns on the perspective of an insider buffeted by particular circumstances. As Burke suggested, "Circumstances (which with some gentlemen pass for nothing) give in reality to every political principle its distinguishing color and discriminating effect."[28] They also, I am suggesting, configure the boundary between the politically included and those politically excluded.

The efficacy of these structures and conventions in moderating the potentially exorbitant and unlimitable claims of an individual who is naturally free is proportional to the degree to which these structures and conventions are taken for granted. Their effectivity derives from a tacit allegiance to a particular ordering of society and through this to a particular set of distinctions that the society incorporates. Social structures and conventions function below the threshold of consciousness and theoretical discourse. As Pierre Bourdieu has suggested "a 'sense of one's place' . . . leads one to exclude oneself from the goods, persons, places and so forth from which one is excluded."[29] Unlike universal anthropological injunctions, conventions and manners are the product of numberless long-forgotten choices that anonymously buffer an individual's act of self-expression. Their anonymity stems, in part, from their embodying the collective sediment of a specific people, a religion, or a family. Conventions and manners are not, and seldom claim to be, universal.[30]

27. E. Durkheim, *The Elementary Forms of Religious Life* (London: Allen and Unwin, 1915), 17.

28. Burke, *Reflections*, 6.

29. Pierre Bourdieu, *Distinction: A Social Critique of the Judgement of Taste*, trans. Richard Nice (Cambridge: Harvard University Press, 1984), 471.

30. In concentrating on the link between political exclusion and social structures and conventions, I am obviously drawing on a rich and predominantly sociological tradition of scholarship. Because these works seldom refer to Locke and the British Utilitarian tradition, and because they do not focus on political exclusion, their importance to this chapter is not adequately acknowledged. I list some of them here to make this acknowledgment explicit: Durkheim, *The Elementary Forms of Religious Life*; Norbert Elias, *The Court Society* (New York: Pantheon, 1983), and *The History of Manners* (Oxford: Basil Blackwell, 1978); Pierre Bourdieu, *Distinction: A Social Critique of the Judgement of Taste*, and *Outline of a Theory of Practice* (Cambridge:

Locke was piercingly aware of the centrality of conventions in his own thought even though, for reasons I have indicated, he seldom fully admits this. He comes closest in the dedicatory epistle to his *Thoughts Concerning Education*,[31] where, after stating that it is a work "fit" and "suited to our English gentry," he explicitly links the education of children with "the welfare and prosperity of the nation." It is, he goes on, a work that will produce "virtuous, useful, and able men in their distinct calling" though most crucially it is designed for a "gentleman's calling."[32]

In the context of studying exclusion there is an obvious reason for focusing on Locke's views on children and relatedly on his Thoughts Concerning Education. Along with "lunaticks" and "ideots," children are explicitly and unambiguously excluded from the consensual politics of the *Second Treatise*.[33] The status of the former two groups—although fascinating for various reasons and one that sustained, with increasing emphasis, Locke's interest throughout his life—is not directly relevant to the issue at hand.[34] In contrast, the exclusion of children—notwithstanding its presumed self-evidence—draws on a central argument of the Second Treatise. Stated simply, the argument involves consent as a fundamental ground for the legitimacy of political authority. For Locke, consent requires, inter alia, acting in view of certain constraints that can broadly be designated by the laws of nature. To know these laws requires reason.[35] Those who are unable to exercise reason either permanently (e.g., madmen and idiots) or temporarily (i.e., children) do not meet a necessary requisite for the expression of consent. By implication, therefore, they can be excluded from the political constituency or, what amounts to the same thing, they can be governed without their consent.

Cambridge University Press, 1977); Stuart Hampshire, "Morality and Convention," in *Morality and Conflict* (Cambridge: Harvard University Press, 1983).

31. John Locke, *Thoughts Concerning Education* (London: Spottiswoode, 1880).

32. Ibid., 56–57.

33. Locke, *Second Treatise*, sec. 60.

34. Locke's concern with madness and its ambivalent relationship to sobriety has been almost wholly overlooked by political commentators. This omission belies the frequency with which Locke returns to this issue, and the political significance he gives it. For instance, the famous chapter "Of the Association of Ideas," which Locke appended to the fourth edition of the *Essay*, is replete with politically charged suggestions regarding the troubling ubiquity of madness and its common root with reason. For an interesting discussion of some of the questions bearing on Locke's views on madness, see Ricardo Quintana's *Two Augustans* (Madison: University of Wisconsin Press, 1978).

35. Locke, *Second Treatise*, secs. 57, 59.

What the argument makes clear is that political inclusion is contingent upon a qualified capacity to reason.[36] Clearly, the precise effect of this claim turns on what, in Locke's view, is involved in developing these requisite capacities, credentials, and associations to be able to reason. The *Thoughts Concerning Education* are Locke's most elaborate response to this crucial issue.[37]

It is impossible to summarize the *Thoughts*. In fact, it is almost as difficult to pick out a few salient themes from the work. This lack of thematic and argumentary order is, however, revealing of Locke's conception of education and, more specifically, of what is involved in learning to reason. The *Thoughts* are replete with the most specific and precise details and instructions. The work reads like a manual, with all the attending minutiae. It ranges over a concern with toilet training, the imprudence of wearing tight-fitting bodices, the appropriate foods to be consumed at breakfast, the importance of knowing how to dance, fence, and ride, the appropriate comportment toward servants and oth-

36. Dahl, *Democracy, Liberty, and Equality*, 208.
37. Apart from reason, there is of course, according to Locke, one other crucial means of access to natural laws—namely, the revealed scriptures of the New Testament. At various points, Locke refers to *reason* and *revelation* as the sources through which the precepts of these laws are comprehended. *Second Treatise*, secs. 6, 25, 56, 57; *The Reasonableness of Christianity*, ed. I. T. Ramsey (Stanford: Stanford University Press, 1989), secs. 231, 239, 242. The precise relationship between reason and revelation and natural laws is a complex one in Locke, as it is in the long history of natural law theorizing. For instance, it is not entirely clear whether Locke views revelation as a means to natural law or whether he also identifies it with the content of these laws. Hence, despite his attempt to offer a rationalistic account of New Testament Christianity—which is designed to suggest its consistency with aspects of pre-Christian and post-Christian ethics—in section 243 of *Reasonableness*, the understanding of the laws of nature is tied to the "knowledge and acknowledgement" of "our Saviour." Similarly, even though Locke presents faith in revelation as a more economical and broad-based venue to natural law by claiming that it obviates the need to carry out "a train of proofs" and "coherent deductions from the first principle" (sec. 243), he also denies that such laws could have been comprehended before "our Saviour's birth."
Clearly Locke places great stock in the significance of faith in revelation. As he says: "[T]he greatest part cannot know and therefore they must believe" (ibid.). My reason for focusing on reason rather than revelation is motivated by the concern with Locke's alleged universalism. To the extent that his argument is universalistic, he is committed to drawing on reason rather than revelation. The reason for this is that despite his attempts to incorporate Confucianism, Islam, Judaism, and other non-Christian ethical systems, the criterion for their exclusion remains particularistic, precisely because it is tied to the extent to which these systems comport with the narrow and doctrinally exclusionary precepts of New Testament Christianity.

ers of "lower rank," and the importance of being able to feign humility, anger, and concern.

The list could easily be extended. But even without that, what is surely remarkable about such a bizarre and contextually detailed index is that it is, on the face of it, presented in support of a capacity that Locke acknowledges to be universal and natural: the capacity to reason. Even on a cursory review, this work suspends the very anthropological guarantees one would have expected Locke, given the claims of the *Treatises*, to have taken for granted. Thus, for instance, Locke puts virtually no stock in the fact that human reason gives us a preconventional access to the precepts of natural law. Instead, the emphasis is wholly on the precise and detailed processes through which this rationality must get inculcated. The purpose of education, as Locke states, is to "[weave] habits into the very principles" of a child's nature, even if the only means to ensure this result involves instilling "fear and awe," including that special fear of a father "who may perhaps disinherit" a child.[38] Similarly, where the contractual logic of the *Treatises* is allegedly driven by the rationality of abstract individuals concerned with enhancing their self-interest, in the *Thoughts* Locke plainly states that "the principle of all virtue and excellency lies in the power of denying ourselves the satisfaction of our desires ... and this power is to be got and improved by custom, made easy and familiar by an early practice."[39] Where in the *Treatises*, Locke, with repeated emphasis, reminds Filmer and his readers that the Fifth Commandment refers to both Adam and Eve, in the *Thoughts* he speaks of the importance of "establish[ing] the Authority of a father."[40]

In the specific context of how to teach children "Reasoning," Locke concentrates, at enormous length, on the importance of the choice of an appropriate tutor or governor. Such a governor, he makes clear, is not to be had at "ordinary Rates."[41] Notwithstanding the considerable expense, when such a governor is found, this is how Locke characterizes his brief toward his pupil:

> To form a young Gentleman, as he should be, 'tis fit his *Governor* should himself be well-bred, understand the Ways of Carriage, and Measures of Civility in all the Variety of Persons,

38. Locke, *Thoughts Concerning Education*, 109.
39. Ibid., 103.
40. Quoted from Nathan Tarcov, *Locke's Education for Liberty* (Chicago: University of Chicago Press, 1984), 94.
41. Locke, *Thoughts Concerning Education*, 94.

> Times and Places; and keep his Pupil, as much as his age re-
> quires, constantly to the Observation of them. This is an Art
> not to be learnt, nor taught by books. Nothing can give it but
> good Company, and the Observation joyn'd together. . . .
> Breeding is that, which sets a Gloss upon all his other good
> qualities, and renders them useful to him, in procuring him the
> Esteem and Good Will of all that comes near.[42]

Breeding, which for Locke is clearly the most salient feature of education, requires an assimilation of the observed social distinctions of society. It cannot be taught through books, and it has no substitute in the
thorough knowledge of Latin, Greek, and metaphysics. It is acquired
simply through an immersion in "good Company" and a recognition of
the "Measures of Civility" that structure such company. Further along
in the same section, Locke emphasizes the need to be "shocked by
some, and caressed by others; warn'd who are like to oppose, who to
mislead, who to undermine him, and who to serve him." In language
that revealingly mirrors the terms used to describe laws in the *Second
Treatise*, these social distinctions are presented as "the only fence against
the World."[43] From even the most casual reading of the *Thoughts*, one
sees that education and, more specifically, reasoning involve understanding a world replete with social and hierarchical distinctions is unmistakable. Far from giving expression to capacities that are universal
because they presume on so little, education is an initiation into the
enormously significant specifications of time, place, and social status.
Locke is explicit in the narrow referent of his own work. In the conclud-
ing paragraph of *Thoughts* he states: "I think a Prince, a Nobleman and
an ordinary Gentleman's son, should have different ways of breeding."[44]

The role of conventions is not restricted to the *Thoughts*, even
though it is in that work that one gets a relatively unguarded glimpse
into their significance. In the *Second Treatise*, for example, Locke, after
repeatedly making the claim in the chapter on paternal power that although a child be naturally free, he only becomes really free when he
understands the laws of England, and that, we are told, happens at the
age of twenty-one. This is also the age when the young adult learns, as
Locke says, "discretion."[45] There is reason to believe that Locke meant
the use of this term in its precise etymological sense, namely the age at

42. Ibid.
43. Ibid.
44. Ibid., 217.
45. Locke, *Second Treatise*, sec. 59.

which one learns to make *distinctions*—distinctions that are invisible in the universal claims. Similarly, in the same chapter, Locke explicitly tells us that inheritance commits one to honor the conventions and conditions under which property was originally acquired. As he says, property is a "strong tie on a man's obedience."[46]

Finally, consider another example from the *Thoughts* that is significant because of its reference to the love of mastery, which according to Locke comes "almost as soon as [we] are born":

> I have told you before that Children love Liberty; and therefore they should be brought to do the things that are fit for them, without feeling any restraint laid upon them. Now I tell you, they love something more; and that is Dominion: And this is the first Original of most vicious habits, that are ordinary and natural.[47]

This love of power, Locke continues, takes two forms: an imperiousness toward others and a desire to have objects for themselves. Furthermore, it is these two forms that are the "roots of almost all the injustice and contention that so disturb human life."[48] The desire for mastery over others requires, for its modification, good manners and an appropriate set of attending feelings. Thus children must be accustomed from an early age to a careful deportment in "language . . . towards their inferiors and the meaner sort of people, particularly servants."[49] The child's "superiority" is to be erased by a feigned denial so as to make "Human Nature" appear equal. The vindication of a sense of our common humanity is thus to be meticulously cultivated in a child by a process that also reinforces the gentleman's scion's notion of superiority.

Terms such as "English gentry," "breeding," "gentleman," "honor," "discretion," "inheritance," and "servant" derive their meaning and significance from a specific set of cultural norms. They refer to a constellation of social practices, riddled with a hierarchical and exclusionary density. They draw on and encourage conceptions of human beings that are far from abstract and universal, and in which the anthropological minimum is buried under a thick set of social inscriptions and signals. They chart a terrain full of social credentials. It is a terrain that the natural individual, equipped with universal capacities, must negotiate before these capacities assume the form necessary for political inclu-

46. Ibid., sec. 73.
47. Locke, *Thoughts Concerning Education*, 102.
48. Ibid.
49. Ibid.

sion. In this, they circumscribe and order the particular form that the universalistic foundations of Lockean liberalism assume. It is a form that can and historically has left an exclusionary imprint in the concrete instantiation of liberal practices.

COLONIAL EXCLUSIONS

In shifting my attention to nineteenth-century India, I must make clear that my purpose is not to chronicle the litany of colonial achievements or injustices. Nor is it to assess the considerable impact that British liberal and utilitarian ideas had on virtually every aspect of public life in India. This shift is spurred by the narrower concern with trying to understand how universalistic doctrines sustained a status quo of unmistakable political exclusion. Given this concern, India's credentials as the site for this exploration are anything but unique. Clearly exclusion occurred elsewhere, and could therefore be studied elsewhere. But if India's credentials for this exploration are not unique, its convenience is perhaps unusual.

It is of course well known that India was of crucial significance to the economic and political ambitions of imperial Britain. It retained this status even after it ceased to be a clear economic asset, as was the case during much of the latter half of the nineteenth century. If for no other reason, its very size gave it the distinction of being the largest "jewel in the crown." What is, however, often overlooked is that behind the exotic paraphernalia of empire and power, India played a sustained and extensive role in the theoretical imagination and exertion of most nineteenth-century British political thinkers. Almost without exception, all the important British political theorists from the late eighteenth century into the twentieth century dealt in extensive and focused manner with India. Edmund Burke's writings on India exceed by a very considerable margin his written attention on any other issue.[50] Although James Mill never visited India—a fact that in his view rendered his understanding of it scientific—he wrote a monumental six-volume history of India. He also worked for several years as the chief examiner of Indian dispatches in the East India Company in London. This was a job that his son held for thirty-five years. Similarly, Bentham not only wrote, with characteristic detail, on issues of legislative design regarding India, but along with

50. To my knowledge the best account of Burke's historical and theoretical involvement with India is Isaac Kramnick, *The Rage of Edmund Burke: Portrait of an Ambivalent Conservative* (New York: Basic Books, 1977), esp. chap. 7.

James Mill, he was the principal architect of the British-Indian judicial and penal systems. Lord Macaulay decisively recast the direction of Indian education, a fact that in Winston Churchill's view lay at the root of the proliferation of Indian nationalist leaders a century later. The list could be extended to include Sir Charles Grant, the Trevelyans, Thomas Carlyle, Walter Bagehot, and, in the twentieth century, the Fabians, Keynes, and of course George Orwell.

However, if the engagement with India was an active and biographically rich one, theoretically it was also a marginal one. The status of India oscillates between being outside the direct purview of the British imagination and being at its very center. Macaulay, for example, looked upon India as "the strangest of all political anomalies" while James Mill, despite years of association, thought of it as "no more than a mere accessory" to British commercial and legal concerns.[51] For J. S. Mill, India was visibly outside the domain of his work on *Representative Government* and *On Liberty*, to which I will return. Ironically, it is this very status of being betwixt and between the liberal and utilitarian imaginations that gives India the attributes of a laboratory from which to view the exertions of theoretical claims that were ostensibly universal.

Because my concern here is with the mediating strategies through which these universalistic doctrines issued in exclusionary practices, I will not address the broad framework either of utilitarianism or of nineteenth-century British liberalism. Instead, to highlight these strategies, the focus will be almost episodical, that is, on the theoretical maneuvers and descriptions by which India was barred from the very institutions that these doctrines professed. The central institution, in this context, is obviously that of representative government.

The nineteenth century brought a significant change in the foundational commitments of the theories being considered. The anthropological minimalism so conspicuous in Locke is, at best, dimly visible on the surface of nineteenth-century utilitarian theorists. Even in a theorist like Bentham, with his fixed conception of human nature, considerations of context and nationality are manifest and evident in the very title of his work, *Essay on the Influence of Time and Place in Matters of Legislation*. With the possible exception of James Mill, no theorist of this period evinces the unbridled theoretical neglect of historical and sociological details of Hobbes or Locke.[52] In John Stuart Mill, such consider-

---

51. Quoted in Stokes, *English Utilitarians in India*, xi.

52. It is on the lack of historical specificity in James Mill's *Essay on Government* that Macaulay focused in his famous and influential review of that work. Mill's universalistic commitment to representative democracy was grounded in the validity of

ations become the basis of a focused and sustained theoretical attention.[53]

The presence of and the theoretical role played by contextual and sociological details raises the important question of what constitutes the precise basis of nineteenth-century universalism. In the case of J. S. Mill, for example, it might be suggested that his attention to matters of civilizational development, his theory of character development (ethology), his explicit commitment to competence criteria, and, more generally, his avowed indebtedness to the "Germano-Coleridgian doctrine" combine to vitiate any pretense to universalism. On this basis, one might argue that liberals such as Mill stand outside the domain that defines the questions pursued in this chapter. The force of this suggestion cannot be fully addressed in this context, because it requires, in part, delineating the theoretical motivations underlying these considerations. If, for instance, these contextual considerations could be identified as modifying responses to the issue of political universalism, then far from being outside, they would instead be central to the claims of this chapter. If instead such considerations are constitutive to the theoretical agenda, then clearly they limit the relevance of my argument.[54] Notwithstanding the importance of these alternatives, in the present context, there is, I believe, evidence of a substantially independent universalistic conception, to which I will return, underlying the liberal view of human beings in *Utilitarianism* and *On Liberty*.

Descriptions are seldom neutral. They affect moral and political

a purely psychological deduction. And it is on this deduction that Macaulay centered his rebuke. The importance of this review and critique can be seen in the enormous influence it had on J. S. Mill: "In politics, . . . I had no longer accepted the doctrine of the *Essay on Government* as a scientific theory, . . . I ceased to consider representative democracy as an absolute principle, and regarded it as a *question of time, place and circumstance*." John Stuart Mill, *Autobiography* (New York: Columbia University Press, 1924), 120; emphasis added.

53. In fact, to the extent that such considerations derive from Coleridge and Wordsworth, they are also linked to Mill's mental recovery. J. S. Mill, *Autobiography*, 110; J. S. Mill, "Coleridge," in *Collected Works*, ed. J. M. Robson (Toronto: University of Toronto Press, 1969), 10:119–63. For a detailed account that weaves together the personal and theoretical significance of Mill's "adjustments," see Robert Denoon Cumming, *Human Nature and History* (Chicago: University of Chicago Press, 1969), 1:6–75, 2:275–307.

54. There is, of course, a complex web of methodological considerations in making a distinction between what is constitutive to a theory and what is merely a modified part of it. Without getting into these considerations, this chapter's section on "Liberal Universalism" represents, at least, one instance where such a distinction is evinced as carrying credibility.

sensibilities, and therefore carry, even when intended innocently, a normative valency.[55] This is particularly true in the context of liberalism, because in presuming on so little—what I have called the anthropological minimum—it professes to accept so much. The putative perimeter of its sympathies is marked by the expansive range of the differences that it tolerates. The limiting point of this perimeter is a form of alterity beyond which differences can no longer be accommodated. The alterity can take many forms. Consider the inaugural statement in James Mill's preface to his work on British India:

> In the course of reading and investigation, necessary for acquiring that measure of knowledge which I was anxious to possess, respecting my country, its people, its government, its interests, its policy, and its laws, I was met, and in some degree surprised, by extraordinary difficulties when I arrived at that part of my inquiries which related to India. On other subjects, of any magnitude and importance, I generally found, that there was some one book, or small number of books, containing the material part of the requisite information; and in which direction was commonly embedded in a large mass of what was trifling and insignificant; and of a body of statements given indiscriminately as matters of fact, ascertained by the senses, the far greater part was in general only matter of opinion, borrowed, in succession, by one set of Indian gentlemen from another.[56]

Mill, by his own admission, is studying and investigating his own country, where usually one book suffices to master subjects of any magnitude. The study of Britain, of its people, its government, its interests, and its laws leads Mill, without discontinuity, to the study of India. But here India's "exceeding difference" sets in and confounds Mill's scholarly ease and equanimity. India casts a dark epistemological shadow in which access is uncertain and, in any case, of apocryphal value. It subverts the otherwise solid distinctions between matters of fact and opinions, between the useful and the insignificant, and between the senses and reason.

The first couple of sentences of Mill's preface perform the double maneuver of the total inclusion of India as part of the study of Britain

55. For a very thoughtful and synthetic essay that deals, among other things, with the political effects of the "starting points" from which differences are described, see Martha Minow, "Justice Engendered," *Harvard Law Review* 101 (November 1987): 10–96.

56. James Mill, *The History of British India*, 1:xv.

and of the simultaneous sequestration of it by a description that renders it all but inscrutable. The themes of inclusion and inscrutability mark strategies to which colonial discourse returns with unfailing regularity. Later in the same preface, Mill variously characterizes India as "impenetrable," "a chaotic mass" resistant to "all logical inquiry," and as a sight where perceptual experience survives at the total expense of reflective judgment. India's exceeding difference does not occasion the need for an engagement with this alterity, for a dialogic encounter between Mill's initial perspective and an alternative self-understanding that confronts him. Rather, it serves to confirm Mill's perspective, and indeed to expand its reach by placing the onus of elucidation on the very point of view from which India appears dense and impenetrable. India's status as an integral part of Britain's political ambit remains thoroughly unquestioned and yet, as a part, it is insistently characterized by its inscrutable and chaotic intransigence.

The significance of designating something as inscrutable can be illustrated by the distinction between something that resists comprehension and something that is inscrutable. The former description permits of a future change in which the object may, finally, become comprehensible. It also places the onus on the comprehending subject and not on the studied object. It suggests a limitation on our knowledge without predicating this on the essentiality of the object. In contrast, inscrutability designates an unfathomable limit to the object of inquiry without implicating either the process of inquiry or the inquirer. It is quite literally a description in which the object is made to appear, as it were, on its own reckoning as something that defies description and, hence, reception. Furthermore, inscrutability clearly places a limit on political possibilities by closing off the prospect that the object satisfies the however minimal conditions requisite for political inclusion. It renders mute the issue of whether this object can satisfy the condition of having reason for Locke, or reasonableness for Rawls. Indeed, drawing on the connection that Hobbes suggests between the capacity to give authority to one's acts and the capacity to be "impersonated" and represented, one might suggest that those who are inscrutable correspond to those inanimate objects that Hobbes claims must be represented precisely because they cannot give authority on their own behalf.[57] Mill's opening sentence, therefore, not only designates India's inert insufficiency but, as part of the study of Britain, also designates Britain as the political compensator for this insufficiency. The textual simultaneity of these two

57. Thomas Hobbes, *Leviathan* (New York: Viking Penguin, 1968), 217–22.

claims recapitulates their political simultaneity in the practice of colonialism.

In the voluminous history of British writings on India, particularly in those that focus on the characters of Indians, the themes of opacity, mystery, and unfathomable inscrutability abound. Lord Macaulay's famous view, expressed early in the nineteenth century, of the Indian as "an enigma of mysterious origin and constitution" had a wide and popular currency. Even that great logician of human character, Sherlock Holmes, is humbled in the presence of "the second floor inhabit[ant] . . . Daulat Ras, the Indian. He is a quiet, inscrutable fellow; as most of those Indians are. He is well up in his work, though his Greek is his weak subject. He is steady and methodical."[58] Clearly, Indian inscrutability trumps the access that could have been gleaned from the presence of those familiar Victorian virtues, the knowledge of Greek and a steady and methodical style. Premodern examples could similarly be added.[59] But this very lack of difference between liberalism and its premodern, nonliberal counterparts in the characterization of differences is revealing. Liberalism's alleged universality is impugned in its descriptive proximity to ideas that claimed no such universality.

If the exclusionary effect of inscrutability is achieved by a crude descriptive fiat in refusing to engage in the particulars of India, the next strategy I will consider represents an almost total reversal. It involves delving into the arcane details of ancient theological, cultural, and historical particulars, and through them, exposing the deficiencies of India's political—although most often psychological—endowments. It presumes on the necessity of a complex set of individual and social indexes as the prerequisite of political inclusion. In this, again, it does not explicitly qualify the universalistic claims; rather, it implicitly raises the ante and thereby the conditions of inclusion. I shall refer to this as the

58. A. C. Doyle, "The Adventure of the Three Students," in *Sherlock Holmes: The Complete Novels and Stories* (New York: Bantam Books, 1986), 1:832.

59. Louis Hartz identifies a similar strategy in the domestic and international limits of American liberalism: "[The American] frame of mind has two axiomatic effects: it hampers creative action abroad by identifying the alien with the unintelligible, and it inspires hysteria at home by generating the anxiety that unintelligible things produce. The red scare, in other words, is not only our domestic problem: it is our international problem as well." Hartz, *The Liberal Tradition in America*, 285.

Inscrutability as a mark of irredeemable alterity is clearly not unique to liberals. Tzevtan Todorov in *The Conquest of America* makes repeated references to Columbus's unfamiliarity with Native Americans as the ground for characterizing them as devoid of distinct norms and languages.

strategy of civilizational infantilism. Despite what might be considered the contradictory emphases of exclusion through inscrutability and exclusion through presumed infantilism, they are often, as in the case of James Mill, deployed in tandem.

In his essay *On Liberty*, J. S. Mill famously defends the principle of liberty as a condition for the mental development of human beings. The application of the principle is limited by three restrictions. First, it applies only to mature adults, although interestingly, like Locke, he allows the law to fix the interpretation of this condition. Second, and for the "same reason" as those required in the first, the principle of liberty has no application to backward societies. And finally, it requires that society not be in a state of war or severe internal turmoil.[60] In elaborating the second restriction, Mill states:

> Liberty, as a principle, has no application to any state of things anterior to the time when mankind have become capable of being improved by free and equal discussion. Until then, there is nothing for them but implicit obedience to an Akbar or a Charlemagne, if they are so fortunate as to find one.[61]

Mill returns to this issue in greater detail in the chapter on "The Government of Dependencies by a Free State" in his work *Representative Government*. The chapter is a striking instance of the embattled commitments of someone who was profoundly invested in liberty and representative government in the face of colonialism. It is also a revealing document on the increasing relevance of cultural, civilizational, linguistic, and racial categories in defining the constituency of Mill's liberalism.

At the outset of the chapter, Mill, having already expressed an indifference to small colonial outposts like Gibraltar and Aden, divides colonized countries into two classes. The first of these classes is composed of countries "of similar civilization to the ruling country; capable of and ripe for representative government: such as the British possessions in America and Australia."[62] The other class includes "others, like India, [that] are still at a great distance from that state."[63] Mill goes on to celebrate England's realization that countries in the first class must be the beneficiaries of "the true principle of government," namely representative government. Indeed, Mill finds the practice of English colonialism toward those who "were of her [England's] own blood and language"

60. J. S. Mill, *On Liberty*, in *Three Essays*, 15–16.
61. Ibid., 16.
62. Mill, *Considerations on Representative Government*, 402.
63. Ibid.

variously "vicious," economically ill-advised, and a betrayal of a "fixed principle . . . professed in theory" regarding free and democratic governance.[64] The populations of these countries are, as he says, ripe and "in a sufficiently advanced state to be fitted for representative government."[65]

Regarding the second class of countries—countries with a population whose civilization, culture, language, and race were different from the British—Mill's attitude is strikingly different and his recommendations correspondingly so. Not only is Mill opposed to dismembering colonialism, he is equally opposed to these countries, being internally democratic. In fact, Mill strongly supports the colonizing country's internal posture within the colony remaining unmistakably authoritarian:

> The ruling country ought to be able to do for its subjects all that could be done by a succession of absolute monarchs, guaranteed by irresistible force against the precariousness of tenure attendant on barbarous despotisms, and qualified by their genius to anticipate all that experience has taught to the more advanced nation.[66]

He goes on: "Such is the ideal rule of a free people over a barbarous or semi-barbarous one."[67] To govern a country with a people different from those of the rulers only allows for "a choice of despotisms";[68] it does not admit of the possibility of democratic representation.

Mill's conclusion is driven by a particular view of India's position in a time line of civilizational and individual development. Reminiscent of Locke's outlook toward children in the *Thoughts*, projected onto a civilizational scale, India is in need of despotism, just as her people are incapable of benefiting from free and equal discussion. The significance of this claim, from the standpoint of this chapter, lies not with its truth or falsity. Similarly, in the present context, the paucity of Mill's evidence in supporting these claims is of little relevance. Instead, their significance derives from the relevance of the anthropological, cultural, psychological, racial, and temporal categories that they evince. It is the sheer descriptive richness that Mill invokes, to justify both his anticolonialism and his colonialism, that is striking and most significant. There is not a hint of any minimalism.

All this might be taken to suggest that Mill lies outside the con-

64. Ibid., 403.
65. Ibid., 408.
66. Ibid., 409.
67. Ibid.
68. Ibid., 410.

straints defined in this chapter. If indeed there is not a hint of minimalism, then, for the reasons I have mentioned earlier, his commitment
to a politically inclusionary universalism would, from the outset, be
qualified in a manner akin to Burke. But such a notion is misguided, for
it overlooks Mill's real anthropological commitments and, in the process, the extent of his break with Bentham. Unlike the latter, Mill does
espouse the "permanent interest of man as a progressive being."[69] Similarly, in defending utilitarianism against the charge that it is a doctrine
fit only for swine, he distinguishes "[h]uman beings [who] have faculties
more elevated than the animal appetites . . . [and who] do not regard
anything as happiness which does not include their gratification."[70]
Again, in contrast with Bentham, for whom each unit of pain should
"count for one and none for more than one," Mill believes that the interests of each should count for one and not more than one.[71] Similarly,
consider the language in which Mill introduces his doctrine of higher-
order pleasures: "Of two pleasures, if there be one to which all or almost
all who have experience of both give a decided preference, irrespective
of any feeling of moral obligations to prefer it, that is the more desirable
pleasure."[72] The distinction between the pleasures turns on the issue of
experience and is thus consistent with Mill's more general commitment
to the notion that people come to recognize that some pleasures are
better than others in the course of their development. Further along, in
the same chapter, when Mill speaks of "a sense of dignity" as the "most
appropriate appellation," it is one that "all human beings possess in one
form or another."[73] Finally, in considering that most critical capacity of
"making a choice," Mill not only identifies it as "a distinctive endow-
ment of a human being" but also links it, again in a manner reminiscent
of Locke, with "the human faculties of perception, judgement, discrimi-
native feeling, mental activity and even moral preference."[74] It is because he holds such a view of human nature and human potentiality that
Mill belongs squarely within the constraints of this chapter.

Mill's exclusion of India and other non-European colonies from

69. Mill, *On Liberty*, 16.
70. Ibid.
71. See Bikhu Parekh, "Bentham's Theory of Equality," *Political Studies* 18
(1970): 478–95. I am thankful to Joshua Cohen and Jane Mansbridge for helping in
clearing up a number of confusions in my earlier discussion of Mill.
72. Mill, *Utilitarianism*, in J. S. Mill and Jeremy Bentham, *Utilitarianism and
Other Essays*, ed. Alan Ryan (London: Penguin, 1987), 211.
73. Ibid., 212.
74. Mill, *On Liberty*, p. 72.

representative institutions is not inconsistent with his ultimate commitments. Despite his break with Bentham, utility remains the unerring ground of Mill's "ultimate appeal." It is this ground that determines the appropriate institutional arrangements for a given situation. And it is by reference to utility that Mill comes to the view that representative institutions are appropriate for Europe and its predominantly white colonies and not for the rest of the world. The bracketing of India, among others, is not therefore the mark of an embarrassing theoretical inconsistency, precisely because at the theoretical level, the commitment to representative institutions is subsequent, and not prevenient, to considerations of utility. My purpose here has been to uncover the specific descriptive grounds through which Mill arrived at the patronizing assessments of civilizational worth that led to India's exclusion.

Where Locke speaks of the identity of our faculties and the commonality of our birth, Mill speaks of the differences of people's cultures, social development, and races. Locke responds to the charge that his state of nature is a historical fiction by referring to "the inconveniences of that condition and the love, and want of Society no sooner brought any number of them [Men] together, but they presently united and incorporated, if they designed to continue together," and that therefore the historical absence of such a state is to be understood by reference to the immediacy of its provenance. Civil government is, as he says, "everywhere antecedent to records."[75] In contrast, Mill makes representative government contingent on a precisely articulated and specific developmental trajectory. Far from being antecedent to records, it requires records of dense and exacting specifications. It should be reemphasized that in making this point, I am not claiming that Mill fully shares the minimalist stipulations of Locke's foundational anthropology, and that therefore the invoking of historical details is somehow in contradiction with Mill's foundational assumptions. My point is simply to highlight the theoretical modifications as a result of which Indians and others get politically excluded.

The theme of the genealogical specifications for representative government is a unifying thread in nineteenth-century British reflections on India. It is evident in the writings of the evangelical tradition, in the work of figures such as Sir Charles Grant, William Wilberforce, and others from the Clapham Sect.[76] It is a conspicuous feature in

75. Locke, *Second Treatise*, sec. 101.
76. Charles Grant, "Observations on the State of Society among the Asiatic Subjects of Britain, Particularly with Respect to Morals: and on the Means of Improving it," in *Parliamentary Papers*, August 1832; W. Wilberforce, *A Practical View of*

Burke's writings on India; indeed, the lack of historical sensitivity is the basis of Burke's most vitriolic objections to Warren Hastings in the course of his celebrated trial.[77] But it is the elder Mill who deploys this theme with the greatest saliency and, it might be added, the greatest antipathy toward Indians. Christopher Hutchins in his book, *The Illusion of Permanence: British Imperialism in India*, indeed argues that the principal substantive motive underlying James Mill's six-volume *History of India* was to provide the historical and developmental case for the permanent subjection of India.[78]

Consider, as a final example of this theme:

> To ascertain the true state of the Hindus in the scale of civilization, is not only an object of curiosity in the history of human nature; but to the people of Great Britain, charged as they are with the government of that great portion of the human species, it is an object of the highest practical importance. No scheme of government can happily conduce to the ends of government, unless it is adapted to the state of the people for whose use it is intended. In those diversities in the state of civilization, which approach the extremes, this truth is universally acknowledged. Should anyone propose, for a band of roving Tartars, the regulations adapted to the happiness of a regular and polished society, he would meet with neglect or derision. The inconveniences are only more concealed, and more or less diminished, when the error elates to states of society which more nearly resemble one another. If the mistake in regard to Hindu society, committed by the British nation, and the British government, be very great; if they have conceived the Hindus to be a people of high civilization, while they have, in reality, made but a few of the earliest steps in the progress to civilization, it is impossible that in many of the measures pursued for the government of that people, the mark aimed at should not have been wrong.[79]

The political exclusion of India is clearly informed by the particulars in which it finds itself embedded. Burke also recognized the great variety

---

the *Prevailing Religious System of Professed Christians* (London: Griffith, Farran, Okeden and Welsh, 1888); J. W. Kaye, *Christianity in India* (London, 1859).

77. Burke, "Speeches on the Impeachment of Warren Hastings," in *Works*, vol. 7.

78. Hutchins, *The Illusion of Permanence: British Imperialism in India*, chaps. 1, 3, 8.

79. Mill, *The History of British India*, 2:107.

and details of India's historical particulars. But for him, this suggested the possibility and likelihood of a similarly different set of destinies. In contrast, James Mill, in speaking the language of civilizational progress, recognizes India's "exceeding difference" only then to husband it within a particular evolutionary path. India's strangeness marks it off from the present, but in the process it gets illuminated by its position on the primitive end of a civilizational schema. Elsewhere Mill, almost to ensure that India not be viewed as an utterly deviant anomaly with a corresponding potentiality, incorporates its present status as part of the prehistory of Britain itself: "The Druids among the ancient Britons . . . possessed many similar privileges and distinctions to those of the Brahmens."[80] Further along he remarks that the written codes of present-day Indians and those of the early Anglo-Saxons are similarly crude.[81]

When viewed from a perspective that includes Locke's anthropological minimalism and both the Mills' detailed essentialistic characterizations of Indians—and particularly Hindus—a revealing duality emerges. In Locke, the grounds on which the inclusionary vision is anchored is the universality of certain purported aspects of our nature. These aspects, by being minimal, extend their reach over a broad, indeed, universal constituency. Ironically, as both the Mills' descriptions make clear, the grounds on which, a century and a half following Locke, people get politically excluded are also aspects of their nature. Human nature, as it were, supports both the inclusionary and the exclusionary vision.

At the outset of this chapter, I referred to two questions that motivated it. The first involved the identification of an exclusionary impulse within the universalistic framework of Lockean liberalism, and the specification of how this impulse gets expressed through the subtle incorporation of exclusionary social conventions. Locke's anthropological minimum is qualified, if not betrayed, by the density of the social norms that are required to support its apparent naturalism. If the education of Rousseau's Emile is an explicit and unmistakable support to the viability of the normative agenda of the *Social Contract*, the *Thoughts Concerning Education* is no less central to the *Two Treatises*. Although, revealingly, in the latter case this centrality is hinted at with elliptical and truncated emphasis.

The second question was to explore the persistence of the exclusionary impulse in nineteenth-century British reflections on India, and through this to suggest the mediating link between the theoretical

80. Ibid., 188.
81. Ibid., 463.

claims and the concrete practices. In the absence of a clear recognition of such mediating links (strategies), the history of liberal theoretical pronouncements and that of liberal practices are liable to pass each other on parallel planes. At a related, although in the present context secondary, level this chapter is meant as a preliminary investigation into the puzzling fact that, in the British case, colonialism was never really justified by a theory commensurate with the political and economic significance of the phenomenon of colonialism. Barring John Stuart Mill, whose theoretical reflections on colonialism are systematic but far from sustained, there is, to my knowledge, no major British theorist in the eighteenth or nineteenth century whose work reflects the obvious cultural and political gravity that colonialism clearly had as a lived phenomenon. The facts of political exclusion—of colonial peoples, of slaves, of women, and of those without sufficient property to exercise either suffrage or real political power—over the past three and a half centuries must be allowed to embarrass the universalistic claims of liberalism.

Finally, and most tentatively, this chapter is meant as a preamble to considering whether the development and consolidation of nineteenth-century social science can be understood as a compensatory response to the anthropological neglect that seventeenth-century Lockean liberalism encouraged. One can imagine that the immediate implications of Locke's anthropological minimalism could have been to devalue and slight the political importance of the study of cultural and historical data. Clearly, by the eighteenth century, this neglect could not be sustained either because the exclusionary exigencies of colonialism required more than mere Lockean conventions or because the experience of colonialism exposed a richer variety of cultural and historical details. It is worth recalling that Haileybury College, where Malthus, Bentham, and so many other pioneers of social science got their start, was explicitly designed to facilitate the understanding and governing of colonial people by the East India Company.[82]

82. There are a number of suggestions on this theme in Arendt's *The Origins of Totalitarianism*. Similarly, Ronald Meek in *Social Science and the Ignoble Savage* (Cambridge: Cambridge University Press, 1976) considers a closely related suggestion focusing on the role of Native Americans in the development of French and British social science.

——◄ T H R E E ►——

Progress, Civilization, and Consent

[A] Greek observing such a culture: he would perceive that for modern man "educated" and "historically educated" seem to belong together as to mean one and the same thing. . . . If he then said that one can be very educated and yet at the same time altogether uneducated historically, modern men would think they had failed to hear him aright and would shake their heads.

FRIEDRICH NIETZSCHE, "On the Uses and Disadvantages of History for Life"

[A] thought must be crude to come into its own in action.

WALTER BENJAMIN, review of *Dreigroschenroman*

History and progress are an unremitting preoccupation of nineteenth-century British liberalism. Yet the political vision that governed that liberalism was, as it were, already firmly universal. Philosophically there is a dilemma here. Either the validity of that political vision could not be swayed by historical considerations or the liberal agenda was in some central way directed at the "reform" and modification of the various histories it encountered, so as to make them conform to that universalistic vision. Because if the particularities and trajectories of the histories and lives to which the empire exposed liberals did not somehow already align themselves with that vision, then either that vision had to be acknowledged as limited in its reach or those recalcitrant and deviant histories had to be realigned to comport with it. Liberals consistently opted for the latter—that is to say, "reform" was indeed central to the liberal agenda and mind-set. To that end they deployed a particular conception of what really constituted history along with a related view of what counted as progress. Moreover, they articulated reasons why such a process of realignment of other extant life forms was consistent with their broader vision. Those reasons and the practices that followed from them make it clear that the commitment to democracy and pluralism were, at best, only provisional motives that allowed—indeed required—enormous temporizing in the face of the "backward" and the unfamiliar.

77

This chapter considers the ideas regarding progress and historical development that inform the broad political structure within which liberals conceived of India in the nineteenth century. Its focus is on James and John Stuart Mill, who successively influenced imperial policy in the two halves of the century. As examiners of Indian dispatches in the East India Company, they were both intimately involved with the minutiae of the government and the company's policies on Indian matters.[1] My focus is less on the policies that they effected and more on how they conceptualized India and its past within the broader terms of their political thought.

As I hope will become clear the conceptualization of India within this framework is itself only an instance of a larger problematic that turns on a commitment to progress. This conceptualization requires an identification of those whose past and present did not align themselves with the expectations of that view of progress,—that is, those who were deemed to be "backward"—and consequently the need and justification of a power to bring about such a progressive alignment.

This is the ambit within which liberal power did, and perhaps must, operate. To call this ambit political is simply to refer to it by the name through which liberalism has chosen to express the imperative nature of its own specific energy. After all, notwithstanding the various specific limitations that are placed on its deployment, ever since Hobbes and Locke the use of political power was conceptually justified the instant it satisfied what were then deemed the directives of progress, namely a concern with the security of corporeal life, the preservation of property, and the maintenance of public order. Whether it be through Locke's understanding of the uses of the "prerogative" or the broad latitude he allows for matters that might involve national security,[2] or simply through a more general Schmittian notion, which liberalism also allows room for, of the sovereign determining the exception, liberals have always associated political power with that capacious imperative for the betterment of life. It is not that this imperative univocally directs liber-

1. The richest account of the policy impact that the Mills had in India, which is also aware of the theoretical position that informed their outlooks, remains, I think, Stokes, *English Utilitarians in India*. The more recent book by Lynn Zastoupil, *John Stuart Mill and India* (Stanford: Stanford University Press, 1994), brings to light some of the vast archival material pertaining to Mill's involvement with India and chronicles the significant changes in Mill's thinking. See also Eileen Sullivan, "Liberalism and Imperialism: John Stuart Mill's Defence of the British Empire," *Journal of the History of Ideas* 44, no. 4 (1983): 599–617.

2. Locke, *Two Treatises of Government*, chaps. 12–16.

alism's programmatic and practical energies. There is after all a tradition of equal longevity and emphasis in which liberals have sought to limit the role of political power from specific issues or "zones," such as the family, religious belief, self-regarding actions, including of course the various specific rights and constitutional protections that liberals have championed as debarred from the interference of the state.

Historically there has been an enduring and pressing tension between these two liberal impulses. The stronger the claims for a particular intervention being progressive, or bettering life, the more it has pressed against the existing norms limiting the use of political power. And in that sense such claims have served to expand, and justify the expansion of, the domain of the political. The important point is that in determining the specific tilt between these two impulses at any given moment the arguments for the betterment of life or progress have always held a strong if not trumping suit.[3] Indeed, the common cant "everything is political," which is not exclusive to liberalism, has served as a powerful engine of progress within the history of liberal practice precisely because the claims of progress have a presumptive appeal on the liberal conception of the political.

I have said in the introduction that the posture of liberal thought toward the world is judgmental. It is a corollary, if not a concrete implication, of this idea that it is also an evangelical posture in which the burning spirit has been that of politics and the eschatology that of progress.[4] What is latent in the liberal conception of the political is a deep impulse to reform the world, and not simply, as is suggested for example by Mill's principle of liberty or the spectrum of rights that are com-

3. While referring to the nineteenth century, Michel Foucault makes the following comment:

> It was life more than the law that became the issue of political struggles, even if the latter were formulated through affirmations concerning rights. The "right" to life, to one's body, to health, to happiness, to the satisfaction of needs, . . . the "right"—which the classical juridical system was utterly incapable of comprehending—was the political response to all these new procedures of power which did not derive, either, from the traditional right of sovereignty. (*History of Sexuality*, vol. 1, *Introduction*, trans. Robert Hurley [New York: Pantheon Books, 1978], 145)

4. This formulation is not meant to glide over the important differences that divide eschatology, or Christian eschatology, from a largely secular conception of progress. The former typically refers to a transcendent and anticipated event breaking into history while the latter is an extrapolation in history of a structure already found in it. See Hans Blumenberg, *The Legitimacy of the Modern Age* (Cambridge: MIT Press, 1983), 27–37.

monly defended, to free individual lives from the unwarranted interference of the world. This view of course diminishes the customary distinction that is drawn between liberalism and other expressions of modern political thought such as Marxism. But here Marxism and liberalism share in a transformative energy and in a view of the world as something malleable through political effort. Their distinctiveness does not vitiate this similarity by virtue of which both are exemplars of a distinctive modern turn of thought.

Given the constitutive nature of this impulse to better the world, there is a necessary tension with other liberal notions such as tolerance, the right to representation, equality, and, crucially for the purposes of this chapter, consent and the sovereignty of the people. In the empire, this latent impulse—this urge to reform and progress—which otherwise so often remains obscured and contested behind a concern with rights and individual freedom, becomes virtually determinative and singular. Here one sees with stark clarity the sense in which the liberal imperialist project was paradigmatically political in the capacious sense, and not as an instance of the various ways that liberals have sought to limit the domain of the political. It has been said of utopian projections that they are attempts to compensate for a deficit of political opportunities so that the imagined becomes a surrogate for what is not immanent.[5] By the mid–nineteenth century, and especially in the context of the empire, this thought assumes a strangely inverted truth such that the utopian comes to be expressed as inexhaustible political opportunity, made possible by a projection on the progressive plane of the future.

The contrast to this perspective, which links the political with the restlessness of progressive activity and where the progressive is itself associated with a broad notion of whatever betters life, is not simply a view that accepts regress, tragedy, evil, or suffering as facts about the world, which it is therefore pointless to try and change. That is to say, the contrast is not simply with the fatalism of Epicurean *ataraxia* (quietude) with its fundamental indifference to the world stemming from the essential inscrutability of its *ratio creandi* (reason for creation). Such a perspective is only one possible contrasting view. But there is at least one other alternative that limits the reach of the political, or, more precisely, is substantially indifferent to the political, but does this by emphasizing the ethical as the more decisive feature of life. But within this perspective there is no a priori limit placed on change nor even the bet-

5. Reinhart Koselleck, *Kritik und Krise: Ein Beitrag zur Pathogenese der burgerlichen Welt* (Freiburg: Karl Alber, 1959), 9.

terment of the world. What is limited is the political as the principal or exclusive instrument to achieve such results. I flag this alternative because, as I hope to make clear at the end of this chapter, it is one that gathers enormous weight, primarily through the influence of Mahatma Gandhi, in dislodging the liberal argument that was grounded on the political conditionalities of historical progress, writ large in terms of civilizational typologies. When Gandhi speaks of progress it is invariably as an ethical relationship that an individual or a community has with itself, with others, and with its deities.[6] Whatever else this does, it cuts through any reliance on history as the register from which alone progress can be read, evaluated, and directed. As an aside it must be pointed out that despite his stature and his influence, Gandhi's voice is the minor key of Indian and most other nationalisms—in part because he was never exclusively or even primarily concerned with nationalism. Nevertheless, it represents a profound and deeply thought response to and critique of the liberal emphasis on history and the primacy of political action, both of which were alloyed in the liberal justification of the empire.

What this chapter seeks to illustrate is the following. For nineteenth-century British liberalism, of which I take J. S. Mill to be the leading exemplar and James Mill a supporting advocate, political institutions such as representative democracy are dependent on societies having reached a particular historical maturation or level of civilization. But such maturation, according to the historiography that the Mills establish and subscribe to, is differentially achieved. That is to say, progress in history itself occurs differentially. Hence, those societies in which the higher accomplishments of civilization have not occurred plainly do not satisfy the conditions for representative government. Under such conditions liberalism in the form of the empire services the deficiencies of the past for societies that have been stunted through history.

This in brief is the liberal justification of the empire. The tutorial

6. There is something quite Hegelian and Wittgensteinian in Gandhi's critique of liberal historicism and in his privileging of the ethical. Gandhi's and Hegel's universalistic ethics stems from an endorsement of a way of life. It is only, as Charles Larmore puts it when referring to Hegel, "by virtue of belonging to this way of life [that] we reason in ethics as we do and judge social practices in the name of universalistic principles." Charles Larmore, *The Romantic Legacy* (New York: Columbia University Press, 1996), 55. This link between Gandhi and Hegel does not close the enormous gap between them when it comes to nationalism. Hegel famously tried to squeeze the moral community into a national frame. This is something that Gandhi fairly consistently resists.

and pedagogic obsession of the empire and especially of liberal imperi-
alists are all part of the effort to move societies along the ascending
gradient of historical progress. The empire, one might say, is an engine
that tows societies stalled in their past into contemporary time and history. But the conception on the basis of which progress is itself established as a summum bonum, and which allows for this particular reading
of history, derives centrally from premises about reason as the appropriate yardstick for judging individual and collective lives.

What is significant in this account is that for both the Mills civilizational achievement, which is paradigmatically the work of collectivities,
is the necessary condition for the realization of the progressive purposes
immanent in history, and hence of its continued progress. Notwithstanding the expressed commitment, both as an ideal and as a process,
to the idea of man-made history and to individual choice, it is the "stage
of civilization" that is taken as the relevant marker of the progressive
possibilities within "the reach" of a given community at any point in
time. The unit of analysis for accessing backwardness and progress is
plainly some understanding of the achievements of a community or collectivity. Within this orientation individual lives, their pains and joys,
the meanings they attach to particular things and events, in short, the
integrity of their life forms, are completely read out of the civilization
or collectivity of which they are deemed to be a part and its standing
within a preestablished scale.

UNIVERSAL HISTORIES

The period from the mid–eighteenth to the mid–nineteenth century is
the high noon of European historiography. It is the century in which
the great, usually multivolume, histories by Gibbon, Ferguson, Hume,
Condorcet, Guizot, Herder, Ranke, Hallam, James Mill, Macaulay, and
Comte were written and published. In their various distinct purposes,
they served the imperatives of nationalism, secularism, the defense of
particular classes, sects, political parties, and imperialism. Despite the
plurality of ends that these grand exemplars vouch for, the underlying
perspective of this tradition is cosmopolitan and global. Even the Romantic movement, especially in its German expression, which has so
often been accused of being parochial in its German *Historismus* and
national in its commitment, evinces a global sweep in the comparisons
that it makes. The same is true for James Mill's *History of British India*,
where the comparisons and contrasts with China, Roman Britain, the
Arabs, and Persia are constant and self-conscious. At least in the writing

of it, and more often than not in the choice of subject matter, by the mid–nineteenth century, European history is firmly global in its orientation.[7] What makes possible and undergirds this orientation is not simply the expanded exposure brought on by increases in trade, travel, wars, and the reach of empires. After all, the singular, the bounded, or the parochial have never had difficulties acknowledging what lay beyond their boundaries. A global orientation, such as that evinced in nineteenth-century historiography and philosophy, requires a global perspective. That perspective, as was discussed in the introduction, derived from an epistemological view that allowed the world to be read abstracted from its concrete aesthetic and emotive particulars and nevertheless issued in a firmness of judgment with respect to those particulars. That perspective draws on, and endorses, what Hans Blumenberg has rightly called a "unity of methodically regulated theory as a coherent entity developing independently of individuals and generations."[8] In the development of that view of theory, Descartes is the crucial figure, and his influence is no less evident in the thought of a group of thinkers commonly designated as empiricists. It is this theoretical orientation that is "usable in any possible world [that] provides the criterion for the elementary exertions of the modern age: The *mathematizing* and the *materializing* of nature."[9]

History, of course, is never merely the narration of the past. By the eighteenth century, and with unveiled clarity in the nineteenth, it is also a chosen battleground on which the Enlightenment carries out its multi-pronged mission against religion, superstition, and ignorance and affirms its conception of progress. For this project, in which the writing of history plays a conspicuous role, education, as an instrument of progress, is a central component. It is not, however, merely the education of the

7. R. G. Collingwood, *The Idea of History* (Oxford: Oxford University Press, 1994); G. P. Gooch, *History and Historians in the Nineteenth Century* (London: Longmans, Green and Co., 1955). For the English tradition see T. P. Peardon, *The Transition in English Historical Writing, 1760–1830* (New York: Columbia University Press, 1933).

The claim of a global or universal orientation does not of course settle the issue of universal understanding. The great twentieth-century German historian Friedrich Meinecke with his penetrating understanding of political ideologies was, I think, prescient in claiming that the Enlightenment had "eine Richtung auf das Universale, die ganze Menschheit Umfassende an, aber ergriff . . . mehr den Stoff als das Innenleben der geschichtlichen Gebilde." Friedrich Meinecke, *Die Entstehung des Historimus.*

8. Blumenberg, *The Legitimacy of the Modern Age*, 31.

9. Ibid., 164. See also Lachterman, *The Ethics of Geometry*, esp. chap. 1.

single individual, the protagonist, for example, of the bildungsroman, but of societies in toto.[10] History and education work in tandem. In the former, one detects the plan of progress for which the latter is the catalytic motor and extension. Even when as with Kant's "An Idea for a Universal History from the Cosmopolitan Point of View" the plan or the teleology can never be affirmed as a scientific law, the idea of a plan to history and the conviction in its progressiveness are never surrendered.

Both notions, namely that of history as having a plan and of that plan representing progress, are combined in the almost compulsive obsession of eighteenth- and nineteenth-century historiography with the pedagogic analogy linking grades in schooling with "stages" of historical development. It is the special achievement of Turgot, Condorcet, and Comte—the first two being profound influences on James Mill, the last on John Stuart Mill—to have mapped the idea of historical progress onto the notion of the stages of human development.[11] By the late nineteenth century, there are of course a plurality of grand narratives, such as evolutionism, utilitarianism, and evangelicalism, that undergird the universalism of the century's historiography. This cosmopolitanism, which is anchored in the problematic of universal history, decisively breaks with the ancient world, where, even when the ideal of cosmopolitanism is present, as with the Stoics, it is not understood within the framework of universal history.[12] Cosmopolitanism without the problematic of universal history generates and aspires to an ethics, but it does not issue in a program of paternalism and interventionist collective action.[13]

It is within this broad framework, committed both to cosmopolitanism and to progress, that late nineteenth-century European political thought also expresses itself. All the major streams of this thought were explicitly and emphatically reliant on history as the ground for their various normative visions. Hegel's articulation of the State as the em-

10. See Louis Dumont, *German Ideology: From France to Germany and Back* (Chicago: University of Chicago Press, 1994), 69–145.

11. Halevy, *The Growth of Philosophic Radicalism*, 251–82.

12. Karl Lowith, *Meaning in History: The Theological Presuppositions of the Philosophy of History* (Chicago: University of Chicago Press, 1949), chap. 1.

13. Here again, as I discuss in the conclusion to this chapter, there is a striking similarity to Gandhi's views. His cosmopolitanism is ethical in a way that neither allows for a reliance on history nor leans on political action as the primary deliverer of progress. Political action, including mass action, such as in the noncooperation movement of the early 1920s, was countenanced only when it remained within a strictly ethical framework anchored, for Gandhi, in a commitment to truth and nonviolence.

bodiment of a concrete ethical rationality represents the realization of a journey of Reason that originated in the distant recesses of "the East."[14] Marx's vision of a proletarian future has its explanatory and political credence in overcoming the contrarian forces that bedevil and spur history. John Stuart Mill's ideal of a liberalism that secures the conditions for the flourishing of individuality, and in doing so maximizes utility, explicitly rests on having reached a point of civilizational progress "when mankind have become capable of being improved by free and equal discussion." "Liberty, as a principle," Mill says, "has no application to any state of things anterior to [that] time."[15] By way of contrast, it is worth noting the change this points to with respect to liberalism's own theoretical origins. Talk of history and civilizational development as a ground for the individualistic foundations of political power and liberal institutions is conspicuously absent in the thought of Hobbes and Locke. Their thought is no doubt universalistic, but despite that, it is substantially indifferent to pressing its judgments on the world. The universalism of this earlier liberalism remains abstract, and the political judgments implicit in it exist as a latent potential.

For Hegel, Marx, and Mill, history is both the condition for the possibility of progress and the evidentiary basis of what that progress should be. As Hans Blumenberg puts it, "[T]he idea of progress extrapolates from a structure present in every moment to a future that is immanent in history."[16] Both the immanence of the future that is present in history and the structure that is exemplified by the present are themselves given the cast of progress by a prior commitment to a rationality that identifies in the past and in the present the progressive extension into the future.

Numerous aspects inform the conception of rationality and the attendant notion of progress. Here I mention only two whose importance is conspicuous to Marx and to Mill, and in a more complex manner evident in Hegel, too. The first is the notion of a history as something that is man-made. Obviously this view informs the Marxian notion of praxis and the liberal commitment to individual choice and consent. The second, which is closely linked with the idea of history as man-made, is that of history's predictability. Both notions attenuate without firmly contradicting the Judeo-Christian notion of a Providence as something superintended by divine purposes, in which human actions

14. Of course because philosophy always "comes too late," in contrast to Marx and Mill, Hegel's reliance on history does not generate a program of action.
15. Mill, *On Liberty*, 16.
16. Blumenberg, *The Legitimacy of the Modern Age*, 30.

and human perceptions are only contingently secure in serving the ends of progress. It is of course possible that the plan of Providence corresponds perfectly with the imperatives of human rationality and the motivations that spur human actions. But such a correspondence would be merely a contingent happenstance of divine ordering. The disjuncture that Enlightenment rationality and historiography introduces into this Judeo-Christian conception is best elaborated by Kant when he speaks of an "a priori possible description of the events that should come to pass" in the future, because the "soothsaying historical narration of what is impending in the future" is theoretically informed by a subject who is at the same time the practical origin of that future—"But how is an a priori history possible? Answer: When the soothsayer himself causes and contrives the events that he proclaims in advance."[17]

The idea that human history is man-made and predictable is itself no guarantee of its being progressive. Nor is the fact that progress is allegedly anchored in history evidence of progress, or of what should count as progress. Notwithstanding the Hegelian, the Marxian, and the liberal attempts to inscribe in the logic of historical development the precise progressive telos of history, and thus as it were read it off from the surface of events, the account of progress must be normatively justified on its own terms. Put differently, one must approach the issue of progress with suspicion, precisely because in the nineteenth century the plurality of agendas that it embodies and of which it is so often a surrogate are naturalized by the powerful and seductive emollient of history, by now wrapped in the paraphernalia of scientific "laws," "rules" of evidence, and the necessary "logic" of development. Whatever one might think of Nietzsche's general derogation of the "excess of history," one cannot, at least provisionally, doubt the suspicion he casts on "that admiration for the 'power of history' which in practice transforms every moment into a naked admiration for success and leads to idolatry of the factual" and in which "talk of a 'world process' [only] justify their age as the necessary result of a 'world process.'"[18] Nietzsche's view implies— and this is easy to overlook given what he is typically associated with— that the world is also made for losers or, at any rate, those who might live within life forms that get designated with losers. To them the excess

17. Immanuel Kant, *Der Streit der Fakultaeten*, 2:2, quoted in Blumenberg, *The Legitimacy of the Modern Age*, 34.
18. Friedrich Nietzsche, "On the Uses and Disadvantages of History for Life," in *Untimely Meditations*, trans. R. J. Hollingdale (Cambridge: Cambridge University Press, 1996), 103–4.

of history, indeed the very reliance on history as a marker of progress or even of what is fated, might very well have been experienced as a ruse that merely denied a life form within which they lived.

Perhaps nowhere is the suspicion for a naked admiration of success, couched in the language of historical necessity, or at any rate of historically sanctioned guidance, more necessary than in the context of the empire. By the nineteenth century every major justification of the raj rests on the dual props of progress for India and a history that makes evident the need for such progress, along with the accompanying claim that such progress can be brought about only through the political interdictions of the empire. If notions such as the legitimacy of conquest, the primacy of the economic self-interest of Britain, or even the imperial right of Britain on account of its rivalries with other European powers undergird Britain's imperial policies, they are expressed in the closed and hushed councils of power, or in the concealed psychological depths of individual men and women. When on occasion, as with Lord Curzon, the viceroy of India, the empire was justified in terms of the bravado of British imperial destiny, it resulted in embarrassment and the tainting of a distinguished career.[19] The dynamism of the empire is so thoroughly wedded to the betterment of the world that it is easy to see why the deployment of power despite its acknowledged and sustained abuses (as for example in the cases of Robert Clive and Warren Hastings), and the often wholesale erasure of extant life forms, could have been countenanced as justified by a higher purpose. The same reason also goes some way to explaining why in a figure like Burke, who has the profoundest suspicions regarding the very project of bettering the world through the radical interventions of political power, the empire finds its severest critic. It is Burke's puzzlement and, ultimately, his humility in the face of the present, and not his reverence for the past, that give him pause in lending his hand to a political optimism that has been a central tenet of liberalism from its very inception.

JAMES MILL AND *THE HISTORY OF BRITISH INDIA*

By the late eighteenth century the empire was a serious matter, politically and morally, and not merely economically. In the numerous public and parliamentary debates regarding the precise relationship of the East India Company to the crown, the issue of the broader historical and

19. See Nicolson, *Curzon: The Last Phase.*

edificatory role of the company is never absent. By the nineteenth century, and conspicuously with both the Mills and Macaulay, the British Empire in India is understood squarely from within the normative framework of liberal thought, along with its reliance on history and civilizational standing, where both were understood as linked to the imperatives of progress.[20] When, as is often the case, as for instance with J. S. Mill, India is singled out for distinctive treatment relative to other outposts of the empire or to Britain itself, it is on account of a distinctiveness again allegedly internal to this broad historical and progressive liberal vision and its reading of India's past.[21] Indeed, the primary and explicit obsession of James Mill's *History* is to establish the civilizational stage to which India's extant condition corresponded. John Stuart Mill, because he did not write a history of India, is less preoccupied with the precise logistics of establishing or presenting the details of such a civilizational hierarchy. Nevertheless, the normative commitments of his thought make it clear that he believed in the existence of such a hierarchy and that it played a crucial role in determining his political outlook on the various parts of the empire; indeed, it played a crucial role in his assessment of political life in Britain and elsewhere.

The concern with civilizational stages is, as I have suggested, the particular form through which the preoccupation with history and progress gets expressed. In the case of the younger Mill, the conception of progress is clear. With respect to the individual it refers to a life in which the "higher quality faculties," which themselves define the fullness of individuality, get expressed. Politically and socially, it refers to the conditions under which individuality finds expression, and these conditions include, barring those that are explicitly excepted and on which I focus, the commitment to representative democracy and other egalitarian institutional arrangements.[22] The combination of a concern

20. John Plamenatz, *On Alien Rule and Self-Government* (London: Longmans, 1960), 102–4.

21. For example in J. S. Mill's discussion in the chapter on "Government of Dependencies" in *Considerations*. Perhaps the most articulate nineteenth-century statement of this broad view is that of Walter Bagehot in *Physics and Politics* (Boston: Beacon Press, 1956). See esp. chap. 2, "The Use of Conflict."

22. Isaiah Berlin, "John Stuart Mill and the Ends of Life" in *Four Essays on Liberty* (London: Oxford University Press, 1969); Richard Wollheim, "John Stuart Mill and Isaiah Berlin: Ends of Life and the Preliminaries of Morality," in *The Idea of Freedom*, ed. Alan Ryan (Oxford: Oxford University Press, 1979), 253–69; Wendy Donner, *The Liberal Self* (Ithaca: Cornell University Press, 1991); John Skorupski, *John Stuart Mill* (London: Routledge, 1989), 248–388; John and Lane Robson, eds.,

with individuality, the choice of life plans, all nested within a democracy realizes the progressive purpose of maximizing utility.[23]

The specific context in which James Mill's *History* was written, and to which it made a decisive and transforming contribution, was an atmosphere of growing admiration for the civilizations of the East. With respect to India, Sir William Jones, the pioneer and champion of Sanskrit studies and India's civilizational richness, was the leading protagonist of this point of view and of the partisans called the Orientalists, who were opposed by the Anglicists. In the early stages of the conflict between the Orientalists and Anglicists, Jones and his epigones had considerable influence on the policies of the company.[24] For example, the company supported Hindu and Muslim places of worship, its troops paraded in honor of Hindu deities, and company offices were often open on Sundays and closed on Indian holidays.[25]

It was this Orientalist view toward Indian civilization and the policies that followed from it that James Mill along with Macaulay decisively revised in the first third of the nineteenth century. They were supported by the powerful Governor General Lord William Bentinck, himself a self-avowed follower of Mill, whose disparagement of India's historical legacy went so far as seriously to consider demolishing the Taj Mahal for the sale of its marble.[26] James Mill's influence in bringing about this sea change, primarily through the publication of his *History*, was enormous. The *History* became the standard and mandatory manual for officials of the company and eventually a required textbook for candidates for the elite corps of senior administrators in the Indian Civil Service. The editor of the 1840 edition of the *History*, H. H. Wilson, in his preface, passed the following judgment: "there is reason to fear that . . . a harsh and illiberal spirit has of late years prevailed in the conduct

---

James and John Stuart Mill: Papers of the Centenary Conference (Toronto: University of Toronto Press, 1976).

23. See Mill, *On Liberty*; and Mill, *Utilitarianism*, in Mill and Bentham, *Utilitarianism and Other Essays*.

24. See Stokes, *English Utilitarians in India*, chaps. 1, 2.

25. Duncan Forbes, "James Mill and India," *Cambridge Journal*, no. 5 (1951): 22. See also Kopf, *British Orientalism and the Origins of the Bengal Renaissance*; and Stokes, *English Utilitarians in India*, xi–80.

26. The plan was finally abandoned because the "test auction" of marble from the palace in Agra proved to be unsatisfactory. See E. Thompson and G. T. Garratt, *Rise and Fulfillment of British Rule in India* (London, 1934), for a discussion of Anglicist attitudes toward India in the 1820s and 1830s.

and councils of the rising service in India, which owes its origin to impressions imbibed in early life from the *History* of Mr. Mill."[27] Indeed, even Macaulay, who despite his scathing review of James Mill's *Essay on Government*, and who had referred to Mill as "my old enemy," praised the *History* in Parliament as "on the whole the greatest historical work which has appeared in our language since that of Gibbon."[28]

As is clear from the statement quoted above by H. H. Wilson, even by the mid–nineteenth century, the severity of James Mill's prejudices against India and especially against the Hindus (in book 2 of the *History*) were recognized. Even by the standards of the times, Mill's views were, to put it mildly, extreme. An entire civilization, with its ancient religious moorings, its artistic and cultural production, its complex legal system, its cosmology, and its science, are dismissed as representing the "rudest and weakest state of the human mind."[29] Mill considers with great seriousness, and no doubt through taxing effort, the ancient scriptures of Hindu mythology, only to conclude that "[t]his is precisely the course which a wild and ignorant mind, regarding only the wonder which it has it in view to excite, naturally, in such cases, and almost universally, pursues."[30] Mill's emphasis on the backwardness of the Indian "mind" anticipates and prepares the way for what becomes the Indian response to this claim. It is to associate the modern not with the social or the political, but rather to index it to thought, especially philosophic thought. In the nineteenth and the twentieth centuries Indians often complimented themselves in language that resonates with a frequent refrain of Marx when he says that the Germans have done in thought what the British have done in fact.

Mill's views regarding India, its past and its present, are so unremittingly dark, often so pathetically foolish in their lack of nuance, that it is hard to believe that even he would have spent over ten years of his life gathering them had he not been motivated by a more serious purpose. It is similarly difficult at this distance, and with the advantage of the postcolonial experience, to imagine how his narrative could have acquired the enormous influence that it did. In this context one should remind oneself that imperial narratives, perhaps all narratives, especially those of power, lose their effectivity in proportion to how complex they become. James Mill's *History* is a vivid example of the truth of Walter

27. Preface to *History of British India*, 4th ed. (1840), 1:viii–ix.
28. Quoted in Forbes, "James Mill and India," 23.
29. Mill, *History of British India*, 1:115.
30. Ibid., 118.

Benjamin's remark that "a thought must be crude to come into its own in action."[31]

Nevertheless, Mill was in fact motivated by a more philosophically serious purpose, and that was to establish on rational grounds a clear scale of civilizational hierarchies. This is how Mill introduces the important and wide-ranging chapter entitled "General Reflections" in book 2 of the *History:*

> To ascertain the true state of the Hindus in the scale of civilization, is not only an object of curiosity in the history of human nature; but to the people of Great Britain, charged as they are with the government of that great portion of the human species, it is an object of the highest practical importance. No scheme of government can happily conduce to the ends of government, unless it is adapted to the state of the people for whose use it is intended. In those diversities in the state of civilization, which approach the extremes, this truth is universally acknowledged. Should anyone propose, for a band of roving Tartars, the regulations adapted to the happiness of a regular and polished society, he would meet with neglect or derision. The inconveniences are only more concealed, and more or less diminished, when the error relates to states of society which more nearly resemble one another. If the mistake in regard to Hindu society, committed by the British nation, and the British government, be very great; if they have conceived the Hindus to be a people of high civilization, while they have, in reality, made but a few of the earliest steps in the progress to civilization, it is impossible that in many of the measures pursued for the government of that people, the mark aimed at should not have been wrong.[32]

Whatever satisfaction ethnographic "curiosity" may get from knowing the precise location of Hindus in the scale of civilization, it is the imperatives of imperial governance that motivate and give urgency to this project. But those imperatives are themselves revealingly presented in impersonal terms, because they are driven by an abstract conception of "usefulness" and "happiness." Mill's sensitivity to the appropriateness of

31. Walter Benjamin, review of *Dreigroschenroman*, quoted in Hannah Arendt, introduction to *Illuminations*, by Benjamin, trans. Harry Zohn (New York: Schocken Books, 1968), 15.
32. Mill, *History of British India*, 2:107.

forms of governance to the forms of society stems from a prior commitment to a univocal conception of progress. In fact, even though it is
tempting to read the above passage as merely an apologia for British
imperial interests, Mill's ultimate interest is neither with the British nor
with the Hindus, but rather with a "civilized" life that represents progress. This is precisely what Mill goes on to make clear:

> The preceding induction of particulars, embracing the reli-
> gion, the laws, the government, the manners, the arts, the sci-
> ences, the literature, of the Hindus, affords, it is presumed, the
> materials, from which a correct judgment may, at last, be
> formed of their progress towards the high attainments of civi-
> lised life.[33]

The reference to induction is very important, and is a clue to a broader
problem that Mill was attempting to solve through his *History*. The
problem was inherited from Bentham. For the latter, the establishing of
the science of legislation had always faced the awkward issue of the effect of prejudices and customs on legislation. Bentham in his *Essay on
the Influence of Time and Place in Legislation* had attempted to address the
issue by considering the case of Bengal: "To a law-giver, who having
been brought up with English notions, shall have learned how to accommodate his laws to the circumstances of Bengal, no other part of
the globe can present a difficulty."[34] Even though Bentham acknowledged that "he who attacks prejudice wantonly and without necessity
and he who suffers himself to be led blindfolded a slave to it, equally
miss the line of reason."[35] Benthamite legislators had to "be possessed
fully of the facts, to be informed of the local situation, the climate, the
bodily constitution, the manners, the legal customs, the religion of
those with whom they have to deal."[36] From Bentham's point of view,
customs, prejudices, indeed the entire array of ethnographic conditions,
were relevant to the science of legislation. Their presence constituted a
problem that had to be "humored," because there was no getting around
customs or the particular facts of a legislative situation. It is therefore
not at all clear that the particulars of a situation were a source of great
worry or embarrassment to Bentham, the father of the science of legislation. But for Mill, in contrast, local conditions, that is, the very facts

33. Ibid., 107–8.
34. Jeremy Bentham, *Essay on the Influence of Time and Place in Legislation*, in
Works of Jeremy Bentham, ed. Bowring, 1:172.
35. Ibid., 180.
36. Ibid.

of history, placed a limit on the scientific aspirations of legislation and theory in general. To this problem of history, Mill offered a philosophy of history as the solution. Following his labors in writing the *History of British India* there would, in a real sense, be no need to engage with the murky facts of history.

This is the problem Mill was attempting to solve and that he believed he had solved.[37] If, in fact, a firm line of civilizational progress, or the "scale of nations," could be inductively established, then the Benthamite legislator-scientist would not have to humor customs or engage with local conditions. A clear scale of civilizational development would tell the legislator precisely what was below and what was above for any civilization under consideration. There would be no need, for example, to get weighed down—as Bentham had, following his study of Montesquieu's theory of climatic relevance—by the consideration of Bengal's climate. For once it had been established that "the savage is listless and indolent under every climate," the issue could conveniently be factored out of the relevant considerations.[38] Ironically the facts of history become the basis for establishing a theory of history and governance, which in turn obviates the need to engage with the facts of history.

As it was, the "induction of particulars" played no role in Mill's scale of civilization. The standard of valuation was not crafted from a view of the particulars of Hindu or any other civilization. It was found readymade in the commitment to the simplicity valorized by Newtonian science, in the principles of laissez-faire economics, in the abhorrence of anything other than deist religiosity, and in the general convictions of utilitarianism. In fact, in his *Essay on Government*, Mill had rejected the "experience test," i.e., induction, and following the lead of Ricardo had expressed a strong preference for deduction as the basis of arriving at an evaluative standard. Halevy is, I think, quite right in claiming that the *History* was in fact part of the Scottish tradition of writing "conjectural history."[39] This form of history had strictly been applied to places, periods, or situations where evidence or documents were lacking, where, in a sense, experience was not at issue, and that therefore allowed and required conjecture to fill in the gaps and to offer an explanatory narrative. It was therefore widely used in geology and archaeology. Mill's conjectures are not on account of the absence of evidence regarding

37. Elie Halevy has suggested that it was Bentham's treatise that in fact led Mill to conceive the project of writing the *History*. Halevy, *The Growth of Philosophic Radicalism*, 277.

38. Mill, *History of British India*, 1:313.

39. Halevy, *The Growth of Philosophic Radicalism*, 274.

Hindu society; rather, they are to service the needs of a science, which on his reckoning would have a minimal reliance on such forms of evidence and which alone could lay claim to a clear and firm law of progress.[40]

The standard for historical development that Mill has in mind has both an endpoint and an engine to move along those who have not got to that point. Regarding the former, he is bluntly Eurocentric:

> [T]he Europeans [of the feudal ages] were superior [to the Hindus of the present] notwithstanding the vices of the papacy, in religion, and defects of the schoolmen, in philosophy. . . . In fine it cannot be doubted that, upon the whole, the gothic nations, as soon as they became settled people, exhibit the marks of a superior character and civilisation to those of the Hindus.[41]

What is more interesting than this predictable claim is that Mill sees in the histories of backward civilizations a potentiality on account of which they can in fact progress. But the actualization of this potentiality typically turns on a force external to those civilizations. Here the elder Mill anticipates an argument that the younger Mill would also use. To repeat an earlier image, progress for Mill is like having a stalled car towed by one that is more powerful and can therefore carry the burden of an ascendant gradient. Kipling's well-known poetic flourish about the white man's burden in the East had its philosophic analogue in the thought of both the Mills and Macaulay. Hindu civilization, for Mill, epitomizes this condition of being stalled in the past. But various aspects of Hindu civilization had prepared it for progressive transformation. Its internally divisive and fractured social and political structure make it ready for unification, its ignorance elicits a yearning for the fruits of knowledge, and even its long association with regressive and repressive tyrants has the salutary consequence of making it receptive to beneficent and progressive successors:

> To retain any considerable number of countries in subjection, preserving their own government, and their own sovereigns, would be really arduous, even where the signs of government were the best understood. To suppose it possible in a country

40. Duncan Forbes graphically expresses this in claiming, "The law of progress, like gravitation, did not admit exceptions, and Mill 'blacked the chimney' not, like Macaulay, for artistic effect, but in the name of science." Forbes, "James Mill and India," *Cambridge Journal*, no. 5 (1951): 29.

41. Mill, *History of British India*, 1:466–67.

where the signs of government is [*sic*] in the state indicated by the laws and institutions of the Hindus, would be in the highest degree extravagant.[42]

This is part of Mill's argument as to why any form of federalism among the various principalities and states in India is an extravagant and retrograde possibility. Mill concludes the argument by pointing to the progressive effects already evinced by Hindu civilization when it has had the benefit of foreign rulers:

> They, who affirm the high state of civilisation among the Hindus previous to their subjugation to foreigners, precede so directly in opposition to evidence, that wherever the Hindus have been always exempt from a domination of foreigners, there they are uniformally found in a state of civilisation inferior to those who have long been the subjects of a Mahomedan throne.[43]

Here Mill closes the circle by deploying the former Muslim rulers as the precursors who establish the evidence for the progressive nature of foreign rule, thus laying the ground for the British, whose superiority, as Europeans, is established over that of the Muslims themselves. For Mill, Hindu civilization is plainly in need of a double tow.

It is of course easy and tempting to dismiss Mill's views on India as utterly driven by a jaundiced set of prejudices that therefore deserve no serious consideration. Apart from the fact that his views were profoundly influential throughout the course of the nineteenth century, and on that account alone should be taken seriously, such a dismissal risks evacuating, on account of Mill's crudity, what is in fact a crucial bedrock of a more sanguine liberalism. It is the perspective, and not so much the details, from which Mill crafts his *History* and the authority he claims for it that matter and which give it its enduring and perturbing relevance. It is a perspective of truth and not of life from which things, beliefs, situations, and ways of being are judged not by reference to the local positivities or the bounded finitude within which experiences occurs. Rather they are judged as forms of knowledge, as truth claims, that when underwritten by Mill's epistemology generate a universal typology in which things must be hierarchical. From this perspective progress is always, even if only implicitly, the only evaluative yardstick.

Mill's *History* is that of things, of people's beliefs, their myths and

42. Ibid., 140.
43. Ibid., 142.

religions, their economic and political institutions and practices. For these things Mill seeks out the laws of their development going back into the recesses of ancient times. Everything is historicized, and everything is part of a general history. Therefore, everything can be compared with everything else. Here all experience is provisional on a future that reveals, only after the fact, and in a sense only to the evaluating historian, the real meaning of an experience. The circumscribed finitude of the present counts for nothing and for that reason sentiments, feelings, the emotive particulars that get experienced in the present, are similarly devalued. Nothing is singular, but everything is an instance of something general, through which alone it acquires its meaning, which amounts to its historical standing.

What Mill's *History* is not is one of human beings and the conditions under which they live their lives. For it denies the conditions for that basic encounter between human beings and societies, that hermeneutic situation, in which the limited view and the narrow perspective—in a word the aesthetics of a situation, as the eighteenth century understood the term—become the filter through which alone human sentiments, in all their nuanced, complex, and experimental fluidity, are appreciated and experienced as real. In such situations rules, laws of development, algorithms of belief, and practice cannot be a substitute for the essential openness suggested by a hermeneutics and perceived predicament. Foucault expresses this eloquently:

> In modern thought, historicism and the analytics of finitude confront one another. Historicism is a means of validating for itself the perpetual critical relation at play between History and the human sciences. But it establishes it solely at the level of the positivities: the positive knowledge of man is limited by the historical positivity of the knowing subject, so that the moment the finitude is dissolved in the play of relativity from which it cannot escape, and which itself has value as an absolute. To be finite, then, would simply be to be trapped in the laws of a perspective which, while allowing a certain apprehension—of the type of perception or understanding—prevents it from ever being universal and definitively intellectual. . . . This is why the analysis of finitude never ceases to use, as a weapon against historicism, the part of itself that historicism has neglected.[44]

44. Foucault, *The Order of Things: An Archaeology of the Human Sciences* (New York: Random House, 1994), 368–69.

Among those weapons that the colonial finite, as it were, uses against the cosmopolitanism of imperial historicism are the dense particularities that make up its life forms, not as provisional planks that must be looked at with a backward gaze but as absolute conditions that are capable of sustaining the richness of experiences. Among these conditions are the possibilities of ethical life where such life does not require being confined in the waiting room of history while some other agency has the key to that room. In this sense one prevalent response to imperial historicism is almost by necessity a form of parochialism, because what has to be valorized is a set of conditions whose normative and experiential credence can be justified without reference to a future or a necessary past and prescribed path of development. But here parochialisms, even nostalgic parochialisms, are just stand-ins for vindicating experiences with which the "backward" can associate real and unconditional feelings.

JOHN STUART MILL: PROGRESS AND CONSENT

J. S. Mill acknowledges at various points in his famous *Autobiography* the immensity of his intellectual inheritance from his father. Yet it is plain that he had little of the latter's programmatic dogmatism and emotional crudeness. In the tradition of nineteenth-century British political thought, it is hard to imagine a figure who could match the breadth of J. S. Mill's intellectual, political, and emotional sympathies or the vigor of his mind. His liberalism is far more capacious than that of any of his contemporaries, and he has none of the imperial arrogance that taints so many of them. In engaging with his thought, one can be confident that one is doing just that and not, as with his father, being thrust up against unreflective prejudices that masquerade as thought. Even when there are important similarities in their views, as is often the case, in the younger Mill those views bespeak an incomparably deeper sensibility of both thought and feeling.

One such similarity is the conviction of progress. It is J. S. Mill's view of progress and its link with political order that I shall focus on, thus sidestepping many of the familiar and important features of his thought. But given Mill's conviction that progress stemmed from a commitment to utilitarianism, attention to the former at least indirectly touches on the utilitarianism with which Mill clearly associated himself to the end of his life.

According to Mill, the principal determinant of progressive change is "the state of the speculative faculties of mankind, including the nature of the beliefs which by any means they have arrived at concerning themselves and the world by which they are surrounded."[45] Thus, for example, he mentions the development of polytheism, Judaism, Christianity, Protestantism, and critical philosophy as "primary agents in making society what it is at each successive period."[46] Furthermore, Mill believed that changes in ideas were substantially autonomous. What he meant by this was that ideas were not merely or even primarily the product of existing circumstances, social arrangements, or relations of power. They stemmed instead from a critical reflection on existing beliefs.

The role Mill imagined himself playing was that of "an interpreter of original thinkers and the mediator between them and the public."[47] He sought to advance a set of ideas that could serve as a public philosophy and would be attentive to the general facts, such as size, complexity, and religious diversity, that characterized his age. The central core of this public philosophy was, of course, utilitarianism. It was the principle of utility that best served the interests of society. Sidestepping many complex issues pertaining to their philosophic relationship, in general terms, Mill accepted Bentham's formulations of utility that "actions are right in proportion as they tend to promote happiness; wrong as they tend to produce the reverse of happiness."[48] Moreover, again agreeing with Bentham, Mill concurred that "by happiness is intended pleasure and the absence of pain; by unhappiness, pain and the privation of pleasure."[49]

The principle of utility was the foundation from which Mill derived a number of secondary principles that were to regulate social and political relations. Among these were (1) the principle of liberty, which restricted coercive interference with the beliefs and actions of individuals so long as they did not harm others (On Liberty); (2) a norm of equal opportunity requiring that careers be open to talent, without regard, for example, to sex (Subjection of Women); (3) a norm of political liberty, implying a broad franchise to participate in politics (Representative Government); (4) the development of worker management in the economy (Political Economy); and (5) limitations on inequality of wealth and income, including inherited resources (Political Economy).

45. J. S. Mill, Logic, 6.10.7.
46. Ibid.
47. J. S. Mill, Autobiography (New York: New American Library, 1964), 174.
48. J. S. Mill, Utilitarianism, chap. 2, para. 2.
49. Ibid.

In all of these works, though most obviously in *On Liberty* and *Considerations on Representative Government*, Mill introduces a caveat that limits the application of these various secondary principles to advanced stages of civilizational conditions. The limitation is not in contradiction to the principle of utility, but rather the opposite. Mill's point is that it is only under advanced conditions that the secondary principles service the ends of advancing and maximizing utility. Hence under conditions of backwardness or for children, the principle of liberty would sanction behavior that would be contrary to utility maximization. Under such conditions, alternative norms are required to remain consistent with the progress associated with utility. These alternative norms or qualifications simply underline the centrality that Mill places on progress.

The clearest statement Mill offers of what he takes backwardness to be is in his essay called "Civilization." The essay was published in *The Westminster Review* in April 1836. Its focus is Britain, and it deals with Mill's perception of the evisceration of the integuments of British society and the impoverishment of the individuality that emerges from it. The way Mill presents his argument is by offering a running contrast between civilization and barbarism:

> Civilization . . . is the direct converse of rudeness or barbarism. Whatever be the characteristics of what we call savage life, the contrary of these, or rather the qualities which society put on as it throws off these, constitute civilization. Thus, a savage consists of a handful of individuals, wandering or thinly scattered over a vast tract of country: a dense population, therefore dwelling in fixed habitations and largely collected together in towns and villages, we term civilized. . . . In savage communities each person shifts for himself; except in war (and even then very imperfectly) we seldom see any joint operations carried on by the union of many; nor do savages find much pleasure in each other's society. Wherever, therefore, we find human beings acting together for common purposes, in large bodies and enjoying the pleasures of social intercourse, we term them civilized.[50]

Mill concludes this binary contrast with the claim that "all these elements [those of civilization] exist in modern Europe, and especially in

50. J. S. Mill, "Civilization," in *Essays on Politics and Culture*, ed. G. Himmelfarb (Gloucester, Mass.: Peter Smith, 1973), 46.

Great Britain, in a more eminent degree . . . than at any other place or time."[51]

The sharpness of the contrast that Mill draws between the savage and the civilized is puzzling and revealing. Because as the essay proceeds, what becomes clear is that it is the savage who has many of the individual qualities that Mill most admires, and which Britons, in his view, are losing. Hence, we are told that it is the savage who has "bodily strength," "courage," and "enterprise," and who is "not without intelligence." It is the savage who "cannot bear to sacrifice . . . his individual will." Similarly, it is the savage who displays a noble and "active" "heroism" in his isolation, the precise opposite of the torpidity, cowardice, and passivity of "modern man" lost in "the crowd."[52] Even the very identification of the savage as isolated has an ambivalent significance in Mill's thought. It is after all precisely worries about the crowd, the masses, the stifling conformitarianism and increasing homogeneity of modern Western society, that provoke the worries that Mill shares with Tocqueville and that explicitly animate the need for a principle such as the principle of liberty.[53] The purpose of the principle after all is to secure "liberty of tastes and pursuits; of framing the plan of our life to suit our own character; of doing as we like, subject to such consequences as may follow; without impediment from our fellow creatures, so long as what we do does not harm them, even though they should think our conduct foolish, perverse, or wrong."[54]

Despite the salutary qualities of the savage, the society or civilization of which he is a member is resolutely denoted as backward or barbarous. There is not a touch of irony in Mill's essay, or in the way he deploys the distinction between the backward and civilized societies. It is this civilizational classification that determines whether or not savages can, for example, be members of independent societies with no need for superintending tutelage; or perhaps even be members of democratic societies, and hence share in the various secondary principles that Mill believed ought to structure such societies. What represents or speaks

51. Ibid., 47.
52. Ibid., 48–59.
53. It is worth noting that a similar ambivalence pervades Tocqueville's *Democracy in America*, where the Native American is consistently characterized in terms that suggest aristocratic individuality in contrast with the leveled-out democratic individuality that Tocqueville worries about. See in particular vol. 1, chap. 1, "The Physical Considerations of America," and vol. 2, chap. 1, "The Three Races that Inhabit America."
54. J. S. Mill, *On Liberty*, 18.

for the savage is the location of the civilization of which he is deemed to be a part, and this in Mill's case turns on a simple binary scale of civilized or backward. Ironically, the very attributes that Mill celebrates in individuals get eclipsed and assigned a negative sign through the civilizational category that Mill encloses individuals within.

The ambivalence that I am pointing to, and which I am arguing gets resolved through the deployment of a philosophy of history or a scale of civilization, is evident in Mill's later work, too. Consider the following well known passage from *On Liberty:*

> The object of this Essay is to assert one very simple principle, as entitled to govern *absolutely* the dealings of society with the individual in the way of compulsion and control, whether the means used be physical force in the form of legal penalties, or the moral coercion of public opinion. That principle is, that the sole end for which mankind are warranted, individually or collectively, in interfering with the liberty of action of any of their member, is self-protection.[55]

This principle professes to secure many of the highest aspirations of Mill's life and philosophy. It distinguishes, through its intended consequences, his own utilitarianism from the more mechanical and authoritarian versions supported by his father and Bentham. It is the root notion of his capacious tolerance of difference and eccentricity. It expresses the deeply held convictions of a man who had been moved and restored to health by Romantic poetry—a man, moreover, who in the high noon of Victorian conventionalism dedicated the work of which this principle is a part to his wife, claiming that she was his intellectual superior. The absolutism on behalf of the individual that the above passage highlights must therefore be taken as deeply felt and sincere.

But consider the sentence that immediately follows the passage quoted above: "[T]he only purpose for which power can be exercised over any member of a *civilized community*, against his will, is to prevent harm to others."[56] The absolutism of the prior quote is instantly qualified by being integrated into an implicit scale of civilizational hierarchies. The forms or expressions of individual life that the principle is intended to secure, facilitate, and champion are now limited by the civilizational standing of the societies of which individuals are members.

55. Ibid. (emphasis added), 14–15.
56. Ibid. (emphasis added).

Mill goes on to elaborate this point by making it clear that "it is, perhaps, hardly necessary to say that this doctrine [i.e., the principle of liberty] is meant to apply only to human beings in the maturity of their faculties."[57] The group of such human beings includes children but also "those backward states of societies in which the race itself may be considered as in its nonage."[58] We now have a principle of liberty whose applicability is limited to those adults who are members of advanced civilizations.

What allows Mill to say that the statement of this limitation or qualification of the principle is "perhaps hardly necessary"? After all, given his express commitments to individuality and the principle he has just articulated, which is meant to secure the most capacious expressions of such individuality, one would least expect that the application of the principle would turn on civilizational and hence on nonindividual criteria. Since Mill has presented the principle as absolute and moreover given the enormous importance of the principle for what he values so dearly, namely well-lived individual lives, the delimitation of the principle by reference to an implicit philosophy of history should, one would have thought, have been a matter of considerable theoretical significance. If, for instance, Mill had limited the reach of the principle to adults, or to those with the capacity to reason (as Locke does), or to those who could meaningfully express themselves, or, more minimally, to those who had a sense of themselves as independent, sentient beings, one could see these limitations as broadly comporting with the aim of the principle, namely to secure the full play of individuality against the intrusion of society. But the limitations that Mill places on the reach of the principle are not narrowly tailored to exclude human beings below a certain threshold that is defined in individual terms. Instead, the exclusion or the limitation operates by explicitly relying on a civilizational, and therefore communal, index. Mill plainly is assuming some version of the objective scale of civilization similar to that crafted by his father, and that, more generally, European historiography of the time presumed.

The delimitation of the principle of liberty by a theory of civilizational hierarchies does not itself constitute a contradiction in Mill's argument. Mill's purpose, after all, in articulating the principle of liberty is to specify the conditions under which that principle would facilitate the maximization of utility—utility being his guiding purpose and the

57. Ibid.
58. Ibid.

ultimate indicator of progress. If, however, under conditions of back-wardness the principle would not lead to the maximization of utility, he is perfectly consistent in denying its applicability and appropriateness. The issue therefore is not one of an inconsistency in Mill's argument. Rather the point is that the particular consistency that Mill gives to his argument is one in which he leans heavily on a civilizational and histori-cal index.

Mill deploys much the same argument in *Considerations on Represen-tative Government*. In that work he makes his commitment to progress even more acute and in the process more narrow. In the second chapter of *Considerations* entitled "Criterion of a Good Form of Government," Mill begins by pointing to those who make a distinction between "Or-der and Progress (in the phraseology of French Thinkers); Permanence and Progression, in the words of Coleridge."[59] For the proponents of this distinction, in addition to progress both order and permanence are important qualities in assessing the form of a political society. Both or-der and permanence refer to those "kinds and amounts of goods which already exist" in a society.[60] Regarding the meaning of progress, Mill says "there is no difficulty." It refers chiefly to the cultivation of "mental activity, enterprise, and courage." And it culminates in "originality or in-vention."[61]

But Mill strongly objects to any idea that order and permanence are in themselves valuable. Whatever "good" qualities they refer to cannot stand apart from the improvement implied by the term *progress*. Perma-nence, which especially troubles Mill, represents precisely those virtues, those conditions of life and living, that, as facts that circumscribe expe-rience, may not need any change, and hence improvement. They ex-hibit, as it were, an internal self-sufficiency, a benign indifference to the future, perhaps to time itself. In this sense they experientially stand outside a historical consciousness because they are rooted in a present, and hence not simply, provisionally in the present. But for Mill the only thing deserving the name *permanence* is progress itself: "progress is per-manence and something more."[62] Mill concludes the discussion of these distinctions with the following remark: "conduciveness to progress, thus understood, includes the whole excellence of a government."

This displacement and jettisoning of the notions of order and per-manence is of considerable importance, because it reveals the broad

59. J. S. Mill, *Considerations*, 158.
60. Ibid., 160.
61. Ibid., 159–161.
62. Ibid., 163.

thrust of Mill's philosophy, in which anything that is not aspiring to improvement or in the process of being improved must on account of that be designated as retrograde. This claim creates the intellectual and political space from which Mill can and does demand that the retrograde become progressive. Progress, Mill claims:

> is the idea of moving onward, whereas the meaning of it here is quite as much the prevention of falling back. The very same causes—the same beliefs, feelings, institutions, and practices— are as much required to prevent society from retrograding, as produce a further advance. Were there no improvement to be hoped for, life would not be the less an unceasing struggle against causes of deterioration; as it even now is.[63]

Life for Mill is ascent, and it has as its opposite any form of stasis. Moreover, the normative injunction to move onward, i.e., progress, at times is not even mentioned because the only alternative would be falling backward. We are left with the stark binary of the backward and the progressive, with nothing in between, nothing that can be bounded, nothing that can be present as a totality. It is the image of being on a sharply ascending mountain where one's only alternative is to have a tight grip on the rope that keeps one moving forward, because any loosening of one's grip would result in a fall. There is therefore a strong obligation to move on. The backward is linked to the future, to progress, to life itself, in such a tight embrace that to give it any latitude is to risk life itself. Moreover, this condition in which the in-between cannot be acknowledged points to the impoverishment of the hermeneutic space that Mill imagines in the encounter with the unfamiliar. If the unfamiliar, the backward, represents simply a threat to life, here understood as progress in terms of the familiar, then the relationship between the two can only be a struggle, a deathly struggle, in which power and not understanding must be deployed. In Mill that power takes the form of paternalism, a paternalism that Macaulay recognized as deeply invested in power:

> Whoever examines their letters written at that time, will find there many just and humane sentiments . . . an admirable code of political ethics . . . Now these instructions, being inter-

63. Ibid., 164.

preted, means [*sic*] simply, "Be the father and the oppressor of the people; be just and unjust, moderate and rapacious."[64]

But what this power does not recognize is that in the in-between is a relationship that constitutes both the familiar and the unfamiliar, the backward and the progressive. It is what Levinas, while explicating the I-Thou relationship in Martin Buber, explains as follows:

> The interval between the I and Thou is inseparable from the adventure in which the individual himself participates; yet is more objective than any other type of objectivity, precisely because of that personal adventure. The *Zwischen* is reconstituted in each fresh meeting. . . . [The] notion of "betweenness" functions as the fundamental category of being. . . . Man must not be construed as a subject constituting reality but rather as the articulation itself of the meeting.[65]

But for Mill the "meeting" between the backward and progressive cannot be an adventure that constantly constitutes a fresh reality because the backward has already, i.e., prior to the meeting, been designated as dead.

There is something deeply agitated about this line of thinking. It cannot stay in place without fearing declension. It is for instance difficult to imagine what Mill's view of "home" would be. After all, home is precisely that space that people imagine themselves going "back to" and where they "relax," i.e., literally stop moving. The idea of a homeland carries similar connotations and is therefore often interchanged with kinship metaphors of motherland or fatherland. It designates a space of permanence, imagined or real.

Once Mill has established the normative primacy of progress, the argument for empire, for tutelage, in a word for progressive superintendence, is all but complete. Given the theory of a hierarchical scale of civilizations and given the injunction to progress, Mill can assert:

> Thus far, of the dependencies whose population is in a sufficiently advanced state to be fitted for representative government. [Mill has been speaking of Canada and New Zealand]. But there are others which have not attained that state, and

64. T. B. Macaulay, "Warren Hastings," in *Critical and Historical Essays* (London: Methuen, 1903), 3:85–86.

65. Emmanuel Levinas, "Martin Buber and the Theory of Knowledge," in *The Levinas Reader* (Oxford: Blackwell, 1989), 65–66.

which if held at all, must be governed by the dominant country, or by persons delegated for that purpose by it. This mode of government is as legitimate as any other, if it is the one which in the existing state of civilization of the subject people, most facilitates their transition to a higher state of improvement. There are, as we have already seen, conditions of society in which a vigorous despotism is in itself the best mode of government for training the people in what is specifically wanting to render them capable of a higher civilization.[66]

THE PROBLEMATIC OF PROGRESS: HISTORY, TIME, AND POLITICS

The central axis on which nineteenth-century liberal justifications of the empire operate is time, and its cognate, patience. It is the historical time of the past and the political time of the future.[67] J. R. Seeley in his influential lectures at Cambridge University, which later were published as *The Expansion of England* (1883), makes this point unmistakable: "The ultimate object of all my teaching here is to establish this fundamental connexion, to show that politics and history are only different aspects of the same study."[68] He went on to explain his point as follows: "What can be more plainly political than the questions: What ought to be done with India? What ought to be done with our Colonies? But they are questions which need the aid of history."[69] The confidence and apparent intelligence of Seeley's linking of history and politics as "aspects of the same study" is liable to dull us, as it did his liberal cohort in the nineteenth century, from seeing the radicalness of the change this view represents with respect to the intellectual origins of liberalism. When Locke invokes history he does it either to point to its political irrelevance or—and this for him amounts to the same thing—to the fact that the testimony of history is unanimous in showing that all governments are formed by the consent of the people.[70] History, that is to say, exposes no special problems that serve as constraints on what is to be done politically. As an aside, it is worth mentioning that some future nationalists would find the thrust and economy of Seeley's and the nineteenth-

66. Mill, *On Liberty*, 408–9.
67. See Homi Bhabha, "Sly Civility," in *The Location of Culture*, 93–101, and "The Postcolonial and the Postmodern," also in *The Location*, 171–97.
68. Seeley, *The Expansion of England*, 133, emphasis added.
69. Ibid., 134.
70. Locke, *Second Treatise of Government*, chap. 8, "Of the Beginning of Political Societies."

century liberal argument, linking the political with the historical, very convenient. In the context of anticolonial struggle it required only that the negative sign attached to the history of the prospective nation be reversed to a positive—"our history makes us ready for political independence"—while in the postindependence context the link between history and the political gave the nationalist state the amplitude of political latitude that was typically sought—"our history requires that the state be powerful and interventionist."[71] What, after all, could give state power, whether imperial or national, greater prestige and room for maneuver than to be responsible for a collective future burdened by a recalcitrant and deviant past?

There is another philosophically more pressing sense in which time plays a crucial role in this broad liberal vision of history. I have suggested that the normative valuations that liberals make, that is of those who are deemed to be "backward" and those who are not, are expressed as historical facts that can be redressed only through the instrument of political intervention and in the register of future time. That is to say, "backwardness" is expressed as a temporal deficit or stasis, which in turn can be made whole, or progressive, only by being hitched to a temporal credit, and through the caboose of politics to the time of the future. Hence even extant examples of "backwardness" get coded as remnants of the past. James Mill's *History* is, for example, replete with instances of practices and beliefs that he acknowledged to be present, that is, as part of the extant life forms of India, but he nevertheless presents them as curious and recalcitrant fossils of the past. The conundrum that this exposes, of a past that is present and a present that is understood as past, is never consciously acknowledged within liberal/imperial historiography. The ideas associated with progress camouflage, as it were, the common meaning of the words that trigger those ideas. Here the evidence lies in the awkwardness that is imposed on language so that neither past nor present mean what they would be understood to mean on a simple temporal reckoning. Instead they represent normative valuations of the backward and the progressive. Here one is reminded of Marx, for he too is left in much the same way—one thinks almost despite himself and despite his account of capitalism—with having to acknowledge those "unconquered remnants"[72] of the past that curiously resist the "despotism of capital."

71. See Partha Chatterjee, *Nationalist Thought and the Colonial World: A Derivative Discourse* (Minneapolis: University of Minnesota Press, 1993), esp. chap. 5.
72. Karl Marx, introduction, in *Grundrisse*, trans. Martin Nicolaus (New York: Vintage, 1973), 105.

But what becomes of the contemporaneous in this view that cannot admit the present as present and that, moreover, cannot see in the present an agentiality, a will, a life form that tenaciously exists against the insistence of a theory that has it designated as dead? If the past and the future are sequentially the sources of liberalism's agenda of reformist action and optimism, it is the contemporaneous that points to the limits of the way liberals like the Mills have typically interpreted the challenge of understanding unfamiliar life forms. For the contemporaneity of these unfamiliar life forms cannot be spoken of in the register of historical time, for that register translates them into the linearity of backwardness and thus immediately conceives of them in terms of an already known future. This mapping codes the life forms, beliefs, practices, and thus the space in which experiencing occurs—that is, the space in which the unfamiliar or the "backward" exist—onto a temporal axis in which their life can be understood only as a provisional or remnant form of extraordinary and spectral survival, like shadows that can be seen despite the absence of their substantiality or ghosts of the past that haunt and are merely hosted by the present. But in this form of survival, experience is either exoticized or denied. In either event this maneuver blocks the search for a hermeneutics of spatially contemporaneous life forms whose differences, at least a priori, exist on the same ontological plane and must therefore be understood in terms of a relationality of heterogeneous spatial simultaneity and not homogeneous temporal linearity.

The appeal of history for liberalism's universalistic political vision has a lot to do, at least conceptually, with the post-Newtonian algebraic continuity that is intuitively suggested in the notion of a continuous, singular, and therefore nondiscrete time. This is true even though, as I am arguing, the liberal conception of time is not, in fact, one of perfect continuity, because the contemporaneous or the present is in constant need of being realigned with the future through the special effort of political intervention. Absent this effort, the present could always have the potential for a dizzying plenitude that could host a multiplicity of developmental trajectories. If such an eventuality appears consonant with the liberal celebration of choice and a variety of life plans, and therefore might be a source of liberal comfort, it is a comfort that they had the confidence to countenance only in the face of the familiar.[73] The

73. What precisely was accepted as the "familiar" is obviously a complex problem and beyond the scope of this work. However, it is important to make clear that the identification of familiarity, like unfamiliarity, did not occur simply through the broad categories of culture, race, religion, or region. The history within Britain of the working-class struggle, women's rights, the status of Jews and Catholics, and, of

PROGRESS, CIVILIZATION, AND CONSENT

language of a progressive history, along with a reliance on a singular and continuous conception of time, serves as an emollient that naturalizes what in fact were often aggressive and violent efforts to suppress multiple and extant temporalities and corresponding life forms.[74]

In contrast to this conception of time, the notion of space—at least after Euler and others challenged the hegemony of the Euclidean version of it, and in doing so returned it to its more experientially self-evident form—is much closer to a vision of discrete and bounded places that can be connected only through the special effort of building bridges—bridges that connect, without the urge to make contiguous or sequential, two or more contemporaneous life forms.[75] In this vision the world is full of islands in which journeys of connection are always, as Hume and the Greek epics remind us, arduous and without assurance of success. Unlike Euclidean space and progressive and continuous time, in this vision transport is not a synonym for journeying for it does not indicate the faults and obstacles encountered in the latter. Here neither reason, language, nor the *ratio* of history gives us the smooth space in which everything is, as it were, already found to be connected. Instead it is a space in which not everything has common boundaries and therefore one cannot make the slippage, no doubt with genuine unselfconsciousness, that allows James Mill to compass the history of his country

---

course, the Irish question in some sense testifies to the fact that notions of history and a developmental temporality play a significant role with regard to these issues, too. Nevertheless, as I have suggested in the introduction, there is a sense in which these issues get settled within the familiar terms of liberal discourse and are therefore importantly different from matters raised within the empire. There is obviously an issue of fuzzy boundaries here, namely the question of where the familiar ends and the unfamiliar begins. With respect to this question I rely on the texts with I deal here because, without fully theorizing this problem, they themselves make clear that empire and issues raised within it occur beyond the point where the boundary is fuzzy.

74. My thoughts on history and time have been strongly influenced by Norbert Elias, *Time: An Essay*, trans. Edmund Jephcott (Oxford: Blackwell, 1987); Emmanuel Levinas, "Time and the Other," in *The Levinas Reader*, 37–58; and Giorgio Agamben, "Time and History," in *Infancy and History: Essays on the Destruction of Experience*, trans. Liz Heron (New York: Verso, 1993), 91–105. Finally, I am indebted to the various writings that touch on these issues by Homi Bhabha and Dipesh Chakrabarty. See esp. Chakrabarty, "Radical Histories and the Question of Enlightenment Rationalism: Some Recent Critiques of *Subaltern Studies*," *Economic and Political Weekly* 30, no. 14 (April 1995): 751–59.

75. See Michel Serres, "Language and Space," in *Hermes: Literature, Science, Philosophy* (Baltimore: Johns Hopkins University Press, 1982), 39–53, for an extremely suggestive reading, primarily of the Greek epics, that explores the notion of spatial discontinuity.

and go on to write the history of India. This is how he introduces his *History:*

> In the course of reading and investigation, necessary for acquiring that measure of knowledge which I was anxious to possess, respecting my country, its people, its government, its interests, its policy, and its laws, I was met, and in some degree surprised, by extraordinary difficulties when I arrived at that part of my inquiries which related to India.[76]

The "extraordinary difficulties" encountered by Mill are those of satisfying the rigorous requirements of writing history—the reading, the investigations, the difficulties of meeting the epistemological standards of producing knowledge. But this standard presumes on a pattern of invariability, an itinerary that history and the historian follow and record. Neither the surprise nor the difficulties that Mill refers to include the recognition of having entered a different space when he arrives at that portion of his inquiries that relate to India. He is, as the single sentence of his prose suggests, simply transported there. In the course of that transposition he comes upon nothing that is closed or only partially open, nothing with an exterior but perhaps an obscured interior, nothing that has a limit or a boundary, in brief, nothing that has a variegated and challenging topology. A few sentences later Mill announces the challenge that he, the historian, the philosopher, and administrator, faces: "[the] knowledge, requisite for attaining an adequate conception of that great scene of British action [i.e., India], was collected no where."[77] The challenge, for Mill, remains squarely epistemological. It is one of finding the right sources, choosing between the multiplicity of conflicting documents, judiciously selecting one's informants: in short, being sure that one is producing knowledge.

What Mill does not recognize, what simply does not strike him, is that this knowledge could refer to a different experiential field, to a different aesthetic, literally to a different perceptual realm and the connections that get made within it.[78] Indeed, as I pointed out in the previous chapter, Mill is self-conscious and insistent on the taint that such perceptual and linguistic contact with India can have on the craft of the historian. The slippage that is evident in the opening passage of Mill's *History* also sets the tone for much that follows in the course of its six

76. Mill, *History of British India*, 1:xv.
77. Ibid.
78. The word *aesthetic* has its etymological origin in the Greek *aisthnesthai*, meaning to perceive.

PROGRESS, CIVILIZATION, AND CONSENT

volumes. Mill does not recognize that a culture or society constructs in and by its own history what Michel Serres has called "an original intersection between . . . spatial varieties, a node of very precise and particular connections."[79] It is in the particularity of the connections and relays that a society makes, and blocks, that its singularity becomes a datum of experience. But Mill will not—in a sense, he must not—for the sake of the history he is writing, come into contact with the singularity of India. That conception of history, as I have suggested, is anchored in a vision of universal history that is itself tethered to an eschatology of progress. In that vision it is not the singularity of India (or anywhere else), or the experiences that are made possible by and that are internal to this singularity, that are significant. Instead, both India and experience have a provisional status that turns on the value accorded to them in a preestablished schema by virtue of their specificity—that is, as instances of this schema—and not on account of their singularity. Within this framework the task of history is to "record" so that it can compare without entering the experience of the backward. For Mill, and for many of his cohort, history is that chosen field that allowed them to imagine the world as a connected and smooth surface, uniformly available to a fixed grid of knowledge.

CONCLUSION

There are many ironic implications of the liberal argument. First, by making the expression of consent conditional on having reached a stage of historical maturation, liberal imperialism never sees, much less acknowledges, its own coercive efforts. As Mill blithely suggests in *On Liberty*, even the despotism of "an Akbar or a Charlemagne" can be a privilege for some societies "if they are fortunate to find" such agents of history to lead them. Because Indians have not reached the point at which they know how to consent or govern themselves, they cannot know or experience coercion or the absence of self-government, which is, after all, nothing other than the frustration of consent. The relativism of this argument allows for an indefinite temporizing so long as such efforts remain within the scaffolding of progress. For liberals, the empire aligns the plural vagaries of history under a singular conception of progress. In a sense this redeems, at least as a possibility, the liberal vision of a cosmopolitan future. Thus it is the past and the future that are the temporalities to which liberalism is most committed. The past,

79. Serres, *Hermes*, 45.

when viewed from the present, always shows its deficiencies; the future, again when viewed from the present, always holds out the promise of realizing Descartes's dream of infinite progress.

A second irony is that despite the expressed liberal commitment to the primacy of the individual, the person who is a member of a backward society or community cannot vouch for him- or herself. He or she is spoken for by the society of which he or she is a member, and that society is itself spoken for by the historiography that establishes the particular stage of historical maturation that that society is deemed to have achieved. The very idea of civilization, as R. G. Collingwood points out, and as both the Mills clearly would have concurred, "is something which happens to a community."[80] This underscores the argument made in the next chapter, namely that notwithstanding the claim that individual consent is the basis of political community, some conception of community must be presupposed or taken for granted as existing prior to the consensual justification of the political community. The moral and political standing of that prior or concealed community—concealed, that is, in liberal thought—makes all the difference to the potentialities associated with the willfully formed community. In effect, the differentials of historical development become the justificatory grounds for the differential rights and privileges granted to individuals. It is indeed curious that John Stuart Mill, who in the context of nineteenth-century European liberalism advocates the most capacious bounds for the play of individuality and eccentricity, should in the context of the empire self-consciously offer arguments whose implications are that we are all confined within the narrow compass of our communal historical pasts and from which we can break out only by attaching ourselves to "the leading strings" of the empire. It is only one of the many revealing ambivalences of Mill's thought that as a committed individualist he should have taken collective histories, rather than individual "case histories," as seriously as he did.

Both of these arguments are challenged in a single blow by nationalism. In denying the differentials of history, nationalism denies the liberal justification of the empire, announces the coercion of the empire as something experienced, and simultaneously makes the new member of the nation a full legal citizen. What nationalism does is repudiate the developmental chronologies of the empire by announcing that the preparatory work for self-governance was done by history long, long ago.

---

80. R. G. Collingwood, *The New Leviathan* (Oxford: Oxford University Press, 1947), 283.

In fact, it displaces history in the name of culture and geography and makes them the evidentiary basis for the readiness of the nation.[81]

In the Indian context, there is the special and almost unique (within nationalist discourse) argument made by Mahatma Gandhi. The terms of the argument have a familiar resonance with the liberal emphasis on civilization as a condition for the possibility of individual and collective self-development. But where liberals associate the term *civilization* with history and the trajectory of its development, for Gandhi the term has a purely ethical and moral meaning. In his 1909 work *Hind Swaraj*, which he himself translated into English, he defines civilization as follows:

> Civilization is that mode of conduct which points to man the path of duty. Performance of duty and observance of morality are convertible terms. To observe morality is to attain mastery over our mind and passions.[82]

As is true of so much about Gandhi, this definition is deceptively simple and almost conceals its own effectivity and relevance vis-à-vis both the empire and the more familiar expressions of nationalism. It accepts the centrality that the liberal argument placed on civilization as a condition of progress and independence. But Gandhi understands the term in ways that make it impossible to rely on history, politics, the tutelage of one community by another, and more generally the work of power as engines and instruments of civilization. Instead, Gandhi's civilization is purely individualistic. It turns on human beings being able to follow the dictates of their duty and their morality. And this Gandhi suggests individuals can do only through enormous effort and self-control. But they can do this—they can, that is, be civilized—even in the earliest and most primitive stages of human development; the fact of greater development, and the history that evidences it, no more or less inclines them to be civilized. Here Gandhi reminds liberals of a value and a truth that he shares with them, but that in his view liberals had lost sight of through the emphasis they came to place on politics and power to the neglect of the ethical—the capacity for moral action of individuals, not some individuals but all individuals.

This in effect was the ethical cosmopolitanism with which Gandhi challenged the political and historical cosmopolitanism of the empire. It allowed Gandhi to countenance the possibility that Indian civilization

---

81. See chapter 4 below.
82. M. K. Gandhi, *Hind Swaraj and Other Writings*, 67.

makes it possible for independent India to grant the full legal rights of democratic citizenship and franchise to 350 million illiterate, substantially impoverished, deeply religious, and markedly diverse individuals. What prepared them for this moment of self-rule were capacities that they had by virtue of being human beings who could act in conformance to their duty. (Of course, and ironically, all this is true only prior to the triumph of the nation, for in the very instance of its success the nation-state typically reappropriates, as Ashis Nandy has argued, the tutelary and developmental language of the empire.)[83]

As a final aside one can see how, at least in part, it is the work of this nationalism that supports and underlies many of the contemporary challenges that multiculturalism stands for. For what the various cultural groups today deny and what nineteenth-century liberalism, in contrast to contemporary liberalism, could assert is the claim of historical and civilizational differentials. The motto of present-day multicultural claims might very well be "We are present in contemporary time and the rights we demand stem from that temporal equality." The "now" that Mill could presume on was a copresence of many differential times, which represented many differential histories, and which it was the work of empire patiently to equalize. Nationalism, which would not "wait," has done that, at least at an enunciatory level. In doing so it has shattered, at least on an international level and perhaps mainly at that level, the pedagogic assumptions on which Lockean and Millian liberalism relied. It is after all only in the last thirty-five-odd years that liberalism has abjured the language of historical backwardness and hesitates even when speaking of a univocal conception of progress.[84]

83. Ashis Nandy, *The Illegitimacy of Nationalism* (Delhi: Oxford University Press, 1994).

84. It is striking, for example, that in a broad-minded and capacious liberal such as John Plamenatz, who at least took the empire problem seriously, writing in 1960, the language of backwardness is still confidently asserted. See Plamenatz, *On Alien Rule and Self-Government.*

Liberalism, Empire, and Territory

One of the remarkable ironies of the link between liberal thought and the British Empire is that the latter's monumental size, the sheer space it occupied on the ground—in brief, its far-flung and immense territory—is seldom raised to the level of theoretical attention by the tradition of the former. The fact, supported by the boast, on account of which the empire was favorably compared even against the sun by claiming that the latter did not set on it, still remained below the threshold of reflection for the empire's most philosophic protagonists. There is nothing in this tradition of thought that compares with Herodotus or Xenophon pondering the effects of the expansion of the Persian Empire on itself and on the Greek Peloponnesus; or with Cicero worrying and reflecting on the predicament of the Roman Empire when one language was no longer adequate to administer it; or with Madison and his fellow Federalists' searching and public deliberations into the modalities by which ancient democratic theory could be modified to serve the needs of an "extended Republic"; nothing analogous to Tocqueville's making the continental expanse of America the point of departure for his reflections on democracy in America. Indeed, there is very little in this tradition by virtue of which it can be seen as seriously reflecting on the question, What—besides power and a congealed state of affairs—made an Inuit in the upper reaches of Canada, a gentleman in a borough of London, a Bhil tribesman in the hills of Rajasthan, and a Maori in New Zealand—all subjects of an empress ensconced in a small island in the Atlantic Ocean?

The space of the empire, along with the myriad political and psychological issues folded into it, is simply not taken seriously by the leading British liberal thinkers of the nineteenth century.[1] It is not, of course, that these thinkers were oblivious to the immensity of the em-

---

1. The one notable and serious exception to this tradition of neglect is Bentham, who in his *Essay on the Influence of Time and Place in Legislation* attempted to address the issue by considering the case of Bengal. "To a law-giver, who having been brought up with English notions, shall have learned how to accommodate his

pire; rather, they did not see that fact as raising questions that could not be integrated within the familiar and well-worn categories of their thought. It is in this denial that the leading thinkers of the age remained strangely but stridently closed to an aspect of the empire that made it distinctive—after all, this was not like any other empire, it was instead, as Charles Duff put it, "the British Government of India, the virtually despotic government of a dependency by a free people."[2] Moreover, in retrospect one can say that the absence of self-consciousness regarding the empire's own locality foretold its fated terminus in the face of nationalism, which, whatever else it did and represented, insisted on the political credence of drawing boundaries.

The temptation to see in this remarkable omission a sign of a deep complicity with the existing state of affairs or a myopia regarding them, such that a basic feature of the empire, its size and variety, could not be interrogated or seen, is simply wrong. Philosophers of John Stuart Mill's intellect and character, and many lesser ones, had no compunctions in holding a candle to deeply entrenched aspects of the status quo by continually casting a searing gaze at it. Neither complicity with the status quo nor a simple myopia is adequate as an explanation for this sustained and significant neglect. Instead, as I argue in this chapter, the issue pertains to a central aspect of liberal thought. It is the manner in which locality or territory is conceived that eviscerates that thought's political and emotive significance and thus renders it inert; it cannot then emerge as a relevant normative issue. This conceptualization both precedes and endures after the imperial phase, and its implications are multifarious.

Indeed, this absence that is so striking in imperial discourse is no less so in contemporary liberal thought. One of the most conspicuous aspects of modern political societies is that they are identified, both internally and externally, with a specific territory.[3] The major political in-

---

laws to the circumstances of Bengal, no other part of the globe can present a difficulty." Jeremy Bentham, *Essay on the Influence of Time and Place in Legislation* in *Works of Jeremy Bentham*, ed. Bowring, 1:172.

However, upon reflection even Bentham considered the issue of time and place, with regard to matters of legislation, only something that had to be "humored" and did not therefore seriously limit the claims or the potential of the "science of legislation."

2. Sir Henry Maine, "The Effects of Observation of India on Modern European Thought" (Cambridge: The Rede Lecture, 1875).

3. There is substantial historical and anthropological evidence to suggest that this is a distinct feature of roughly post-fifteenth-century politics. For broad historical accounts that consider the changing relationship between political power and

struments, the laws, the institutions, the obligations and benefits that states impose and grant, the determinants of membership, indeed the political constitution of a society, are territorially delimited. Moreover, societies typically invest considerable material and symbolic resources in the security and celebration of the territory with which they are identified. They guard their borders, carefully monitor entry and exit, and in things like national songs and anthems they most often valorize their land and geography.

Subjectively, citizens think of themselves, in no doubt complex ways, as "coming from" or "belonging to" a specific, territorially demarcated place. In this they give expression to an important ground that they share with their fellow citizens and cohabitants. They invest that ground with qualities that express their individual and collective identities as in the familiar American songs "My Country 'Tis of Thee, Sweet *Land* of Liberty" and "America the Beautiful." Clearly the cartographic practice of indicating distinct political societies with sharply different colors has its analogue in the cognitive realities of most citizens.[4]

Yet, despite this, political theorists in the Anglo-American liberal tradition have, for the most part, not only ignored the links between political identity and territory, but have also conceptualized the former in terms that at least implicitly deny any significance to the latter and

rule and territory, see, for instance, Norbert Elias, *Power and Civility*, trans. Edmund Jephcott (New York: Pantheon Books), 91–117; Georges Duby, *The Three Orders: Feudal Society Imagined*, trans. Arthur Goldhammer (Chicago: University of Chicago Press, 1980); E. L. Jones, *The European Miracle: Environments, Economics, and Geopolitics in the History of Europe and Asia* (Cambridge: Cambridge University Press, 1981); Jean Gottmann, *The Significance of Territory* (Charlottesville: University of Virginia Press, 1973); and Robert David Sack, *Human Territoriality: Its Theory and History* (New York: Cambridge University Press, 1986). In the anthropological literature there is the classic statement by L. H. Morgan that formulates social evolution in terms of the shift from consanguinity to contiguity; see Morgan, *Ancient Society*, ed. Eleanor Leacock (Gloucester, Mass.: Peter Smith, 1963).

4. This is not to suggest that other sources of belonging such as blood ties, ethnicity, common language, race, and of course constitutional preference have not played a significant role. Clearly they have. But this fact does not, by itself, invalidate the role of territory for at least two reasons: first, because there is no reason why there could not be more than one source to this sense of national identification; and second, because it is seldom the case that any one or some combination of these alternative sources has functioned without also having an explicit territorial referent. For instance, in the United States, where, according to the widely held and celebrated Jeffersonian tradition, political identity resides in the shared commitment to certain "self-evident" normative liberal principles, references to territoriality date back to at least John Winthrop's "City on the Hill" sermon delivered on the deck of the Arrabella in 1630.

to the links between the two.[5] The implications of this neglect are considerable, both in their historical and contemporary effects. They are also revealing of the important ways in which liberalism conceptualizes political identity and the struggles that inform it. The issue of political identity and territory relates, for instance, to the now well acknowledged though historically long-standing silence and incomprehension of liberal thinkers in the face of nineteenth-century European nationalism and concurrent and subsequent anticolonial nationalist struggles.[6] It is similarly implicated with problems of subnationalism, self-determination, border changes and conflicts, regional unification, and even the global phenomenon of international immigration and refugee populations, which feature the porous nature of territorial boundaries. And plainly the defense of borders and the territory that they enclose is a crucial consideration in interstate wars and in the justification of the wide latitude that national security concerns typically receive. Relatedly, in the twentieth century, it is clear that something about territory makes it taboo for states to sell it, or to deploy it as a fungible liquid asset in their relations with other states. Barring conditions such as in the former Yugoslavia or the immediate aftermath of the Second World War, territory simply is not a bargaining counter that states can use in international conflict.[7] Territory remains, notwithstanding the various changes that sovereignty is undergoing, the most tangible and symbolic expression of sovereignty and political unity.[8]

5. The reason for the restriction to "Anglo-American liberalism" is that consideration of territoriality, either directly or indirectly, via notions such as climate and geography, are plainly evident in the work of, for instance, French liberals such as Montesquieu, Tocqueville, and Durkheim. Which is not to say that the specific omissions that I point to vis-à-vis the Anglo-American liberal tradition are absent in the French, only that it is less plainly the case with respect to this latter, or more generally the Continental, tradition.

6. Isaiah Berlin, "The Bent Twig," in *The Crooked Timber of Humanity* (New York: Knopf, 1991), 238–61.

7. James D. Fearon conceptualizes this fact as part of a group of situations where feasible bargains between states are indivisible. See Fearon, "Rationalist Explanations for War," *International Organization* 49, no. 3 (summer 1995): 379–414.

8. In a wide-ranging and insightful article, John G. Ruggie explores how contemporary international relations theory simply assumes the distinctly modern form of territoriality as something that is "disjoint, fixed, and mutually exclusive" (p 168). In doing so the prevailing theory ignores the historical peculiarity and the corresponding theoretical inflections of the process by which the differentiation of states came to assume this form. Ruggie, "Territoriality and Beyond," *International Organization* 47, no. 1 (winter 1993): 139–74. See also John Herz, "The Territorial State Revisited: Reflections on the Future of the Nation State," *Polity* (fall 1968): 32–59.

The issue therefore is not that territory, as a fact that underlies political arrangements, is ignored. Indeed, it is obvious that we would not recognize either inter- or intrastate political arrangements and deliberations without explicit or implicit reference to this fact. Rather the problem, at one level, is that the ubiquity of its significance is belied by the lack of theoretical attention paid to it.[9] At another and more relevant level the theoretical assumptions of liberalism do not readily comport with the very considerations that give territory its political salience. This points to a tension between the facts of political life and the dominant theory through which we interpret and seek guidance in transforming that life. The argument of this chapter is that, with respect to political identity, the theory diverges so starkly from the pattern of human feelings and extant political practices that it does not appreciate and hence cannot guide those feelings and practices without significantly modifying itself. Moreover, the neglect of the role and significance of territory has diminished the liberal appreciation of the manifold constituents of political identity, and for this reason, it has often both narrowed liberal sympathies in the face of alternative and unfamiliar ways of organizing political communities and also colluded in their violation. Liberals have failed to appreciate that territory is both a symbolic expression and a concrete condition for the possibility of (or aspirations to) a distinct way of life, and that in the modern epoch it gathers together many of the associations through which individuals come to see themselves as members of a political society.[10] To invoke a metaphor

9. This has a corresponding effect on the literature. I know of no nonlegal treatise within the liberal tradition that considers the issue of territory with any degree of sustained seriousness. Of course historians, geographers, international lawyers, and scholars of international relations have written extensively on matters that directly relate to this issue. The reason for this is clearly that in these fields the fact of territory (both in the sense of something that *exists* and in the historical sense of something that is *made*) simply cannot be evaded. Among contemporary political theorists William Connolly is the only one of whom I am aware who has considered issues of territoriality with the seriousness that they deserve. See the very insightful chapter "Democracy and Territoriality" in Connolly, *The Ethos of Pluralization* (Minneapolis: University of Minnesota Press, 1995), 135–63.

10. There is an irony in this neglect; it reveals political theory as proceeding at a tangent to the emerging practices with which it was broadly coterminous. Just when, in the popular imagination, the associations between territory and political identity were being consolidated and were replacing older notions that had linked the latter with monarchical authority and genealogy, Anglo-American liberalism denied the significance of any such links. The link between land, map making, and political identity and the manner in which these connections subtly challenged and displaced royal absolutism has been illustrated with regard to Britain in Richard

prevalent in early liberal theorizing, territory is the *body* of the polity, which, not unlike the human body, marks the perimeter within and through which its identity is constituted and the specific expression of its autonomy is molded.

This chapter has three broad purposes. The first is to explain the historical and conceptual basis of the liberal neglect of the political significance of territory. In the Lockean liberal tradition, on which I focus, discussions of political identity—or in Locke's language the basis of political society—have been anchored in the idea of individual consent and the presumed priority of rational, individual self-interest in consensually and contractually establishing political society. In terms of elaborating the significance of territory to political identity this orientation in effect involves elaborating on, and explaining the reasons for, an absence. Discussions of territorial political attachments are on the surface simply absent from Locke's *Treatises*.[11] I therefore illustrate this first purpose indirectly through Locke's famous discussion of the origins of private property. The substantive point that this first section establishes is that Locke characterizes the human encounter with nature and the earth as one that is sentimentally inert at both an individual and collective level. The fact that people live and interact together in a world that is "commonly held" is of no political import. Such interactions neither engender communal sentiments nor stem from a sense of locality. Finally, they also do not create identities based on a functional interdependence mediated by nature or the earth. Moreover, nothing in Locke's analysis suggests that the human encounter with nature has any such potential. For this reason there is no attempt to give conceptual or political credence to any "prepolitical" sense of belonging or togetherness that is braced by the links with nature or the earth. Locke's discussion of private property vividly illustrates the conceptual moves through which territorial attachments are bleached of any potential political weight in the course of establishing his ostensible purpose, namely, to give an account of the origins of private property.

The second purpose is to draw out some of the political implications of this neglect. The implication on which I focus is the Lockean and nineteenth-century liberal resistance to recognize the distinctiveness of political societies and hence the physical and emotional

---

Helgerson, *Forms of Nationhood* (Chicago: University of Chicago Press, 1992), esp. chap. 3.

11. I say "on the surface" because there are all sorts of indications that suggest that Locke is in fact presuming, but without elaborating on, some kind of territorial cohesion. See the discussion on pages 130–132 on borders and tacit consent.

boundaries that link and separate them. Precisely because the Lockean conception of political identity rests on individual consent, this is of special poignancy in instances where plainly the basis of political society, both subjectively for individuals and for the collectivity, is not, or was not, such consent. The main point of this, the second section, is to highlight how in the absence of a conception of belonging or territorial togetherness, liberals were unable to recognize and appreciate the political integrity of various nonconsensual societies.

Finally, I conclude by pointing to the manner in which the above claims cast some light on the puzzling fact of the liberal endorsement of the British Empire during the eighteenth, nineteenth, and even early twentieth centuries.[12] It is no exaggeration to say that the liberal justification of the British Empire in the eighteenth century, but most conspicuously in the nineteenth, was premised on the presumed nonexistence of extant "native" political societies. It is a view on which Bentham, James Mill, Macaulay, J. S. Mill, and a host of other thinkers were in complete agreement. Such societies were at best only in a state of "becoming."[13] What is remarkable is that this view is embedded in a constellation of ideas that were committed to representative government and the primacy of a citizenly identity. The view endures with added emphasis into the nineteenth century, when notions of autonomy and self-governance come to predominate over the explicit idea of individual consent.

The most far-reaching implication of the denial of extant political societies is the long-standing and even contemporary difficulty that liberals have had in acknowledging the motives and tenacity of European and anticolonial nationalism. In the case of the British in India, by the

12. Here again I not making the claim that this fact *alone* explains or exhausts this puzzle.

13. This view has considerable tenacity and persists in the thought of several contemporary scholars. Louis Dumont for instance sees in the pervasiveness of caste ideology the fundamental reason for India's political disunity. Similarly Burton Stein justifies this view by reference to parochial peasant mentality, and J. C. Heesterman finds in the renunciatory emphasis of local religions the unstable grounding to political institutions. See Louis Dumont, "The Conception of Kingship in Ancient India," appendix C to *Homo Hierarchicus*, rev. ed., trans. Mark Sainsbury, Louis Dumont, and Basia Gulati (Chicago: University of Chicago Press, 1980); Burton Stein, *Peasant State and Society in Medieval South India* (Delhi: Oxford University Press, 1980); and J. C. Heesterman, *The Inner Conflict of Tradition: Essays in Indian Ritual, Kinship, and Society* (Chicago: University of Chicago Press, 1985). All three of these scholars are discussed in some detail in Ronald Inden, *Imagining India* (Oxford: Blackwell, 1992), chap. 5.

mid–nineteenth century, the presumed absence in India of the basic integuments of nationhood (or nationhoods) becomes the justificatory
cornerstone of imperial practices and ideology. It informs the entire
spectrum of liberal and progressive reforms in which the empire is no
longer justified on the basis of the rights and the needs of the metropole,
but rather on grounds of the political inadequacies of the colonies. Underlying such denials and claims of inadequacy is the more fundamental
theoretical resistance to the possibility that political identity can be
forged from associations and attachments that are local, contingent, and
hence, from an Archimedean point of view, historically arbitrary; which
is to say that these identities emerge from and gather together local
historical genealogies. For liberals such as both the Mills, as I have argued in the previous chapter, the existence of political societies is predicated on civilizational and developmental narratives. Indeed, during the
nineteenth century the political and normative thrust of liberalism is
squarely predicated on a philosophy of history that completely displaces
the earlier heuristic of the hypothetical state of nature. But for nationalists in anticolonial struggles, the local and the contingent (contingent,
of course, only in terms of liberal narratives) are crucial normative resources. Even when nationalists invoked the language of liberal universalism they alloyed it with the textured realities of a locally imagined
and physical landscape.[14] And geography was often their most powerful
tool.[15] And even though there has always been great complexity and
normative variety in the terms through which nationalists have articulated the "we" on whose behalf they profess to speak, nevertheless de-

14. In subsection 346 of the *Philosophy of Right*, Hegel makes the following
statement, which also appears to suggest the link between the contingencies of local
and geographical conditions with national identity:

> History is mind clothing itself with the forms of events or the immediate
> actuality of nature. The stages of its development are therefore presented
> as immediate natural principles. These, because they are natural, are a plu-
> rality external to one another, and they are present therefore in such a
> way that each of them is assigned to one nation in the external form of
> its geographical and anthropological conditions. (Hegel, *Philosophy of
> Right*, 217)

15. In this context it is worth mentioning that the Indian nationalist and statesman Jawaharlal Nehru always visualized India as defined by the sweep of monumental geographical icons. In his autobiography *Discovery of India*, and in numerous other
works, Nehru typically conceives of India as a land demarcated by the Himalayan
arch of the north, the Indus River system of the west, the great river deltas of the
east, the southern peninsula, all under the umbrella of the monsoons from the east
and the west.

mands for political autonomy have insisted on the requirement of a separate territory.

As part of the second and third purposes I point to Burke by way of contrast with the Lockean tradition. For Burke, territory, or *place*, is a fundamental condition of collective and individual political identity. Moreover, it constitutes the ground through which notions such as duty, obligation, order, and freedom come to have the political meaning that they do. In this Burke extends, perhaps beyond recognition, Machiavelli's understanding of sovereignty in terms of a prince's control or rule over a specified territory. Burke's extension is to have seen *place* as anchoring both individual and collective identity, not just for the narrow instrumentality of rule or control, but in the more complex and psychologically deeper sense in which identity draws on entrenched feelings and memories and, through them, to prospective hopes. Images of anchoring, depth, and entrenchment understandably provoke fears of confinement and of an identity that must intransigently remain in the *place* where it belongs. Burke would challenge such an interpretation and the locational rigidity that it ascribes to his views. But his challenge would emphatically caution against the opposite assumption, one he would call speculative, in which identities are crafted from a presumed absence of entrenched feelings and associations and an amplitude of willful choice. That alternative is fraught with the destructive horror of Jacobin and imperial arrogance and naïveté. It is, in part, because Burke views *place* as linked with specifically political attributes that he was able to recognize alternative ways of forming political societies, including the incipient expressions of the energy and imagination that culminated in nineteenth- and twentieth-century nationalism. Moreover, it is inter alia this very appreciation that informs his deep—and in the eighteenth century profoundly lonely—critique of the British Empire.

Nature, a Worthless Inheritance

The ostensible purpose of Locke's discussion of property in the *Second Treatise* is to explain how human beings legitimately subdivided into units of private property a world that had been granted to them by God "in common."[16] To this end Locke puts forward his well-known idea of private property originating from the mixing of human labor with a nature held in common and of labor being the principal source of value.

---

16. Locke, *Second Treatise of Government*, ed. Peter Laslett (New York: Mentor Books, 1960), sec. 25, p. 327.

The explanation and the legitimacy for parceling what was given in common into privately held property stems from labor making things in general, and land in particular, valuable. Because "every man has a *Property* in his own *Person*" and since this property is exclusive of others, "mixing" it with a portion of commonly held nature makes that portion "properly his."[17] Conceptually the idea is that the mixing of something that is clearly *mine* (i.e., my labor) with something that is held in common makes the relevant portion of the latter *my* property.

The plausibility of Locke's argument crucially and explicitly relies on two claims that he treats as facts: first, that nature in itself is all but worthless; and second, that individual labor is the overwhelming source of value, more precisely use value. This latter claim is made more conspicuous and significant through its contrast with the worthlessness of nature. Only by treating these two claims as background facts does the mixing of human labor into a portion of commonly held nature establish exclusive private property rights. In their absence, there would always be the possibility that acts of human labor simply enriched the commons or, as Locke might have thought, such acts merely wasted themselves into the commons without having established any exclusive right to a portion of it.[18] Such a possibility is blocked by the force of the two claims. Because labor is the preponderant source of value, mixing it with nature in a sense extends the domain of the body. This is the domain that Locke, notwithstanding his view of human beings as "being all the Workmanship of one Omnipotent, and infinitely wise Maker,"[19] associates with having property in one's "own person" and with exclusivity— "[t]he *labor* of his Body, and the *Work* of his Hands, we may say, are properly his."[20] Private property, at least in its origin, thus involves the dual features of marking something that was held in common, i.e., making it distinct—a sort of tactile signature—and simultaneously imbuing it with value and in the process making it worthy of being possessed.

Locke's characterization of nature and specifically of the earth is resonant with familiar though strangely subverted metaphors. The earth, our common inheritance, a gift from God no less, turns out to be in its given form worthless, an inertial wasteland: "Nature and Earth furnished only the almost *worthless* materials, as in themselves."[21] Nature, "the common Mother of all," is infertile until she is "subdued" for

17. Ibid., sec. 27.
18. See ibid., secs. 40, 41, and 42.
19. Ibid., sec. 6.
20. Ibid., sec. 27.
21. Ibid., sec. 43 (emphasis added).

the "benefit of life" through labor's seminal infusion.[22] A common and capacious divine gift is redeemed only by laborious acts of human "improvement"; acts that "enclose . . . from the Common" and only thus make it distinctive and valuable.[23] There is a strained quality to the way Locke deploys these metaphors. They appear to point in one direction on account of the familiar associations on which they draw, and yet these associations get vitiated in Locke's conclusions. The metaphors and the ideas that they bear are in fact a clue to the radical changes that Locke, among others, is introducing into the medieval conceptions of God, Nature, and the earth, along with the human relationship to all of them. Locke's starkly impoverished view of nature as inert and incapable of imposing any constraints on human sociability hints at the extent to which political society was to become with him, as it already was for Hobbes, the outcome of an artificial and constructive endeavor. There is no teleological or regulative residue left in the idea of a pre-given nature; instead, the task of political reason is to revive the original situation, an *imitare creationem*, and this under the novel conditions of not merely formless matter but worthless matter.

What is most revealing, both in itself and in its implications, is that even though the earth was given and held in common, neither the reception from God, the holding, nor the fact of its being common has any individual, social, or political significance. To the extent that social relations, shared sentiments, and individual and collective identities relate to this common inheritance, they do so through a posture of reciprocal indifference. The initial commonness of the earth does not inform subsequent social norms or forms of shared and collective identification, just as the latter, when they do exist, do not draw on the antecedent condition of commonality.[24] Similarly, to the extent that labor is the ex-

22. Ibid., sec. 28. This characterization, of a feminine *nature* that is barren and a distinctly masculine *labor* that is the source of all fecundity, is strangely at odds with Locke's view of the conjugal bond in which both mothers and fathers are recognized for their contributions to the birth and development of children. See *Second Treatise*, chap. 6, "Of Paternal Power."

23. Ibid., sec. 32.

24. Locke, of course, believed that the effects of property accumulation were naturally limited by a circumstantial fact. He stated, "[N]or was *appropriation* of any parcel of *land*, by improving it, any prejudice to any other man, since there was still enough, and as good left. . . . For he that leaves as much as another can make use of, does as good as take nothing at all" (*Second Treatise*, sec. 33). To this, he adds, in sec. 36, the normative constraint that a person should not accumulate more than what he or she can make use of, i.e., a proscription against wastage.

It may appear that by placing these constraints on the appropriation from the commons, Locke is trying to ensure that the fact of initial commonness guides subsequent social norms. This view strikes me as mistaken for the following reasons.

pression of individuality, the latter conceptually precedes the experience of commonness and the encounter with nature. Despite the imprimatur of divine origins and generosity, this original commonality serves only as an axiom that gives coherence to Locke's anti-Filmerian conflation of property rights and political power and to his query into the origins of private property.

In its commonly held form the earth is worthless in its materiality and inert in its sentimental force. These two aspects are clearly related. The earth, as Locke imagines it in his chapter on property, and of which he takes America to be paradigmatic, is all but a vacant space. Its emotive passivity is suggested by the examples that he offers of early human labor vis-à-vis the earth—picking apples and acorns, hunting deer, and fishing. These are all examples of activities that are adequately carried out by individuals in relative isolation and where the resistance or vitality of nature is muted. When Locke imagines nature, it is not through images of monumental majesty, fecundity, intriguing symmetry, or threatening unpredictability. Nature simply does not constitute a horizon of constraint. Moreover, it is a nature with no distinguishing markers, nothing set apart, nothing enclosed, no points where societies naturally congeal, in the process often narrowing and deepening their bonds and horizons. The claim that nature is worthless obscures or levels out all of these features. Correspondingly, there are none of the human emotions of fear, wonder, kinship, reverence, and humility through

---

First, because the stipulation of leaving "enough, and as good" land is one that Locke himself believed would not become operative because he did not imagine the relevant scarcity as being imminent (see secs. 33 and 36). Second, the proscription against wastage is, according to Locke, overridden by the introduction of money (see sec. 48). (As an aside, this condition does not seem especially effective as a limitation since wastage stems from either perverse irrationality, e.g., just letting perishables rot, or from markets not clearing. Clearly the former kind of wastage could occur even within a monetized economy and the latter kind need not occur in a nonmonetized barter economy, just as it could occur in a monetized economy.)

Finally, and most importantly, there is a distinction between constraints that guide the acquisition and administering of private property and of such constraints simultaneously also drawing on the antecedent fact of commonality as a normative ideal. The constraints that Locke has in mind, to the extent that they are constraints at all, are plainly of the former kind. Put differently, it seems clear that even if the world had not been commonly held Locke would have had the same sort of constraints in place. His constraints are driven by considerations of fairness and efficiency and do not, as such, feature the political or normative significance of an initial condition of the world being held in common.

I am grateful to Joshua Cohen for pointing out the importance of addressing this issue.

which so much of early mythology sought to explain both the urge and sentiment of collectivity along with its special link to nature.[25] And therefore, not surprisingly, the commonality of nature turns out to be just the inert initial condition attached to an intrinsically worthless gift leaving no individual or collective emotive trace. We, individually and collectively, are not touched by a natural world that is not a construct of rational human contractual artifice. Locke's argument regarding the inertness of nature and the earth in general carries over to considerations pertaining to the formation of specific political societies and their relationship to the land they occupy. No additional argument is offered for this; and on Lockean grounds none is needed. What we have here is the uniformity of Euclidean space, where in principle each unit is a congruent and translatable replica of any other unit.

The implications of this sentimentally impoverished characterization of commonality and the encounter with nature are far-reaching and extend well beyond issues of private property. In fact, through the discussion of the origins of private property Locke reveals the considerations that are deemed relevant, and those that are not, to the articulation of individual and political identity. There are four broad and closely linked implications that are relevant.

The first implication relates to collective political identity. By divesting a nature given and held in common of any emotive force, Locke blocks an important moment of commonness from furnishing a sense of collectivity, and thus being a collective experience, and, hence, the constituent of a potential political identity at this the foundational point in his argument.[26] The initial commonality of the world, which after all bears the imprimatur of divine design, generates absolutely no sentiment of a shared political asset and through that of a shared political identity. It is this sharing in which both individual and collective identities emerge through an imbrication with nature that Locke's account strikingly, even though implicitly, denies and cannot accommodate. Nothing in the account suggests that nature, or some portion of it, constitutes the ground for experiences, which from the very outset become habitual; and therefore nothing in Locke's interpretation suggests that

25. For an interesting recent discussion of political and cosmological ideas associated with geographical space, see Mary W. Helms, *Ulysses' Sail: An Ethnographic Odyssey of Power, Knowledge, and Geographical Distance* (Princeton: Princeton University Press, 1988).

26. I call it the foundational point in view of comments such as "[the] great and *chief end* therefore, of men uniting into Commonwealths, and putting themselves under Governments, *is the Preservation of their Property.*" *Second Treatise*, sec. 124.

to inhabit nature is an expression of a crucial fit or placement in it. Similarly, nothing in the argument allows for such a fit or placement to furnish a partial definition of a society in the sense of establishing a boundary that thus expresses the society's distinctiveness. Of course, in terms of Locke's argument the reason for this denial is straightforward. Given Locke's view regarding the material worthlessness of nature, it follows as a practical inference that the sharing of it would hardly generate significant bonds or sentiments of association. Therefore, hereafter, until the articulation of the contract, and through it the consensual formation of political society, collective identity is an absence.[27] That is to say, individuals are deemed to lack a sense of themselves as constituting a people or in Locke's words constituting "one body."[28] The fact that perhaps those who consent are already in a real sense "together" and separate from others is a politically irrelevant fact. Locke's views on nature make clear the depth of the association between the idea that political society has its only basis in the social contract and that all other forms of collective identity are extraneous to the formation of such a society and plainly not a substitute for it.[29]

27. It might be thought that this claim overemphasizes the significance of the contract by underappreciating the role of Locke's commitment to natural laws. Clearly, Locke accepted the standard and classical view that natural laws were a preconventional moral anchor whose precepts were regulative of individual and collective actions such as those of the legislature. But adherence to this claim does not imply that natural laws are the basis, or even the partial constituents, of collective identity. In fact, given Locke's nonstandard and highly individualistic view, in which he typically (though not always) associates natural laws with individual reason and not with accepting divine positive laws along with their solidaristic implications, there is little warrant for the view that natural laws serve as the basis of a preconventional collective identity. Put differently, individuals and members of communities are indeed to be guided and constrained by the moral status of natural laws. But they do not by virtue of this guidance and constraint become members of communities in that they have a shared sense of themselves as forming a community.

28. *Second Treatise*, sec. 87.

29. Perhaps the most telling indirect evidence of the extent to which Locke divests nature and location of any emotive and political weight is the manner in which he draws upon the Old Testament. Locke invokes Scripture to establish the claim that the world was given to humankind in common (see *Second Treatise*, sec. 25, and more extensively *First Treatise*, chap. 4, 191–207.) More generally, he presents the argument for private property as following from, and being consistent with, Scripture (see in particular *Second Treatise*, secs. 26, 31, 32, and 34). But the way Locke goes about this and the reading he implicitly offers of the Scriptures simply abuses the facts. It requires overlooking or, more precisely, denying the conspicuous centrality of the role of nature and natural events in the narrative of the Old Testa-

The second implication pertains to individual identity. By rendering nature, and the encounter with it, sentimentally inert, Locke denies locational attachments as having any individual significance in relation to political identity. The sentiments implicit in a person "coming from" or "belonging to" a *place*, and of those sentiments being constitutive of his or her identity, are all deemed politically irrelevant. Similarly, even though Locke's is an exploration into the origins of private property, the original human encounter with nature is not a mirror on our inadequate singularity, or on the natural eventualities that lead us to cooperate with each other, and still less a spur to our undeveloped cognitive competence. Indeed, given the enormous weight that is attached to labor being the source of value, it is striking that neither the encounter with nature nor the experience of commonality is deemed relevant to establish the intersubjective context through which valuableness acquires its meaning and labor comes to be interpreted as expressive of individuality. The discussion of private property makes clear that individuality along with its value-infusing capability are plainly being presupposed as antecedent to the encounter with nature. In fact, Locke's characterization of the original human encounter with nature is so completely lacking in any sentimental trace that it is hard to imagine this encounter as relevant to individual identity of any sort beyond, of course, that which relates to the creation and acquisition of private property.

A third implication of Locke's view is that by imagining nature as a physically and emotionally vacant space, with no binding potential, he makes it all but conceptually impossible to articulate the origins and the continued existence of distinct political societies or nations. By not acknowledging natural or geographical distinctions along with their corresponding emotional attachments as having any political value, Locke and much of the subsequent British liberal tradition cannot give credence to the claims of territoriality that undergird most political

ment. One cannot comprehend the moral, and certainly the political, meaning of the Scriptures as a text if one overlooks the role of the Flood, Exodus and exile, wandering, the parting of seas, and, most importantly, the very idea of the Promised Land of Israel. These events with their conspicuous physicality are deeply linked with Jewish faith as constituents of Hebraic moral and political identity. They feature a sensibility that is completely divergent from one in which nature is viewed as worthless and in which the encounter with it is emotionally vacant. In the Old Testament it is plainly the case that nature and natural events are not simply background for a monumental drama but rather vital protagonists that inform the details of its meaning. Yet, in Locke's implicit reading of the Old Testament, all of this is missing and based on his explicit proposals none of it would be possible.

identities and all nationalisms.[30] This is not to suggest that such claims exhaust or are even the most important features of national identity. Clearly, this is often not the case. But even when national origins and identities reside in something else, such as common ethnicity, language, religion, a real or imagined history, or a shared commitment to certain normative principles, such claims when they are politically intended are projected territorially. Put differently, whatever the real or purported basis of nations, they all claim sovereignty over some specified territory. Territoriality is, at least—but nevertheless crucially—emblematic of a distinct political identity, and hence not surprisingly it has served as a marker of a people's sense of autonomy, especially when that autonomy has been denied or compromised by imperial or statist power.[31]

Finally, a specific extension of the previous point is that Locke's account cannot give significance to nor account for the fact that political societies have territorial boundaries. He cannot, for instance, explain or justify why the physical boundary of Britain should be limited by the English Channel and not, for example, by the Rhine. To say that those within the extant boundaries have consented to the government in Britain only begs the question on Locke's contractual grounds, because it does not address the issue of how those boundaries acquired their delimiting status in the first place. Given Locke's argument, it appears that the only conceptual resource available to account for the territorial boundaries of a state is to say that those boundaries correspond to an aggregate of the private properties of those who have contracted to form that particular political society and government.[32] But this account suf-

30. See Charles de Visscher, *Theory and Reality in Public International Law*, trans. P. E. Corbett (Princeton: Princeton University Press, 1957), 197–98; and R. Y. Jennings, *The Acquisition of Territory in International Law* (Manchester: Manchester University Press, 1963), 2. For a more recent discussion of these issues, see Anthony Smith, "States and Homelands: The Social and Geopolitical Implications of National Territory," *Millennium, Journal of International Studies* 10, no. 3: 187–202.

31. Here again Locke's interpretation of the Scriptures is revealing for what it ignores. In terms of political significance, the Old Testament clearly presents separate territory as a necessary condition for the freedom and independence of the Hebrews. Upon reaching the Promised Land, the link between territoriality, political structure, and sovereignty is immediately felt and extensively discussed in the Book of Judges and the Book of Kings. These discussions, among other things, underline what is in any case obvious, i.e., that in the narrative of the Old Testament the encounter with nature and specifically with land is a crucial ingredient of a distinctive Jewish collective and political identity. But in Locke, political structure, legitimacy, and sovereignty must be articulated without reference to nature and geography.

32. See *Second Treatise*, sec. 38.

fers from at least two serious weaknesses. First, it is wholly inaccurate as an account of the boundaries of real states. Such boundaries typically include various commons or privately unclaimed lands, and thus do not in fact correspond to the private properties of their citizens.[33] This was plainly the case in seventeenth-century England, and this fact does not appear to have confused Locke regarding the boundaries of the country in which he liveds. Moreover, citizens and states think and act in ways that suggest that their identities are implicated with the preservation of something that is not territorially congruent with the aggregate of private properties. The second weakness is that if, following Locke, the explanation for the territorial boundary of a political society is that it corresponds to the aggregate of the private properties of those who have contracted to form such a society, then there is no normative reason why, for example, property owners across the channel, by expressing such contractual affiliation, could not simply demand changes in the boundaries of Britain.

But such normative simplicity flies in the face of reality in the double sense of neither explaining it nor realistically guiding its transformation. The boundaries of states are plainly the product of an ongoing complex historical palimpsest in which military conquest, matrimonial alliances, language, ethnicity, geographical delineation, and various factors other than the contractual preferences of property owners have had their effect. Some of these factors give expression to the deep affections and emotive attachments through which a people have a sense of belonging and a corresponding sense of themselves as members of a distinct political community. In other instances, boundaries were imposed that did not correspond to such affections, and where only with time and often coercion did such a correspondence materialize. And in yet other instances such correspondence never materializes. My point is not to offer a theory of how the boundaries of states get established and change. Instead, it is to point to the fact that boundaries—like territoriality more generally—are emblematic of the distinctiveness of communities and political societies. In one sense the boundaries of states are merely physical lines on the ground akin to the fences that Locke associates with private property, but in another sense the former reflect a distinctive cognitive or emotional reality of their members in which the physical considerations demarcate a positive collective identification.

33. The only exception to this appears to be cases where a single authority (typically a monarch) claims the entire domain of the state as its private property.

And in this sense the boundaries of states are only partially analogous to those of private property.[34] Unlike the latter, they are expressive, through a complex cognitive operation, of a link between people who are often disparately situated on many registers of self-description but who nevertheless share a sense of belonging.

This discussion of Locke's views regarding property and nature at one level simply confirms the standard interpretation of some of his central political ideas. Locke is of course associated with the conviction that the basis and legitimacy of political associations stems from their voluntary nature and that the social contract facilitates the formation of such an association. He is similarly identified with political views that are in the main secular and, if not expressly anti-Scriptural, at least anti-Adamic, and so we should be surprised to see the gravity of a divine gift ignored. But in confirming this well-accepted view of Locke, I hope to have drawn out some of its less obvious implications. To establish the initial conditions whereby the Lockean contract can be the foundational basis for the formation of political society, Locke erases any trace of belonging or togetherness by virtue of which individuals may have already acquired a sense of themselves as constituting a people along with norms of political accountability and legitimacy. In this regard the emotionally evacuated characterization of the encounter with nature is especially revealing. Clearly for Locke the parceling of nature into private units is the condition for the possibility of political unity, because no such unity is deemed to exist by virtue of the experience of nature itself. It is with the same conceptual brush that Locke presents nature as *terra nullius*, a vacant land, and various alternative forms of political order and unity as merely prepolitical stages of the state of nature.[35]

TERRITORIALITY AND POLITICAL SOCIETY

There is a sharp contrast between the Lockean neglect of territory or place and the associations that Burke links to these very categories. For

34. This is, perhaps, what Heidegger means by the statement "a boundary is not that at which something stops but, as the Greeks recognized, the boundary is that from which something *begins its presencing.* . . . Space is in essence that for which room has been made, that which is let into its bounds." Martin Heidegger, "Building, Dwelling, Thinking," in *Poetry, Language, Thought,* trans. Albert Hofstadter (New York: Harper Colophon Books, 1975), 154. This essay abounds in philological examples that strike me as deeply Burkean in their sensibility.

35. See James Tully, *An Approach to Political Philosophy: Locke in Contexts* (Cambridge: Cambridge University Press, 1993), for a very informative and persuasive description of various seventeenth- and eighteenth-century forms of Native American political society.

Burke the discussion of place starts with a distinction between place conceived in territorial terms and its significance when conceived in social terms. The former refers to physical space, land, rivers, monuments, borders; the latter refers to social position, origins, distinctions of status and even reputation. Both senses of the term are essential to Burke's understanding of social order, as well as the individual and collective identities that relate to it. And both are tightly intertwined. In fact, the way in which Burke imagines social position and related categories such as class and title reveal them to be inextricably rooted in territoriality. The sentiments and the feelings that get expressed in the deference or etiquette that one might show to a person by virtue of his or her social station are themselves implicitly, and often explicitly, linked with the physical place with which one associates their standing. The braiding of these two aspects is further underlined, for Burke, by the fact that the dislocation of one is invariably accompanied by the dislocation of the other. But the deeper insight that unifies Burke's understanding of place, as both territorial and social, is a profound distrust of any orientation that proceeds from a conception of experience as something not shared with others. It is this that makes it impossible to imagine Burke treating the commonness of the earth—the fact that it was given and held as a shared asset—with the psychological and material instrumentality with which Locke views it. For Burke, this monumental fact, especially given its divine imprimatur, even if it were not taken literally, would have served as a guiding metaphor for his understanding of individuals and society and the experience of both. It could never have been merely the axiom that gave coherence to an account of the origins of private property and lent additional credence to the critique of Filmer's patriarchalism.

Burke never fully elaborates in a systematic or detailed manner the logic of the psychological or cognitive operations through which place comes to acquire its crucial relation to identity. There are passages in which the "instinct" for a "love of country" is presented as "natural" and akin to the love that parents have for their children. The justification for such metaphysical or psychological assumptions should not detain us here. For what is abundantly clear is that for Burke the link between place and identity is a psychological one in which feelings (such as love) and cognitive associations and not merely preferences, such as those that get mobilized in the expression of consent, are galvanized. It is because of the presumed depth and tenacity of such feelings that Burke takes territoriality to be constitutive of individual and collective identity and associates its denial with the cavalier horror of imperial and Jacobin excesses.

Burke makes repeated references to territoriality in his speeches. He urges his fellow parliamentarians to imagine India, before all else, in the richness of its concrete geographical particulars: "But before I consider of what nature these abuses are . . . permit me to recall to your recollection the map of the country which this abused chartered right affects."[36] Burke proceeds to do precisely that. He presents the Commons with a systematic and detailed geography of the subcontinent. In his speech on the Nabob of Arcot's debts, he laments the unavailability of a map he had hoped would be ready to lay before the Commons; in its absence, he decides to use his own.[37] Burke painstakingly tries to convey a sense of the territory, and by the analogy he draws, it is clear that he wishes that sense to be almost tactile for his audience:

> The Carnatic is a country not much inferior in extent to England. Figure to yourself, Mr. Speaker, the land in whose representative chair you sit; figure to yourself the form and fashion of your sweet and cheerful country from Thames to Trent, north and south, and from the Irish to the German sea . . . Extend your imagination a little further.[38]

Burke is, in a sense, transporting the Carnatic into the Commons to have it felt and experienced as something so commonplace as to be the object of sweet and cheerful sentiments. But if this transposition serves Burke's purpose of generating sympathy among his colleagues for the Carnatic, he is nevertheless under no illusions of the distinct reasons through which the monumental geography of the Carnatic generates the affections and loyalties of its own inhabitants:

> These are not the enterprises of your power, nor in a style of magnificence suited to the taste of your minister. These are the monuments of real kings, who are the fathers of their people,— testators to a posterity which they embrace as their own. These

36. Burke, "Fox's India Bill Speech," 5:387. The context of this remark and the speech in general is the parliamentary consideration of various alleged abuses by the East India Company along with the question whether the charter granted to the company in 1600 constituted a political charter like Magna Carta. The implication of this would have been that the company had independent political authority. Burke's position is that the charter is a limited commercial charter, giving the company the monopoly right to trade but no political power.

37. Burke, "Speech on the Nabob of Arcot's Debts," in *Writings and Speeches* (Oxford), 5:521.

38. Ibid., 520.

are the grand sepulchres built by ambition,—but by the ambition of an insatiable benevolence, which not contented with reigning in the dispensation of happiness during the contracted term of human life, had strained, with all the reachings and graspings of a vivacious mind, to extend the dominion of their bounty beyond the limits of Nature, and to perpetuate themselves through generations of generations, the guardians, the protectors, the nourishers of mankind.[39]

What Burke is attempting to convey, here and elsewhere, is the sense of a place known to its inhabitants, and in which that knowledge, at least partially, prescribes the content of who they are. His panegyric of the Carnatic may only strike someone who, like Burke, imbues real kings with the august status of being a father of their people. And if this is so, clearly the richness, perhaps one should say the sentimentality, of Burke's description, and not the actual events described, bear out the point he is making. But in any case, the description suggests the centrality that Burke at least attaches to these spatial links and the connections that they embody.

Of course, an irony here points out the limitations and broader purpose of what Burke is attempting. Had Burke found the map for which he wished, it still would not have conveyed the sensibilities that he hoped to capture and transmit. That map would have been emotionally flat, a two-dimensional trace—the product in all likelihood of a surveyor's or geologist's efforts. It would have lacked the phenomenological depth and details of ascending hills, receding valleys, or wells shared by a village community, along with the feelings they engendered. In a word, it would have lacked the three-dimensionality of experience that Burke's prose is at pains to capture. So instead Burke must strain against and stretch his own medium. Words must stand in for pictures that themselves are only to be a substitute for a conversation that the empire vitiates. In the process of these complex substitutions—the Carnatic for England, the speaker of the Commons for "real kings," sentimentality for experiences—the sympathy for Indians that Burke wishes to convey gets transformed from a perceptual reality into an ethical position in which he must insist on sympathy for the unfortunate natives. The map represents the sign of that frustrating transition and substitution between an ethics that is anchored in the proximity of what is seen and shared—an ethics that the empire destroys and makes all but impossible—and an ethics that must in the face of that destruction resort to

39. Ibid.

narrative as its only substitute. When Burke, with a pleading insistence, tries to "approximate" for his fellow parliamentarians the "feelings" of the "unfortunate natives," he is left with nothing more than the power of his narrative—a narrative that can never be unequivocal in its meaning and certainly not in its emotive impact. But Burke is not burdened by the priority of logic over rhetoric. He knows that in the challenge of facilitating what amounts to a conversation across boundaries of strangeness there is no shortcut around the messiness of communication, no immanent truth on which words can fix, no easy glossaries of translation—instead there is only the richness or paucity of the vocabularies we use to describe ourselves and those we are trying to understand. The space within which Burke's voluminous narratives on the empire operate is therefore never precise in the sense of representing a reality whose contours and destiny are understood as already programmed, decoded, and known in advance. Despite the eloquence and rhetorical force of his words and the stakes he attaches to the debates in which he is involved, there is always something provisional in his narratives. He expects to be surprised and to be puzzled. But precisely because of the provisional nature of the conversation in which he is involved, he is more deeply committed to the gravity of the ethical and political choices that arise from such a contingent encounter. There is something deeply plaintive about Burke addressing the speaker of the Commons, saying "Figure to yourself."

The frequency with which Burke invokes and portrays the geographical coherence of India or subdivisions within it is too extensive for an appropriately nuanced sense of it to be easily conveyed. His descriptions range from the minute hillocks and rivulets that bound a village to the panoramas from which he makes global comparisons. Consider the following:

> If I were to take the whole aggregate of our possessions there, I should compare it, as the nearest parallel I can find, with the empire of Germany. Our immediate possessions I should compare with the Austrian dominions, and they would not suffer in the comparison. The Nabob of Oude might stand for the King of Prussia; the Nabob of Arcot I would compare, as superior in territory, and equal in revenue, to the Elector of Saxony. Cheyt Sing, the Rajah of Benares, might well rank with the Prince of Hesse at least; and the Rajah of Tanjore (though hardly equal in extent of dominion, superior in revenue) to the Elector of Bavaria. The Polygars and the northern Zemindars, and other great chiefs, might well class with the rest of the Princes,

Dukes, Counts, Marquisses, and Bishops in the empire; all of whom I mention to honor, and surely without disparagement to any or all of those most respectable princes and grandees.

All this vast mass, composed of so many orders and classes of men, is again infinitely diversified by manners, by religion, by hereditary employment, through all their possible combinations. This renders the handling of India a matter in an high degree critical and delicate. But oh! it has been handled rudely indeed. Even some of the reformers seem to have forgot that they had any thing to do but to regulate the tenants of a manor, or the shopkeepers of the next county town.[40]

The mosaic of princely Indian states manifests the diversity and social coherence of the German states. Where they suffer in size, they exceed in revenue. In comparing the landed nobility (zemindars) in India with their counterparts in Europe, Burke means to disparage neither but to honor both. The former inhabit and partially constitute a complex social structure, with all the relevant features—religion, classes, hereditary orders. One could easily mistake the comparisons that Burke is making as motivated by what, in the previous chapter, I have called the problematic of universal history. Comparisons are a repeated and familiar trope of this genre of history writing. With regard to India, James Mill, for example, constantly deploys them as a means for establishing and illustrating the scale of civilizational development that is so central to his broader purpose. But Burke's purpose in offering this comparison of similarities is markedly different. It is, as he goes on to say, "to awaken something of [the] sympathy" for India that his compatriots feel for such august territories, orders, and complex societies in Europe. Burke's purpose, far from being hierarchical or predicated on a prior structure of generality, is to create a lateral plane, and beyond that, it is to position that plane at the level of sentiments so that they serve as motives for understanding and for actions. To treat the inhabitants of such places as the transient tenants of a manor is to deny or overlook the solidity of the attachments and sentiments that such places engender. And Burke leads us to assume that for the inhabitants of India, this panoply of historically sanctioned titles, states, and classes engenders the same feeling of "honor" as it does in him.

40. Burke, "Fox's India Bill Speech," 5:390. James Mill, in his *History of British India*, is also prone to make comparisons with European states and circumstances. But consistently in those comparisons, the appropriate analogy is between contemporary India and some distant, usually pre-Christian, moment in European history.

For Burke, these are places to which people *belong*. Put differently, places give to people a sense of where they come from, and in this they indicate if not an origin then at least a sense of the path they have traveled, including something of its future course. The East India Company, with its imperial and commercial perspective on such matters, disorders the spatial complex that represents the accretion and effects of a long history and the feelings that are attendant on it. It inflames the territorial pretensions of Indian princes by selectively dispensing patronage and protection (as it did in provoking and sanctioning the feud between the nabob of Arcot and the rajah of Tanjore). It combines and recombines old states to form new ones, as though geography were simply the demarcations on a map that could be redrawn in the Company House in London. Its officers, like Hastings, assume traditional Indian titles and the privileges that they think go with them, as though these were hollow vestments that could be filled with novel content at will. The company does what the Jacobins did by "breaking all connection between territory and dignity, and abolishing every species of nobility, gentry, and church establishments."[41] The company and the Jacobins, in part by the ineradicable impulse they have to conquer and expand, and because they must destroy and dislocate to survive, put

> an end of that narrow scheme of relations called our country, with all its pride, its prejudices, and its partial affections. All the little quiet rivulets, that watered an humble, a contracted, but not unfruitful field, are to be lost in the vast expanse, and boundless, barren ocean of the homicide philanthropy of France.[42]

41. Burke, "Thoughts on French Affairs," in *Further Reflections on the Revolution in France*, ed. Daniel E. Ritchie (Indianapolis: Liberty Fund, 1992), 211–12. Burke's preoccupation with the domestic and international territorial consequences of the French Revolution are extensive. He speaks of the revolutionaries in *Reflections* as

> treat[ing] France exactly like a country of conquest. Acting as conquerors, they have imitated the policy of the harshest of that race. The policy of such barbarous victors, who condemn a subdued people, and insult their feelings, has ever been, as much as in them lay, to destroy all vestiges of the ancient country, in religion, in polity, in laws, and in manners; to confound all territorial limits . . . to put up their properties to auction; to crush their princes, nobles and pontiffs; to lay low everything which had lifted its head above the level." (*Reflections*, 297–98)

In "Thoughts on French Affairs" (215) he goes through every European nation to consider the extent to which they are vulnerable to the "armed doctrine" of the Jacobins.

42. Burke, "Letters on a Regicide Peace," in *Writings and Speeches* (Taylor), 5:393.

They are committed to the mobility of relations between places as though the sentiments that were imbricated in those relations were simply rootless and floating affections that did not stamp individuals and communities. To recall an image that Burke uses to characterize the company officials and the Jacobins, they are like birds of prey in whom the expedient of conquest and the wholesale transformation of society has replaced the feeling of belonging and destination: "the truth is, that France is out of itself,—the moral France is separated from the geographical."[43] This idea captures what is so often lost in the typical portrayal of Burke as one whose views on morality could be summarized in the adherence to an abstract natural law of Christianity. Such a portrayal misses the crucial tension—a tension that Burke himself often glides over—between the abstraction of this familiar position and the locational specificity that he emphasizes and that supplies the felt integuments of morality. Burke is much closer to what Richard Rorty eloquently describes when he writes, "[Our] identification with our community—our society, our political tradition, our intellectual heritage—is heightened when we see this community as *ours* rather than *nature's*, *shaped* rather than *found*, *one among many which men have made*."[44] Burke's cosmopolitanism, what I have earlier referred to as the cosmopolitanism of sentiments, is the painstaking product of bridging the last clause of this quotation with what precedes it. That cosmopolitanism is never assured because it emerges, if at all, from the glacial process of understanding that *our* society is *one among many which men have made*.

There are two relevant underlying themes in Burke's views on the British Empire. The first is the *instrumentalism* that governs the imperial mindset and informs its practices. This is what is implicit in Burke's characterization of the empire as an adolescent fantasy come to life; young boys greedily amassing wealth, power, and status with no sense of the reciprocity and social basis of such attributes.[45] The empire is superficial. Its economic, political, and ultimately psychological investments pertain only to the surface of things. In this it compares unfavorably even with other empires of the region.

> But the difference in favour of the first conquerors [the Arabs, Tartars, and Persians] is this; the Asiatic conquerors very soon abated of their ferocity, because they made the conquered country their own. They rose or fell with the rise and fall of the

43. Burke, "On the Policies of the Allies," in *Writings and Speeches* (Taylor), 4:421.
44. Rorty, *Consequences of Pragmatism*, 166 (emphasis added to the last clause).
45. Burke, "Fox's India Bill Speech," 5:461.

territory they lived in. Fathers there deposited the hopes of
their posterity; and children there beheld the monuments of
their fathers. Here their lot was finally cast; and it is the natural
wish of all, that their lot should not be cast in a bad land.[46]

Our relationship to territory is indicative of, and gathers together aspects of, a broader commitment to human fellowship and ultimately
even to oneself. By making India "their own" country these other conquerors put themselves in a particular relationship with it. It is a relationship from which, in Burke's view, moral and political consequences
follow; because for him both morality and politics are precisely forms
of knowledge and action that stem from an investment that combines
the past, present, and future. It is the same idea that Burke expresses in
the more familiar words of the *Reflections* in a context where his concern
is more directly with the convulsions of revolutions. Of course, for
Burke the empire was in fact no less revolutionary than the activity of
the Jacobins:

> One of the first and most leading principles on which the com-
> monwealth and the laws are consecrated, is lest the temporary
> possessors and life-renters in it, unmindful of what they have
> received from their ancestors or of what is due to their poster-
> ity, should act as if they were the entire masters; that they
> should not think it amongst their rights to cut off the entail or
> commit waste on the inheritance, by destroying at their plea-
> sure the whole original fabric of their society; hazarding to
> leave to those who come after them a ruin instead of an habita-
> tion—and teaching these successors as little to respect their
> contrivances, as they had themselves respected the institutions
> of their forefathers. By this unprincipled facility of changing
> the state as often, and as much, and in as many ways as there
> are floating fancies or fashions, the whole chain and continuity
> of the commonwealth would be broken. No one generation
> could link with the other. Men would become little better than
> the flies of a summer.[47]

In contrast with the other conquerors of India but similar to the Jacobins, the British rulers of India are lacking in that depth that transforms
the crude and ferocious impulses of conquest into the nobler and more
sympathetic sentiments that link parents and children. To sustain this

46. Ibid., 401.
47. Burke, *Reflections*, 91–92.

disengagement and maintain the distance that would collapse if they made India "their own" country, the British must lean heavily on notions such as pride, arrogance, and, in the nineteenth century, civilizational superiority. In speaking, as the British were wont to do, of *our* empire, *our* colonial subjects, *our* dependents, the possessive adjective merely affirmed an attitudinal and moral distance that it semantically appeared to deny. At best such attitudes and forms of speech were a sentimental pretense. Put differently, for Burke such expressions were merely paternalistic; they carried none of the real sentiments that he imagined bound parents and children in a moral embrace and were therefore antithetical to, and a monitor against, instrumentalism. In contrast with Locke and both the Mills, the metaphor of kinship, in Burke, does not primarily refer to a pedagogic relationship, in which power, however it is veiled, must be acknowledged as constitutive of that relationship. Instead Burke braids the parent-child relationship with the reference to land and country because they all supply the conditions of that continuity that he deems essential to individuals and communities having a moral identity. For the same reason, where Burke likens "casting in one's lot with the land" to the hopes and respect that parents and children have for each other, Locke and his eighteenth- and nineteenth-century epigones might very well have only imagined extractive possibilities from which no emotive connections followed.

The second theme is what might be called the theme of *belonging.* Here again the idea is elaborated through the image of parental links and locational attachments.

> Next to the love of parents for their children, the strongest instinct, both natural and moral, that exists in man, is the love of his country. . . . All creatures love their offspring; next to that they love their homes: they have a fondness for the place where they have been bred, for the habitations they have dwelt in, for the stalls in which they have been fed, the pastures they have browsed in, and the wilds in which they have roamed. We all know that the natal soil has a sweetness in it beyond the harmony of verse. This [is the] instinct, I say, that binds all creatures to their country.[48]

Like parental love, belonging is an instinct. But unlike the former, the latter develops as though through concentric circles of broadening loca-

---

48. Burke, "Impeachment of Warren Hastings," in *Selected Writings and Speeches*, ed. Peter J. Stanlis (Chicago: Regnery Gateway, 1963), 409.

tional attachments, culminating in a bond with one's country. Burke elaborates that bond in the language of kinship and the sentiments of love, habit, and recognition that are common to it. In this he prefigures the ubiquitous familial genealogies that nations imagine for themselves.[49] But there is another, perhaps less obvious, interpretation to this and similar passages. It is one in which Burke is elaborating the conditions of our individual and collective identities along with their preservation, and revealing those conditions to be, from the very outset, bound up with locational reliances and the sentiments that follow from them. The homes where we are bred, the stalls in which we are fed—these are literally the conditions upon which our survival as corporeal and sentient beings depends. To abstract away from these conditions and attachments is to impoverish the understanding of self-preservation and identity of precisely that which gives them their enduring centrality. The British Empire, through the East India Company and in the person of a figure like Hastings, was, in Burke's view, committed to just such an abstraction. It abused the material needs of its subjects and violated the sense of belonging that was an integral part of those needs. In this sense subsequent anticolonial nationalism, at least in its professed aims, hoped to redress both the material and what Partha Chatterjee has aptly called the "inner" aspects of identity.[50] It performed this dual task by insistently affirming a sense of belonging and demanding a political cast for it.

Through all these examples Burke's point is to emphasize that the integrity of individuals and groups, or personality and social order, is derivative of social context. Spaces, both territorial and social, define that context. Feelings and sentiments are forged within spatial associations. Nevertheless, those bonds and feelings can of course be destroyed not merely by the instrumentality of the company or the violence of the Jacobins, but also by a theory that assumes a perspective from "nowhere," or by a noble lord who through a sudden revolutionary enlight-

49. A lot has recently been written on the gendered and familial ascriptions of homelands, nations, and their putative founders. See for instance Lynn Hunt, *The Family Romance of the French Revolution* (Berkeley and Los Angeles: University of California Press, 1992); Partha Chatterjee, *Nationalist Thought and the Colonial World;* Andrew Parker, Mary Russo, Doris Sommer, and Patricia Yaeger, *Nationalisms and Sexualities* (New York: Routledge, 1992); Thongchai Winichahul, *Siam Mapped: A History of the Geo-Body of a Nation* (Honolulu: University of Hawaii Press, 1994); Suruchi Thaper, "Women as Activists; Women as Symbols: A Study of the Nationalist Movement," *Feminist Review* 44 (summer 1993): 81–96.

50. Partha Chatterjee, *The Nation and Its Fragments* (Princeton: Princeton University Press, 1993), chap. 2.

LIBERALISM, EMPIRE, AND TERRITORY   143

enment forgets his own "position" and past.[51] The Burkean "night-
mare," as David Bromwich insightfully points out, "is not a loss of
profitable markets, or of the energy of enlightened persons who can
exploit such markets, but rather the passing from sight of old places
consecrated by use and custom."[52]

Here it is worth noting the contrast with Rousseau's views on nature
and the implied understanding and significance of those views regarding
the distinctive basis of political societies. The most obvious point of
contrast is that for Rousseau nature is not an indistinct, empty vessel
into which human labor infuses value and in the process draws the only
boundaries that Locke acknowledges, those that stem from the demar-
cating of private property. For Rousseau, nature has both density and
variety.[53] It imposes constraints on the form that human associations
take and affects both the cognitive potentialities that get triggered and
developed and the motivations that characterize human behavior. Apparently innocuous natural circumstances such as the height of trees and
the agility and ferocity of animals lead to, and explain, incipient forms
of social cooperation, cognitive development, and the shape of human
motivation. More complex phenomena such as volcanoes and ensuing
fires, differences in soils and climates, the variability in the existence of
iron ore, earthquakes that result in the formation of islands—all of these
circumstances are relevant not only to the explanation of inequality
(Rousseau's express concern in *The Second Discourse*), but also to the formation of distinct political identities. The integration of these phenomena into his analysis of the origins of political societies allows Rousseau
to draw implications such as "differences in soil, climates and seasons
could force [people living on islands] to inculcate these differences in
their lifestyles" and "clearly among men thus brought together and
forced to live together, a common idiom must have been formed sooner
than those who wandered freely about the forests of the mainland."[54]

There is an element of contingency to these implications; it relates
to the general significance that Rousseau attaches to the role of *chance*
in the account that he offers regarding the development of political societies. At one level the idea of chance is meant simply to capture the fact

51. See Burke, "Letter to a Noble Lord," in *Writings and Speeches* (Taylor),
5:198.
52. Bromwich, *A Choice of Inheritance*, 58.
53. In this discussion of Rousseau's views I am drawing primarily from the
second part of J. J. Rousseau, *Discourse on the Origins of Inequality*, trans. Donald A.
Cress (Indianapolis: Hackett, 1987).
54. Ibid., 60, 63.

that from a physical standpoint there is no telling when or where, or what natural exigencies will arise. But the incorporation of this element of natural contingency into the understanding of political development suggests for Rousseau that there is, by virtue of the role of natural circumstances, an ineradicable specificity to the formation of political identity. This is why the account he offers in the *Second Discourse* is "a hypothetical history" that eschews the idea of a unique and general foundation for the basis of political identity. In effect, Rousseau deploys the category of chance as a stand-in for the myriad histories, natural and otherwise, that intertwined to give a people a sense of belonging and of constituting a unified body.

CONCLUSION

Within the Lockean liberal tradition the distinction between the political identity of a society and the conditions for that society being deemed politically legitimate is altogether absent. The very move through which the latter is acknowledged also brings into being and is the necessary condition for the existence of the former. Hence the unanimity among those who contract and consent to form political society is also the very thing that in Locke's view gives that society its political legitimacy.[55] This conflation of conditions is of enormous concrete significance because it allows certain issues to get settled in Locke's argument at a point that, if there were greater openness regarding what constitutes political identity or political society, would be precisely where considerations of history and geography would become relevant. Moreover, their relevance would constitute a constraint on the normative issue of legitimacy. But for Locke the very act of forming political society through contract, i.e., the renunciation of what he calls the "natural powers" of individuals, simultaneously establishes a "community," governed by "settled standing rules, indifferent, and the same to all parties," and moreover the same act makes "it easie to discern, who are, and who are not, in *political society* together."[56]

55. Locke does, of course, allow for the possibility that duly established legislatures could violate the terms of the "trust" on which they receive their authority from the people. But such instances indicate the illegitimacy of governments, which can, as Locke is well known to have countenanced, even lead to their possible dissolution. In contrast, political societies, since their existence and legitimacy stem solely from a unanimous agreement, can only shrink (if some members choose to return to the state of nature) or perhaps, even disband (if all members assert such a choice); but they cannot have another basis.

56. Revealingly all this occurs in the course of a single paragraph: Locke, *Two Treatises*, sec. 87.

The economy of Locke's argument rests on a presumed unproblematic silence and irrelevance of history and geography in struggling for and constituting a distinct polity and its boundaries and hence in partially settling the issue of membership.[57] In this silence resides a profound evasion regarding the complexities to which societies and communities are typically prone and from which nations in the modern era are crafted.[58] Here Locke inaugurates and exemplifies a broader liberal cast of mind. It presumed on the coherence and distinctiveness of the European nation in a way that folded the very things that were central to the constructive efforts of subsequent nationalists into what was taken for granted or presumed on. And hence those constructive possibilities—the very features that are crucial to establishing a distinct society—are absent or invisible from liberal theory as constructive options. Yet in newly emerged postcolonial polities with their experiences of ad hoc colonial melange or precolonial provincialism, the issue of a distinct political identity is not only deeply vexing but also one in which considerations of history and geography are inescapable. It is precisely these sorts of contestations that attend the emergence of nations, stamp their identities in ways that are seldom, if ever, wholly matters of their choosing, and constrain their normative and state-building agendas. For instance, in the case of prepartition India the historical concentration of Muslims in the west and in the delta region of the east, along with water needs and therefore the locations of the Indus, the Ganges, and the Brahmaputra Rivers, become at least partially determinative of where the borders of India and Pakistan got established. And clearly all those issues have, it appears, indelibly marked the subsequent identities of India and Pakistan. Similarly, the fact that India was a multiethnic, multireligious, and multilingual society was

---

The closest that Locke gets to acknowledging an alternative basis to political society is when he admits that patriarchal families "by degrees grew into a commonwealth, and fatherly authority continued on to the elder son" (sec. 110). This, coming from Locke, is a puzzling claim, because it calls into question his vociferous critique of Filmer in the *First Critique* and in any case does not square with his numerous statements sharply distinguishing the power of a paterfamilias, in both extent and duration, from that of a legislature. See secs. 2, 64, 65, 71, and 86.

57. I say "presumed" because the contractual basis of political society obviates the need to be explicitly antihistorical and antigeographical.

58. Partha Chatterjee has insightfully elaborated the logic and the implications of this liberal undertheorizing of community and by implication the imperatives of nationalism. See Chatterjee, "Response to Modes of Civil Society," *Public Culture* 3, no. 1 (fall 1990): 102–19; and *The Nation and Its Fragments* (Princeton: Princeton University Press, 1993), chap. 11.

clearly critical in the constitutional choice of establishing a federal republic.[59]

The point is that even though Locke acknowledges the distinction between political identity and political legitimacy, by collapsing the conditions requisite for the two he erases their effective differences and is blinded to the complexities that attend the former and, by its connection, the latter, too. The result, as Partha Chatterjee has rightly pointed out, is that one is left with "two extreme positions: on the one hand, abolishing community altogether and thinking of rights as grounded solely in the self-determining individual will, and on the other, attributing to community a single determinate form, delegitimizing all other forms of community."[60] Indeed, and this goes beyond the issue of territory per se, there is very little in Locke, and more generally in the liberal tradition, that casts any light on the plethora of concerns that bear on political identity and the variety of communities to which it typically relates. In this is summarized the long-standing liberal myopia, as distinct from its normative reservations, with regard to nationalism in general and anticolonial political aspirations in particular.

It is the distinctiveness and political valency of locational attachments, the sources of which are no doubt complex and manifold, that the Lockean position cannot appreciate and thats, in the imperial context, often implicated that position with a profound political insensitivity and supplied the justification for imperial power. There is a revealing irony in this theoretical neglect of the role, and significance, of boundaries and geography to political identity. So often when British political thinkers have imagined an ideal polity they have given it the physical form of an island state, one in which nature and geography serve as unmistakable markers of a distinct political identity. But by presuming on such natural/political boundaries, they have failed to recognize their more general significance as expressions of distinct political identity.[61] In sharp contrast with Burke, those who held to the Lockean cast

59. On the issue of history as a fundamental ground for national and political self-definition, see Chatterjee, *The Nation and its Fragments*, introduction and chap. 4; on the issue of how historical facts serve as normative constraints, see B. N. Rao, *The Making of the Indian Constitution* (New Delhi: Orient Longmans, 1960).

60. Chatterjee, *The Nation and Its Fragments*, 230.

61. Among political works the most obvious examples of this presumption are Francis Bacon's *New Atlantis* and Thomas More's *Utopia*. In a more popular genre, it is evident in works such as R. L. Stevenson's *Treasure Island* and William Golding's *Lord of the Flies*. See also Gillian Beer's superb article "The Island and the Aeroplane," in *Nation and Narration*, ed. Homi Bhabha (London: Routledge, 1990), 265–90. Of course the classic and most emblematic expression of this is in Shakespeare's *Rich-*

of mind in the late eighteenth and nineteenth centuries in India were confident of the obvious fact that the societies they saw and administered were not based on contractual consent; from this fact, they drew the inference that these societies also lacked all political integrity, along with similarly distinctive norms of accountability and legitimacy. This confidence has its analogue in Locke's own seventeenth-century judgment in which he implied that, because Native Americans lacked the appropriate form of private property, they therefore also lacked political society.[62]

Of course, political identity and a sense of distinctiveness may have many sources, such as a common religion, ethnicity, race, or, as the German Romantic tradition tended to emphasize, a common language.[63] To the extent that these various sources vitiate against the singularity and primacy of the consensual basis of political society, Locke's views run contrary to them. I have suggested that Burke's perspective is more general, in that it potentially subsumes these various sources of unity,

---

ard II. The force of Gaunt's idealization of England lies in braiding her genealogical and political blessings with her sharply distinct geographical contours:

> This Royal Throne of Kings, this sceptred Isle.
> This earth of Majesty, this seat of Mars
> This other Eden, demy paradise,
> This fortress built by Nature for self,
> Against infection, and the hand of war:
> This happy breed of men, this little world,
> This precious stone, set in the silver sea,
> Which serves it in the office of a wall,
> Or as Moate defensive to a house,
> Against the envy of less happier Lands,
> This blessed plot, this earth, this Realm, this England.

William Shakespeare, *Richard II*, 2.1.42–52.

62. *Second Treatise*, secs. 14, 36, 49, and esp. 108. For a discussion of the contextual and textual deployment of America in Locke's writings, see Herman Lebovics, "The Uses of America in Locke's *Second Treatise of Government*," *Journal of the History of Ideas* 47 (1986): 567–81; and John Dunn, "The Politics of Locke in England and America in the Eighteenth Century," in *John Locke: Problems and Perspectives*, ed. John Yolton (Cambridge: Cambridge University Press, 1969), 45–80. More recently, James Tully has written a very learned and thoughtful piece that considers the ways in which Locke's ideas were intended to undermine the acknowledgment of Native American forms of political society. See "The *Two Treatises* and Aboriginal Rights," in *An Approach to Political Philosophy: Locke in Contexts* (Cambridge: Cambridge University Press, 1993), 137–76.

63. For example, J. B. Fichte, *Addresses to the German Nation*, trans. R. F. Jones and G. H. Turnbull (Chicago: Open Court, 1922), esp. address 13 and pp. 223–36.

including the Lockean one, without giving any one of them an a priori
primacy. For Burke, territory or location is both a metaphor and an important physical fact that captures the psychological and emotional condition of individuals viewing themselves as members of a distinct society. It is this sense of belonging, in which there is an ineradicable
element of contingency and arbitrariness, and which Burke understood
could take numerous forms, that he credits as being the basis of political
society. Of course, with Burke the word *basis* carries no originary and
foundational connotations. There is a veil over origins, and neither territory nor anything else gives us access to what lies behind it. For this
very reason Burke is not troubled by the question of whether the sense
of sharing in something common precedes the sense of territorial belonging, or vice versa. And for the same reason, like Rousseau, he does
not sharply distinguish between the accidents of history and those of
geography. Both history and geography, notwithstanding the contestations that attend them, facilitate the creation of that sense of bounded
togetherness, through which itself the notion of sharing in something
comes to be effective and available to normative and institutional modification.

Hence Burke's objection to the Lockean position is not directed
against its contractualism per se, but rather against the primacy it gives
to the consensual contract as the only legitimate basis to the formation
of political society. Through this emphasis Locke gives himself the latitude whereby he came to overlook the manifold conditions, including
the role of borders, by which political societies come to exist and de-
velop an investment in their distinctiveness. As I have argued, with
Locke there is no concrete basis on which to articulate the familiar distinction between political identity and the structures of political legitimacy. Even though Locke famously acknowledged differing types of authority and societies such as those between a husband and a wife,
parents and children, and masters and servants, he also claimed that
"each of these, or all together came short of *Political Society*."[64] The
Lockean social contract, in being the normative ground for the formation of legitimate political society and authority, is apparently indifferent not only to the societies Locke himself acknowledges but to any
alternative form of political identity.[65] Here again this radical sequester-

64. *Second Treatise*, sec. 77.
65. I say "apparently" because, I believe that Locke's political society does in
fact rely on conventional and customary social practices that he does not officially
acknowledge. This is especially the case in the education that is deemed necessary

ing of the social from the political is fraught with imperial implications. By the eighteenth century, and with added emphasis in the nineteenth, the typical liberal view on India associates it with the turgid constrictions of familial, religious, ethnic, and other various complex social ties. But none of these individually, nor all of them together, is taken as evidence of a political bond or society. Indeed, the reverse is more often the case.

In my reading of Burke, location or territory has a special salience, but only because, in his view, it captured an emotional attachment or sense of belonging that he deemed central to collective and political identity. It is precisely this sensibility that informs (though by no means exhausts) nationalism in its various anti-imperialist and other efforts. By the mid–nineteenth century the dominant tilt among British liberals was to repudiate any link between a sense of territorial belonging and nationhood. The classic statement of this view is in John R. Seeley's enormously influential work *The Expansion of England*, a book of lectures originally delivered at Cambridge University in 1881 and 1882. For Seeley "the fundamental fact then is that India had no jealousy of the foreigner because India had no sense whatever of national unity, because there *was* no India and therefore, properly speaking, no foreigner."[66] Similarly, John Strachey, a leading colonial administrator and liberal intellectual, responded to the question "What is India? What does the name India really signify?" with:

> The answer that I have sometimes given sounds paradoxical, but it is true. There is no such country, and this is the first and most essential fact about India that can be learned. . . . India is a name which we give to a great region . . . there is not, and never was an India, or even a country of India, possessing, according to European ideas, any sort of unity, physical, political, social, or religious; no Indian nation, no "people of India," of which we hear so much.[67]

This view was shared, despite nuances of differing emphasis, by Bentham, James Mill, Macaulay, and J. S. Mill. And it supplied the intellec-

---

for the inculcation of reason. See my *The Anxiety of Freedom*, esp. the introduction and chap. 4.

66. Seeley, *The Expansion of England*, 161. For extensive references to the absence of geographical unity, see the chapter entitled "How we Govern India," 172–86.

67. John Strachey, *India: Its Administration and Progress*, 4th ed. (London, 1911), 1–5.

tual and normative grounds for the liberal justification of the British Empire.[68]

In contrast, Burke's critique of the empire in India and America, and his only slightly concealed advocacy of the political independence of the latter, derives from his identifying in these places a sentiment of attachment to something that was "held in common." A distinctive sense of sharing in a common territory is one especially significant instance where, in his view, such sentiments get developed and evinced. It is worth recalling that Tocqueville in the first chapter of *Democracy in America*, entitled "Physical Configuration of North America," also partially located the distinctive basis of American nationhood and democracy in the sentiments engendered by its geography. It is this attachment and belonging that demarcate and partially define the political community by articulating the way in which members share in it. Bhikhu Parekh, in a recent article, eloquently states this idea in a way that captures the Burkean and Rousseauian intonations to which I have pointed.

> A political community is a territorially concentrated group of people bound together by their acceptance of a common mode of conducting their collective affairs, including a body of institutions and shared values. It is a public institution shared by its members collectively, as a community. It is not shared by them in a way that we might share a piece of cake, but in a way that we share streets, parks, the institutions of government, and so on. And it is common to them not in a way that having two eyes is common to all human beings, but in a way that a dining table is common to those seated around it. The identity of a political community lies in what all its members share not individually but collectively, not privately but publicly, and has an inescapable institutional focus.[69]

The perspective from which Burke identifies territoriality as being significant is one in which a political community embodies the kind of

---

68. The liberal denial of India as constituting a nation is itself a conclusion that follows from many subsidiary arguments. Crucial among these arguments is the claim that Indians have not reached the point of being able to consent to their political governors and can therefore not constitute a political society of "their own." I consider some of these arguments with a special focus on J. S. Mill in "Empire and Consent" (unpublished).

69. Bhikhu Parekh, "Discourses on National Identity," *Political Studies* 42 (1994): 492–504.

sharing that Parekh articulates. It represents a commitment to what is publicly and commonly shared or held and therefore takes seriously the process, itself often locationally implicated, through which such sentiments of sharing get engendered. Its emphasis is on what is publicly and commonly held and not on the individual characteristics that are common. And for this reason the interpretation of Burke that emphasizes the centrality of territoriality is sharply at odds with a view of a political community that features the importance of common ethnicity, race, or other individual attributes such as temperament or even reason. In this, Burke is the spiritual precursor to Rousseau, who in his work on Poland made clear that his purpose was to identify norms and institutions appropriate to Poland rather than address the question of who was, in the appropriate sense, a Pole. Throughout much of the nineteenth century, most British liberals were preoccupied with qestions such as who is a Punjabi, a Bengali, or more generally an Indian, and not with questions such as what is Punjab, or Bengal, or India.

A final word on what is distinctive about territory. At a subjective level, as I have mentioned, it constitutes the ground for a host of experiences that become habitual to us and are suggested in the idea of "inhabiting" a place or by the German word *Gewohnte*. In this respect the ties of territory are at least broadly similar to those of language, ethnicity, and shared beliefs and customs, because clearly these other attributes also engender the shared familiarity of habits. But in another sense territory is without analogue. Clearly in the postnationalist era, states feel the imperative to claim to be able to preserve and defend a distinctive way of life. But simultaneously, they are aware that such claims to distinctiveness are themselves weakened in this era. Ethnicity, religion, and language, the very attributes that nations in the stage of their formation so often tout, cease to be the markers of distinctiveness. States cannot protect or police the borders of their languages, and still less the religious commitments and interethnic links that their citizens increasingly cultivate. (Despite this, of course, states often try, and they are seldom totally indifferent to such matters.) But they can try to protect their territorial borders. In an odd sort of way territory becomes the last resort (last not in a temporal sense, because the imperative to distinctiveness is there from the beginning) of political autonomy and sovereignty. In this, of course, is revealed something of its hollowness and centrality. Nationalism, as Harold Laski rightly points out, is after all "urgently separatist in character," and for that reason can often be expressed only in the symbolism of flag and map waving.[70] It is a politics of recognition, in which sovereignty, independence, and the right of self-determination sometimes amount to no more than having a *place* in the United Nations.

70. Harold Laski, *A Grammar of Politics* (New Haven: Yale University Press, 1929), 220.

---◄ F I V E ►---

Edmund Burke on the Perils of the Empire

[F]ree governments have been commonly the most happy for those who partake of their freedom; yet are they the most ruinous and oppressive to their provinces.

DAVID HUME, "Politics as a Science"

It is but too true, that the love, and even the very idea, of genuine liberty is extremely rare.... [T]here are many, whose whole scheme of freedom is made up of pride, perverseness, and insolence. They feel themselves in a state of thraldom, they imagine that their souls are cooped and cabined in, unless they have some man, or some body of men, dependent on their mercy.... This disposition is the true source of the passion, which many men, in very humble life, have taken to the American war. *Our* subjects in America; *our* colonies; *our* dependents.

EDMUND BURKE, *Writings and Speeches* (Taylor)

When placed alongside his major contemporaries and the political theorists who followed him in the nineteenth century, Burke's views on the empire stand out for numerous reasons. First, his views were well developed and complex, appropriate to the turgid vexations of the reality to which they pertained. Moreover, these views were integral to his broader political thinking. In this regard it is worth noting that notwithstanding its extent, longevity, and unmistakable domestic and international significance, the British Empire was for most of its existence a phenomenon without a commensurate theoretical elaboration and justification. This was especially true among political theorists; the major British political thinkers of the eighteenth and nineteenth centuries did not write books that elaborated in any detail on the notion of empire or its cognate practices—such as having subjects rather than citizens. From both a normative and an explanatory standpoint, major British political theorists were largely untroubled by the empire.[1]

---

1. This condition remains substantially true even today. Indeed, with the exception of John Plamenatz's *On Alien Rule and Self-Government*, published in 1960, and the second part of Hannah Arendt's *The Origins of Totalitarianism*, and despite

153

From the seventeenth to the nineteenth century the fact of the empire serves as an occasionally tenebrous and often spectacular background that is held together by a hardened though implicit social consensus. It is a consensus that occasionally gets frayed at the edges and in those instances provokes discussion of, for example, issues of free trade, the precise relationship of the East India Company to Parliament, and the moral and administrative probity of some officials. But for the most part, the consensus is seldom pierced, even by the activity of self-conscious theorizing. By the second half of the nineteenth century, when this consensus and indifference begin to abate in the writings of John Stuart Mill and Walter Bagehot, for example, the empire is still only a marginal concern. It was, in part, with an eye to this curious insouciance that the influential historian and social scientist J. R. Seeley commented, "We seem, as it were, to have conquered and peopled half the world in a fit of absence of mind."[2] Burke's writings and parliamentary speeches are a conspicuous and impressive exception to this tradition of neglect, presumption, or absentmindedness.

Related to this is the significant fact that Burke reflected on and wrote about various major sites of the empire—Ireland, America, and India. At the forefront of these reflections is an awareness that following the Seven Years' War (1756–63) the British Empire was neither predominantly Protestant nor Anglophone. It now included French Catholics in Quebec and millions of Asians who were neither Christian nor white. Burke was alone in asking how traditional British liberties could be reconciled with "that vast, heterogeneous, intricate Mass of Interests, which at this day forms the Body of the British Power."[3] He was alone

the current explosion of historical and literary postcolonial studies, imperialism has received very little attention from political theorists and philosophers in the post–World War II period. In reviewing Plamenetz's On Alien Rule and Self Government, Brian Barry rightly pointed out that this work was hardly reviewed or read when it was first published. This is a fate that certainly endures, despite the very considerable stature and influence of its author in the sixties and seventies. See Brian Barry, Democracy, Power, and Justice (Oxford: Clarendon Press, 1989), 156–87.

2. Seeley, The Expansion of England, 12. The failure of British political theorists to incorporate considerations of the empire into their normative frameworks is all the more puzzling in light of the fact that virtually all them were actively and substantially involved in the administration of the empire.

3. Burke, Sheffield Archives, Wentworth Woodhouse Muniments 9/23, quoted in David Bromwich, "The Context of Burke's Reflections," Social Research 58, no. 2 (1991): 328. On changes occurring in the British Empire in the late eighteenth century, see Linda Colley, Britons: Forging the Nation 1707–1837 (New Haven: Yale University Press, 1992), 101–93; P. J. Marshall, A Free Though Conquering People: Britain and Asia in the Eighteenth Century (London: Allen and Unwin, 1968); and Jack P.

in recognizing what a century later Seeley believed his contemporaries were still unwilling to admit, namely, that by the eighteenth century, "the history of England [was] not in England but in America and Asia."[4] Burke's writings make it undeniably clear that he reflected with great seriousness on situations in which the exercise of power and authority was implicated with considerations of cultural and racial diversity, contrasting civilizational unities, the absence of geographical contiguity and consensual government, and alternative norms of political identity and legitimacy. These are issues that today receive considerable attention within academic and popular discourse but were largely muted in eighteenth- and nineteenth-century British liberal thought. Burke was the singular exception. The left-wing critic Harold Laski rightly commented that "[on] Ireland, America, and India, he [Burke] was at every point upon the side of the future" and that "he was the first English statesman to fully understand the moral import of the problem of subject races."[5]

Finally, there is the initially surprising fact, given the common conception regarding Burke as a conservative defender of the traditional British political establishment, that he viewed the British Empire with deep reservations and vociferously challenged most of its earlier and extant practices. He opposed the injustice of the system of Protestant control in Ireland, and recognized without regret the inevitability of American independence and saw the capriciousness and legal pedantry on which George III's hollow power relied and rested. Finally, and most importantly for this chapter, he saw through the abusive distortions of civilizational hierarchies, racial superiority, and assumptions of cultural impoverishment by which British power justified its territorial expansionism and commercial avarice in India and elsewhere. In the tenacity with which he pressed his objections to these ideas and practices, Burke is unmatched by any British statesmen or political thinker of the eighteenth or nineteenth century. None of the well-known liberals or socialists of the nineteenth century expresses anything like Burke's indignation and searching critique of the empire. The British Empire and its principal early instrument, the East India Company, certainly had their

---

Greene, *Peripheries and Center: Constitutional Developments in the Extended Polities of the British Empire and the United States (1607–1788)* (Athens: University of Georgia Press, 1986).

4. Seeley, *The Expansion of England*, 13. Seeley was the most influential and widely read historian of the empire. Stokes, *The English Utilitarians in India*, is still, I think, the best detailed overview of the writings and influence of British political thinkers on India from the late eighteenth to the early twentieth century.

5. Laski, *Political Thought in England from Locke to Bentham*, 149, 153.

critics. But no such critic would have, as Burke did, press that criticism
by calling into question the very possibility of "drawing up an indictment against a whole people."[6] Constructing such indictments, including those based on single criteria such as race, geography, climate,
religion, origins, or cranial dimensions, was a minor cottage industry among eighteenth- and nineteenth-century European intellectuals.
None would have sensed, as Burke did, that in the distant and often
exotic spectacle of the empire, there lurked an intimate internal threat:
"in order to prove that the Americans have no right to their liberties,
we are every day endeavoring to subvert the maxims which preserve the
whole spirit of our own."[7] And again in a remarkable statement made
during the impeachment trial of Governor Warren Hastings he said,
"Today the Commons of Great Britain prosecutes the delinquents of
India [i.e., Hastings and his associates]: tomorrow the delinquents of
India may be the Commons of Great Britain."[8]

Perhaps most importantly in this context, no other statesman or
thinker expresses the depth of pathos, the pained embarrassment, the
capacious compassion, and the sustained moral revulsion for the cruelty,
torture, deprivation, and injustice that the company was perpetrating.
Burke is virtually alone in owning up to this as an indictment of Britain's
moral and political rectitude. There is scarcely a page in the thousands
that Burke wrote and uttered during the Hastings trial, in the speech on
the debts of the nabob of Arcot, in the Fox India Bill speech, or in his
numerous other writings on India and the British in which a simple but
piercing concern with brutality, exploitation, the humiliation of women,
the avarice of the company and its parliamentary patrons, the corresponding effect of destitution and the arbitrary use of unjust power is
not an illuminated feature of the background that he is aware of, and the
implications of which he is at pains to convey to his audience. Notwithstanding the significant differences in their views, Harold Laski with
characteristic insight commented that "[t]he essential Burke is, no
doubt, a great and generous man, the springs of whose compassion were
as wide as they were deep."[9] Consider the following statement uttered
in the House of Commons, where Burke was surrounded by the very
people to whom the statement makes reference:

6. Burke, "Speech on Conciliation with America," in *Writings and Speeches*
(Taylor), 2:136.

7. Ibid., 130.

8. Burke, "Impeachment of Warren Hastings," in *Writings and Speeches* (Taylor),
10:450–51.

9. Harold J. Laski, *The Rise of European Liberalism* (London: Unwin Books,
1936), 129.

This was the golden cup of abominations; this the chalice of the fornications of rapine, usury, and oppression, which was held out by the gorgeous eastern harlot; which so many people, so many of the nobles of this land, had drained to the very dregs. Do you think that no reckoning was to follow this lewd debauch? that no payment was to be demanded for this riot of public drunkenness and national prostitution? Here! you have it here before you.[10]

The metaphor and imagery of the empire as a debased and coerced orgy is frequent in his writings, as are the sentiments with which Burke concluded this speech:

Whoever therefore shall at any time bring before you [i.e., the Commons] any thing towards the relief of our distressed follow-citizens in India, and towards a subversion of the present most corrupt and oppressive system for its government, in me shall find, . . . a steady, earnest, and faithful assistant.[11]

If one ignores or deflates the significance of such lucid moral lyricism as expressing no more than the righteousness or sensitivity of one man's opinions, and therefore deems them unworthy of theoretical attention, one places theory at an embarrassing remove from human pain and suffering. The claim that such a distance allows us to be theoretical or gives us a perspective that is political, or objective, hardly exonerates the moral indifference. It is an enduring tribute to Burke, the man and the thinker, that his sympathy and ire and ultimately his political thought are garnered by thinking through and feeling with tactile intensity specific episodes replete with proper nouns, an imagined inhabitation of real places, and an engaged imbrication in vital traditions. As I hope this chapter will make clear, it is what Raymond Williams referred to as this "style of thinking" that is essential to understanding Burke's views on the empire.[12]

It is of course true that Burke did not oppose the empire in the sense of calling for its immediate dismantling. He was far too deferential to such weighty and established practices, to countenance what for him would have amounted, in that context, to a "revolutionary" and therefore morally, politically, and psychologically retrograde alternative.

---

10. Burke, "Speech on the Nabob of Arcot's Debts," in *Writings and Speeches* (Oxford), 5:543.

11. Ibid., 552.

12. Raymond Williams, *Culture and Society* (London: Chatto & Hindus, 1958).

Much of what he says about the British rule in India is squarely within the framework of a plea for good government; none of it is a plea for Indian self-government. He is substantially concerned with the moral and political probity of those, like Governor Warren Hastings and Paul Benfield, who violated the norms of good government and in doing so abused power and the public interest. But to conclude from all of this that Burke was merely an enlightened imperialist, an apologist laboring to secure the empire on surer and more commendable foundations, would be thoroughly to miss the tenor of his thought and the significant challenge that he presents to the empire and to the ways of thinking and acting that sustained it.

The important point is not whether Burke was or was not an imperialist in an explicit or declared sense. In the eighteenth century that question had not surfaced to self-consciousness and had scarcely any of the associations that it has acquired following the nationalist struggles and the decolonization of European empires in this century. Even in the case of American independence, which most closely resembles twentieth-century nationalism, the announced anti-imperialism is muted, as is evident from the almost deferential tone of the Declaration of Independence.

Regarding the empire, the relevant questions in the eighteenth and nineteenth centuries were, what were the relationships on which the empire was predicated, and which it fostered, and how were these understood? Did it, for instance, rely on and entrench a worldview in which considerations of blood and essentialized conceptions of national and cultural destinies got braided with the exercise and purported legitimacy of imperial power? Was that power furthermore reliant on a "progressive" view of history in which somehow India, and more generally the East, got coded as ossified and confined in their "traditions" and therefore were "backward" or stunted in a civilizational infancy? Did this conception of historical development underappreciate the coherence of extant lived social forms and thus make them merely unstable stages in the realization of an alleged cosmopolitan moral and political ideal? Did the category "traditional" itself serve to blanket India such that local life forms and institutions were bleached of their coherence, flexibility, and contingency—in short, of their possible vitality? By the nineteenth century virtually all normative theorizing is explicitly grounded in some account of universal history, pace Hegel, Marx, and Mill. For liberals this was obviously a departure from the equally explicit antihistorical orientation of Hobbes and Locke, where the normative foundations rested on an account of human nature that was at least ostensibly indifferent to civilizational accomplishments and cultural values. Finally, do the protagonists of the empire hold to an overly narrow conception of political order that implicitly sanctions imperial interventions by obscuring or distorting alternative extant forms of political order in India?

It is these questions that allow the empire to be a mirror on late eighteenth- and nineteenth-century British political thought. And it is through their interrogation that one gets a sense of how familiar liberal concerns with issues of toleration, popular sovereignty, and limits on the exercise of legitimate power got played out under conditions of multifaceted and lived pluralism. These are the very questions that inform Burke's thinking. More generally, what animates Burke's views on the empire and his political thought is an alternative understanding regarding the basis of political power and individual and political identity—including the issue of membership—and via these concerns an alternative conception of public interest. It is this alternative understanding that this chapter illustrates and that I contend is at the root of Burke's prophetic view of the empire.

Theoretical Underpinnings

Burke was deeply moved by various aspects of Indian social order and civilization, but most particularly his concern centered on India as a site of British political adventure and expansionism. The specific question that this chapter considers is what was the political basis of Burke's concern for India and, relatedly, what were the grounds for his deep reservations toward British imperial practices in India? Burke's views on this question are closely linked to his thoughts on political identity, the basis of legitimacy, and the practices through which both can be undermined. It is commonplace to think of these latter issues as best elaborated in Burke's writings on the excesses of the French Revolution. As an aside, I hope to make clear that for Burke, the British Empire, especially in India, was nothing less than a revolution, with all the psychological naïveté and theoretical arrogance that he associated with the revolution in France.

In his writings on India, as in his work on the French Revolution, Burke is primarily concerned with established communities that are threatened. The greed and financial corruption of the empire, the capricious brutality with which Governor General Hastings and his associates abuse their office and power, the arbitrary and feigned concern that Parliament occasionally shows toward these and other abuses—in all these and numerous other instances Burke's ire and sympathy are provoked in substantial part by a concern for a threatened community. Even when his attention is fastened on individuals, as in his famous description of Marie Antoinette fleeing from her bedchamber or as in numerous descriptions of Indian men and women, the pathos he invokes is through the relations and circumstances that coalesce in these individuals as members of a besieged community. The same is true of those who are the objects of his pitiless scorn and condemnation. Warren Hastings, Paul Benfield, the duke of Bedford, and the Jacobins are mainly judged as members and instruments of one community involved in unsettling the integrity and coherence of another.

The argument of this chapter follows from this concern with threatened communities. Because Burke's primary sympathy is directed toward communities, it is important to consider how Burke identifies communities or, more generally, where he sees social order as residing. Given the British imperial context, this concern has two distinct components. The first relates to the factors that incline Burke to the conclusion that India does constitute a political community, and the second relates to the practices of the colonial engagement that threaten it.

Regarding the first consideration, Burke draws attention to certain long-standing and prevailing locational attachments and historical associations by virtue of which India constitutes a political community and Indians have a sense of themselves as individuals. As has been explained in the preceding chapter, one of the striking features of Burke's views, in part because it contrasts so starkly with the classical liberal tradition, is the political and psychological significance he attaches to places. Individuals "belong to," "come from," and "live in" places. For Burke, these philological emblems capture a fundamental aspect of individual and collective identity. If language is revealing of our nature, as it most certainly is for Burke, we both possess places and are possessed by them. For Locke and the classical liberal tradition, only the former is the case—a relationship that is captured in the view of property as the mere extension of individual will via the value-infusing capabilities of labor working on a "worthless Nature."[13] In contrast, for Burke, places partially constitute who we are, and in doing so, they are, at a minimum, normatively relevant to the institutions and social arrangements that we envision. We do not simply live in places; we also *inhabit* them in the sense that they supply, from the very outset, the conditions for the expe-

13. See chapter 3 for a more extensive discussion of this issue and the relevant citations from Locke.

riences that become habitual to us. In the language of social science one might say that places represent that juncture within which structure and agency are imbricated. This point also illustrates that Burke's valorization of the habitual is not merely an obeisance to practices that derive from the preestablished and hence facilitate the reproduction of the past. Rather, the emphasis on habits, and by implication on locational attachments as an important ingredient of the habitual, represent Burke's commitment to the idea that political and moral theories are only as credible as the psychological account that undergirds them. The normative force of history and location stems from their psychological centrality to identity formation. And for this reason they supply at least some of the desiderata on which political institutions and social practices must rely.

The contrast between the significance that the liberal and Burkean positions attach to place is indicative of a broader difference, one of considerable importance in their differing assessments of the empire. By viewing place and history as constitutive of human identity, Burke takes identity as something partially, though importantly, given and hence not wholly an artifice of individual choice. Moreover, what is given is also shared to the extent that places and history engender common sentiments and individuals view them as such. This sharing has an irredeemably historical aspect to it, in that it precedes individual will formation by being a ground for it. In fact, for Burke history and place have the same psychological valency. Indeed, the account of place and history is fundamentally a psychological one that, for instance, is broadly consonant with Freud's views. One can imagine Burke responding simultaneously to Hobbes's claim at the beginning of the *Leviathan* that human artifice can "imitate" and outdo Nature and to Locke's claim that "in the beginning all the world was America," i.e., materially and sentimentally inert, with the assertion that they are dangerously false and irrelevant. Burke would respond that swe are constrained from the beginning, and human artifice is always mediated by those constraints. It follows that any reference to a beginning prior to such constraints is irrelevant to social and political life and therefore not a foundation for them.

One implication that Burke draws from these claims is that the existence of political society does not turn exclusively on such individual capacities as reason, will, and the ability to choose, but also on the presence of a certain *shared order on the ground*. In the imperial context this is of crucial significance. Admittedly, this is a vague notion because the order on the ground may not, and in all likelihood will not, give us determinate conceptions of institutional arrangements, how power is to be exercised, and a host of other important issues. Nevertheless, for Burke this order is crucial to establishing or settling at least one important claim: do a group of people form a political community, that is, do they have the requisite sense of sharing in something common, beyond the merely contingent sharing that overlapping individual interests or preferences may produce? With respect to India and America, Burke's answer to this question was emphatically affirmative. Indeed, the vagueness of such a notion itself points to the plurality of conditions that might satisfy the requirements for a political community. This is where Burke unmistakably parts company with classical liberals like Locke, Bentham, the Mills, and Macaulay. The latter tradition, as has been mentioned, is virtually unified in its view regarding the absence of political community in India and, more generally, in the colonies. This absence and the redress that the empire purportedly supplies for it is the mainstay of the liberal justification of the empire: India is in a condition of tutelage. Like Lockean children, it is born to freedom but *not yet* capable of exercising it. The empire is a promissory note of future release conditional on following a specific trajectory of development.

This liberal assessment is undergirded by the archetypical narrative of individual consent as the basis of political society. That narrative features a particular view of the individual as one whose identity is mobile in the sense of being substantially free of involuntary and constitutive linkages. His or her reason, will, and interests are literally contained within the body. Aspirationally, these are directed toward some form of the ideal of autonomy. This familiar view has attended liberalism both as a point of celebration and a critique from its very inception. Its various elaborations have included Locke's rational individuals, anxiously holding onto the last remnants of a faith that once confidently assumed that the rationality and divinity of the natural moral order made it isomorphic with individual rationality, Kant's acutely self-conscious suspicion of anything that might be tainted with heteronomous links, and J. S. Mill's celebration of individual eccentricity and progressive nature in choosing "life plans" as something sharply antithetical to the habitual.

The critical mirror that Burke holds up to these views, especially in the imperial context, though elsewhere too, is both psychological and political. In terms of the former, he contends that inheritances are in some crucial measure involuntary and that they bind us (which of course is different from confining us in the present through the inescapable mediation of location and the past. Psychologically, we are always in medias res. In terms of politics, Burke's point is that the existence of political society and the form of institutional arrangements must be conditional on it because of the force of the former point. By reference to these two claims, he sees political society and order in India and not just the prospect of it through the tutored development of individual capacities.

As to the second question, that of which practices threaten the extant political community in India, Burke sees British practices as fracturing and recombining, for reasons of commercial and political greed, these locational and historical attachments and willfully denying these considerations that have given India a sense of social order. The dislocation stemming from such actions does not merely affect India. In fact, Burke is constantly concerned with how, in order to effect these dislocations in India, the British have to put into risk the very things that have historically given Britain a sense of social order and political cohesion.

I hope to make clear how for Burke these questions ultimately turn on how individuals and communities come to have a confident sense of themselves and thus secure the conditions for their freedom, and how in the clutches of certain ways of thinking and behaving they risk dispossessing themselves of this sense. Finally, I want to suggest that Burke's communitarianism picks out the very concerns that have been salient to identifying nations and subsequent nationalist claims. His sympathy for India stems from his deploying concepts through which India's potential nationhood was evident to him centuries before it was to most Indians. Given this fact, or rather what Burke prefigures would be a fact, he was anticipating what Benedict Anderson has called the "inner incompatibility between empire and nation."[14] For Burke, this incompatibility was necessarily debilitating both to India's nationhood and to Britain's pretended imperial nationhood.

There is one other broad aspect of Burke's writings on India that I simply flag at this point; it is more relevantly and extensively discussed alongside James Mill's *History of British India* and J. S. Mill's account of civilizational progress. Burke, as I have mentioned, was deeply engaged with India's history and civilizational coherence. Furthermore, there is a specific quality to this engagement that sets it apart and casts a general hue on his views on the empire. It is this perspective on India's history and more generally on India itself—as distinct from his specific assessments—that is unique. It is the perspective of a spectator—concerned, at points sympathetic, at others critical—but always mindful of a dis-

14. Anderson, *Imagined Communities: Reflections on the Origins and Spread of Nationalism* (London: Verso, 1983), 39.

tance, not simply physical but more importantly emotional, that separates him from those whose story he is recounting. It is a history he had studied with great diligence and passion. But Burke is painstakingly aware that neither of these qualities makes it his history, nor do they guarantee that it will become transparent to him. History as experienced is more than the knowledge of that experience.

This feature of acknowledging a history and a set of concerns of which he has no part has significant implications. First, it suggests that inheritances are specific and bounded. To this idea Burke will add that political order and society are crafted within boundaries and only rarely set outside the boundaries themselves. Second, the spectatorial perspective indicates a position from which something can be viewed without being able to touch or meddle with it. This represents a restraint that Burke sets on the use of power, in this instance imperial power. He will not countenance power arrogating to itself the right to meddle with other peoples' history, especially when those histories have produced a social coherence of their own. Finally, what has far-reaching implications regarding this point is that it eschews a general ethical or political viewpoint (such as an abstract account of human progress or even an abstract account of human nature as in Mill's notion of man as a progressive being) as serving as a surrogate for power. Something of this idea is suggested in a remark Burke makes in parliament: "[I]f we are not able to contrive some method of governing India well which will not of necessity become the means of governing Great Britain ill, a ground is laid for their eternal separation, but none for sacrificing the people of that country to our constitution."[15]

This idea has its basis in a deep, even reverent humility that Burke feels in the face of differences—cultural, economic, and political. If that is the case, the humility touches and surrounds his thought in a way that permits him to accept those differences as lived possibilities even when they sharply contrasted, as the norms in India no doubt did, with the practices with which Burke was at home. Here Burke expresses a tolerance that is grounded on an acceptance of his own limitations and his own possible obtuseness to other practices, and it is therefore a deeper tolerance than that of his liberal compatriots, even when they made toleration the focus of their theoretical attention. In contrast to the darkness that James Mill and others ascribed to India, Burke sees and accepts that darkness as perhaps stemming from the limits of his own circumscribed vision.[16]

15. Burke, "Fox's India Bill Speech," 5:438.
16. See chapter 2.

I have framed my reading of Burke in political terms. This calls for some justification regarding which I make two related points. First, there is a tendency among those who have written on Burke's views on India and his critical evaluation of the empire to ascribe these views to a rather personalized quality stemming from Burke's character, personality, and circumstance. James Prior, an early biographer, saw Burke as personally motivated by "a detestation of any thing like oppression or injustice."[17] Alexander Bickel viewed Burke's thoughts on the different sites of the empire as unified and supported by an abhorrence of uncontrolled and arbitrary power.[18] More recently, Conor Cruise O'Brien has argued that Burke's mature writings on India and his concern for the suffering there are driven by a psychological need to atone for his earlier indifference to the sufferings of Ireland, and for his own and his father's related betrayal.[19] According to this account, Burke's involvement with India is a displaced and complex extension of a concern for his native Ireland. With a different emphasis, though still within this family of personalized interpretations, there is H. N. Brailsford's general comment that "[o]f Burke one must ask not so much What did he believe? as Whom did he pity?"[20] There is a lot in Burke's personality and the circumstances of his life that gives some credence to these and similar views. For instance, the immoderate tenacity with which Burke pursues Warren Hastings may hint at causes that require a psychological perspective fully to fathom them. Similarly, both his language and his views suggest that he often braided Ireland and India in his mind's eye.

And yet—and this is the second point—these personalized interpretations tend to muffle if not entirely overlook the important ways in which Burke's views on India, and more generally on the empire, are illustrative of and integral to his political thought. Burke's interest in India is not merely that of a scholarly Orientalist such as the pioneering Sanskritist Sir William Jones. He is not drawn to it by its civilizational and cultural riches or by the spectacle of its alluring peculiarity. India implicates British power. It is to illustrate and reform features of that

17. Prior, *The Life of the Right Honourable Edmund Burke* (London: Henry G. Bohn, 1854), 248.

18. Bickel, "Constitutional Government and Revolution," in *Edmund Burke: Appraisals and Applications*, ed. Daniel Ritchie (London: Transaction Publishers, 1990), 135.

19. O'Brien, *The Great Melody: A Thematic Biography and Commented Anthology of Edmund Burke* (Chicago: University of Chicago Press, 1992), 271–72.

20. Brailsford, *Shelly, Godwin, and Their Circle* (London, 1913), 20, quoted in David Bromwich, *A Choice of Inheritance*, 51.

power, along with the ideas and presumptions that sustain it, that Burke is led to a consideration of India's civilizational and cultural integuments. His sympathy for India as possessing a political and cultural coherence of its own is undeniable. But—and this is what is usually overlooked—Burke's sympathy is informed by a commitment to concepts and ways of thinking that pick out and give credence to that coherence. Therefore, to understand the basis of that sympathy and the attending worries regarding the British colonial engagement is to go beyond questions of India and British colonialism per se. His writings on India are neither an exception to his general social, moral, and political views nor are they merely a mundane instance of those views. They are, in his own estimate, the most sustained and consummate expression of these views and his thinking more generally.

THE BACKGROUND OF INVOLVEMENT

Burke's involvement with British-Indian affairs begins in 1767, the year he first entered Parliament, and concludes in his public role in 1795, two years before his death. He was the principal and in many instances the sole author of eleven parliamentary reports on India. The breadth and depth of his knowledge of India were legendary and are plainly evident in his writings. He was also the author of numerous parliamentary bills regarding Indian affairs, including the famous Fox India Bill. In sheer volume, his writings on India constitute a majority of his published works by a substantial margin. Neither the French Revolution, his native Ireland, America, nor parliamentary reform—all of which were causes on which he felt passionately—invoked the febrile intensity and gravity of purpose that India did for Burke.

Burke often simultaneously brought to mind the threat posed by the French Revolution along with that of the British in India, and at these moments it is always the latter that provoked greater concern for its actual and potential effects. In 1796, Burke wrote to Lord Loughborough: "Our Government and our Laws are beset by two different enemies, which are sapping its foundation, Indianism, and Jacobinism. In some cases they act separately, in some they act in conjunction: But of this I am sure; that the first is the worst by far."[21] Again in 1796, and toward the end of his life, when the deservedness of a state pension that Burke had been granted was being challenged by the duke of Bedford,

---

21. *The Correspondence of Edmund Burke,* ed. Thomas Copeland (Chicago: University of Chicago Press, 1958–78), 8:432.

he emphasized and prioritized a lifetime spent dealing with public issues:

> In truth, the services I am called on to account for are not those on which I value myself the most. If I were to call for a reward, (which I have never done,) it should be for those in which for fourteen years without intermission I showed the most industry and had the least success: I mean in the affairs of India. They are those on which I value myself the most; most for the importance; most for labour; most for the judgment; most for constancy and perseverance in the pursuit. Others may value them most for the *intention*. In that, surely, they are not mistaken.[22]

Part of what makes this statement remarkable is that it dates from a time when in the popular imagination he had been vindicated in many of his prophecies regarding the turns that the French Revolution would take and his reputation was most celebrated and associated with that event.[23]

Ten years earlier, while he was in the midst of the Hastings trial and as his unremitting intensity on Indian matters began to be the subject of public caricature and party concern, he wrote to Mary Palmer: "I have no party in this Business . . . but among a set of people, who have none of your Lilies and Roses in their faces; but who are the images of the great Pattern as well as you and I. I know what I am doing; whether the white people like it or not."[24] The statement is remarkable both for the capaciousness of Burke's own sympathy and for his brazenly direct way of pointing to the narrowness that informed prevailing prejudices.[25] Our familiarity today with such an exposing remark as "whether the white people like it or not" muffles the incredible and complex sensibility from which alone, in the eighteenth century, it could stem, and the thunderous effect it must have had on Mary Palmer at least.

Over India, Burke lost personal friendships, political allies, and patrons such as Fox, strained beyond repair his association with his party, and became the object of lampoons in which he was often portrayed as a

22. Burke, "Letter to a Noble Lord," in *Writings and Speeches* (Taylor), 5:192.
23. The fourteen years referred to here pertain only to the period of Burke's involvement with the Hastings impeachment.
24. *Selected Letters of Edmund Burke*, ed. Harvey C. Mansfield (Chicago: University of Chicago Press, 1984), 381.
25. David Bromwich has referred to this last sentence as "one of the most startling and admirable things ever said by a human being." David Bromwich, review of *The Great Melody*, by Conor Cruise O'Brien, *New Republic*, 1 March 1993, 37.

monk with obscure and fanatical designs.[26] There was indeed something
excessive in the tenacity that Burke brought to bear on Indian issues.
His opening speech to the House of Lords imploring them to impeach
Hastings went on for seven days; his closing arguments went on for
nine. A plausible case can be made that the reason for which the greatest
British parliamentarian of the eighteenth century was only offered a position in the privy council and never in the cabinet, and that too as pay-
master general, was because of his apparently inexplicable obsession
with the link between his people and those who had neither lilies nor
roses in their faces.[27] And yet, despite the price he had paid for this
obsession, Burke was unrelenting. A few months before his death, he
wrote to his young friend and literary executor, French Laurence:

> Let not this cruel, daring, unexampled act of publick corrup-
> tion, guilt, and meanness go down—to a posterity, perhaps as
> careless as the present race, without its due animadversion,
> which will be best found in its own acts and monuments. Let
> my endeavors to save the Nation from that Shame and Guilt,
> be my monument; The only one I ever will have. Let every
> thing I have done, said, or written be forgotten but this. I have
> struggled with the great and the little on this point during the
> greater part of my active Life; and I wish after my death, to
> have my Defiance of the Judgments of those, who consider the
> dominion of the glorious Empire given by an incomprehensible
> dispensation of the Divine providence into our hands as noth-
> ing more than an opportunity of gratifying for the lowest of
> their purposes, the lowest of their passions—and that for such
> poor rewards, and for the most part, indirect and silly Bribes,
> as indicate even more the folly than the corruption of these
> infamous and contemptible wretches. . . . Above all make out
> the cruelty of this pretended acquittal, but in reality this barba-
> rous and inhuman condemnation of whole Tribes and nations,
> and of all the abuses they contain. If ever Europe recovers its

26. See David Bromwich, "The Context of Burke's *Reflections*," *Social Research*
58, no. 2 (1991): 313–54.
27. Conor Cruise O'Brien in his monumental thematic biography of Burke
supplies the evidence for such a case, even though the thrust of his interpretation
and explanation of Burke's concern with India involves Burke associating India with
his native Ireland. See O'Brien, *The Great Melody*, 257–384, 579–92. Also see Prior,
Life of the Right Honorable Edmund Burke, 243–75.

civilization that work will be useful. Remember! Remember! Remember![28]

His intensity of commitment was to a largely lost cause in which one might say (as the House of Lords did) that even if every charge Burke was urging was true, and acknowledged as such, one would have little more than one corrupt governor-general, who had embezzled from the most profitable company in the world, allowed some prisoners of war to be tortured, countenanced the humiliation of an Indian begum, and perhaps directed the murder of one local official: in brief, he had abused his high office. The gravity of the matter is not, at least obviously, commensurate with the efforts and consequences of the previous decade and a half. And so one is led, as most commentators have been, to explain such immoderate effort and commitment by reference to some obsessional pathology that, because it underlies the labor, impugns, or at least limits the significance of, the product.

But this and similar interpretations overlook (as the lords did) that, for Burke, these efforts were nothing less than an attempt to "save the nation" and to make possible a redemption of European civilization despite its inhumanity toward whole tribes and other nations. They involved the "Shame and Guilt" of Great Britain. But whatever the reasons, the most substantial portion of Burke's political writings focused on the single issue that he hoped would be his only "monument," the defeat of the enemy he believed was far more dangerous than Jacobinism, the matter on which he "knew" what he was doing and insisted irrespective of whether his peers and compatriots liked it or not, the effort for which with forlorn emphasis he pleaded to be remembered— with regard to that concern, contemporary political theorists and interpreters have been all but completely silent. With the important and recent exception of Conor Cruise O'Brien's *The Great Melody*, there are to my knowledge not a single book and no more than a handful of articles published in the West during the last sixty years that give substantial attention to the political significance of Burke's writings on India.[29] The strategy of exonerating this indifference by reference to an

28. Burke, *Correspondence*, 9:62–63. This letter is representative of Burke's intensified preoccupation with Indian matters in his last years. For excerpts from some of his correspondence, see O'Brien, *The Great Melody*, 461–593.

29. Another recent book that has two nuanced chapters on Burke's Indian writings is Sara Suleri, *The Rhetoric of English India* (Chicago: University of Chicago Press, 1992). Suleri's reading belongs to a distinguished tradition that has interpreted Burke primarily through literary concepts. For reasons that have to do with the force of

alleged obsessional pathology simply abuses the facts. Burke was too self-conscious a writer and a thinker for such explanations to be at all credible. In any case, the concern with India spans his entire career and is intertwined and conceptually consistent with most of his other works.

What this indifference to Burke's Indian writings vitiates is a fuller understanding in the broadest sense of Burke the political thinker and more specifically as a thinker who offers us a rich and complex political and psychological interpretation of culture and social order. Perhaps most importantly, his writings on India are the most sophisticated and moving elaboration on the idea of sympathy—the means through which one develops in oneself a feeling for another person or collectivity of persons. In this final regard, Burke was no doubt following the lead and insights of his contemporary David Hume. Burke's writings on India are, in fact, a poignant example of an analysis that deploys what Hume distinguishes as the "understanding" in its function as perceiving the relations between things, and "moral sentiments" as the register of the feelings associated with the perception of such relations.[30] Burke's efforts in his writings and speeches on India can be seen as an extended tutorial to his compatriots to help them perceive certain relations both between things within India and between things in India and Britain so that the moral sentiments appropriate to such relations would be awakened in them.

BRAIDED CONCERNS: BRITAIN AND INDIA

Burke's writings on India are marked by a constant duality of purpose: a concern on the one hand for the effects that imperial practices will have on Britain and, on the other, for the effects they will have on India. The two concerns are tightly intertwined. The oppression of India re-

---

Burke's writing, the most interesting work on Burke has often come from literary theorists. In recent times, the exponents of this style would include Raymond Williams, *Culture and Society: 1780–1950* (New York: Columbia University Press, 1983), 3–20; David Bromwich, *A Choice of Inheritance*, 43–79, and *Politics by Other Means* (New Haven: Yale University Press, 1992), 133–64; A. C. Goodson, "Burke's Orphics and Coleridge's Contrary Understanding," *The Wordsworth Circle*, summer 1991, 29–41. Suleri's book, the only one of this group that deals in a focused way on Burke's Indian writings, offers an interpretation that links his concept of the sublime from his *A Philosophical Inquiry into the Origins of Our Ideas of the Sublime and Beautiful* to his characterization of India as resisting representation "in the English language." Suleri, *Rhetoric*, 26.

30. David Hume, *A Treatise of Human Nature*, ed. L. A. Selby-Bigge (Oxford: Clarendon Press, 1978), bk. 3, secs. 1–2, pp. 455–80. See also Sheldon Wolin, "Hume and Conservatism," *American Political Science Review* 48 (1954): 999–1016.

bounds with similar effects on Britain; the British delinquents of India will become the commons of Great Britain. In terms that resonate with the utterances of later nationalists, Burke constantly drives home the point that the empire is doubly implicating. At the beginning of his speech urging his fellow parliamentarians to pass the Fox India Bill, he says, "I am certain that every means, effectual to preserve India from oppression, is a guard to preserve the British constitution from its worst corruption."[31] At the end of the speech, he reiterates the coupled nature of his concern: "I am happy to have lived to see this day; I feel myself overpaid for the labors of eighteen years, when, at this period, I am able to take my share, by one humble vote, in destroying a tyranny that exists to the disgrace of *this nation*, and the destruction of so large a part of the human species."[32] Elsewhere, he speaks of the dereliction of power exercised over Indians as leading to the "annihilation" of British liberties.[33]

Burke's reasons for believing in this mutuality of imperial consequences are more specific than a generalized view, such as that oppression does not pay or that the weak have weapons that the strong would do well to acknowledge in the exercise of their strength. No doubt Burke held such views, especially in a form that suggested some Christian notion of justice. Burke's more precise and urgent reasons for being worried about this mutuality—and this is the heart of the matter—is that the conditions that secure British liberties are threatened by the extension of British power in India. Similarly, the exercise of that power undermines the conditions that are requisite for the expression of Indian liberties. The various specific objections to British behavior in India that Burke details—the peculation of company officials, the political greed involved in making allies and enemies among Indian princes for the purpose of extending British dominion, the cavalier instrumentality that underlies respecting or overriding local traditions, and similar attitudes toward the hierarchies of the Indian social structure—all provoke the same general concern. They are instances in which the secure and stable conditions that undergird the liberties of two societies are threatened.

This braided concern is vividly portrayed in the collective biography that Burke sketches of British functionaries in India, and the trajectory of their effects on British and Indian society. They are, we are told,

---

31. Burke, "Fox's India Bill Speech," 5:385.
32. Ibid., 451, emphasis added.
33. Burke, "Speech on Amas Ali Khan," in *Writings and Speeches* (Oxford), 5:468.

"young men (almost boys)" who govern "without society, and without sympathy with the natives." But what for Burke is more telling: "they have no more social habits with the people than if they resided in England."[34] They are, in a sense, commercial mercenaries, unmarked by the burdens and privileges of any society, but nevertheless called upon to exercise political power over the natives. In a brilliant and horrifying image, Burke describes them as "birds of prey" that swoop down, "wave after wave . . . [with] nothing before the eyes of the natives but an endless, hopeless prospect of new flights . . . with appetites continually renewing for a food that is continually wasting."[35] They make their fortunes long before either "nature or reason have any opportunity to exert themselves for remedy of the excesses of their premature power."[36] Having preyed on India, they return to England for another feeding frenzy:

> Their prey is lodged in England; and the cries of India are given to sea and winds. . . . In India, all the vices operate by which sudden fortune is acquired; in England are often displayed, by the same persons, the virtues which dispense hereditary wealth. Arrived in England, the destroyers of the nobility and gentry of a whole kingdom will find the best company in this nation, at a board of elegance and hospitality. Here the manufacturer and the husbandman will bless the just and punctual hand, that in India has torn the cloth from the loom, or wrested the scanty portion of rice and salt from the peasants of Bengal. . . . They marry into your families; they enter into your senate; they ease your estates by loans; they raise their value by demand; they cherish and protect your relations which lie heavy on your patronage; and there is scarcely a house in the kingdom that does not feel some concern and interest that makes all your reform of our Eastern government appear officious and disgusting; and, on the whole, a most discouraging attempt. . . . Our Indian government is in its best state a grievance.[37]

The empire effects its power through the creation of a class of individuals who are rootless and who afflict the societies they touch with a similar contagion. Lacking society themselves, they unsettle the norms of both British and Indian society. Burke may have been thinking in terms

34. Burke, "Fox's India Bill Speech," 5:402.
35. Ibid.
36. Ibid.
37. Ibid., 403.

of rather concrete historical facts. As evinced by the life and career of Robert Clive, who is commonly thought of as the founder of the company's dominion in India, the colonies, and especially India, had become a place where men and boys of humble and dislocated roots went not just to make a fortune but also to "acquire British society." Having destroyed the nobility and gentry in India, plucked the rice and salt from the Bengali peasant, they return to England with the monetary and social profits of that endeavor and insinuate their mercenary logic into the historically sanctioned estates that anchor British society. They make money the medium of social and political circulation and order; they buy power and social standing, and in doing so subvert what for Burke are the traditional and historically appropriate foundations of each. They are, in this sense, like the Jacobins. Unlike the latter's explicit commitment to start anew, the British functionaries in India insidiously, and hence more dangerously, uproot and level out the conditions that make Britain whole.[38] Burke is always attentive to a social dynamic internal to the company that has far-reaching domestic implications in Britain:

> Another circumstance which distinguishes the East India Company is the youth of the persons who are employed in the system of that service. The servants have almost universally been sent out to begin their career in active occupation and in the exercise of high authority, at that period of life which, in all other places, has been employed in the course of rigid education. To put the matter in a few words,—they are transformed from slippery youth to perilous independence, from perilous independence to inordinate expectations, from inordinate

38. Speaking of the French revolutionaries, Burke constantly identifies them as "totally abolishing hereditary name and office [and] levelling all conditions of men (except where money *must* make a difference)." Burke, "Thoughts on French Affairs," in *Further Reflections*, 211. The image of the British as birds of prey is precisely the one that Burke uses to portray the French revolutionaries:

> The Revolution harpies of France, sprung from Night and Hell, or from the chaotic Anarchy which generates equivocally 'all monstrous, all prodigious things,' cuckoo-like, adulterously lay their eggs, and brood over, and hatch them in the nest of every neighbouring state. These obscene harpies, who deck themselves in I know not what divine attributes, but who in reality are foul and ravenous *birds of prey*, (both mothers and daughters) flutter over our heads and souse down upon our tables, and leave nothing unrent, unrifled, unravaged, or unpolluted with the slime of their filthy offal. (Burke, "Letter to a Noble Lord," 5:187)

expectations to boundless power. Schoolboys without tutors, minors without guardians, the world is let loose upon them, with all its temptations, and they are let loose upon the world with all the power that despotism involves.[39]

The theme of the youth of company officials is significant even beyond the specific points Burke makes in regard to it. It offers a vivid contrast to the familiar characterization of liberal theorists who spoke of the childlike nature of Indians. J. S. Mill's image of Indians as still in need of "leading strings"[40]—the strings used to help children to learn to walk—is a thematic that Macaulay and others lifted and amplified as a general warrant for the necessity and justification of the empire. The theme also recapitulates a terror that Locke in *The Thoughts Concerning Education* spoke of in regard to children who did not obey and who had an overdeveloped sense of their own difference and whose will had therefore to be bent by force. For Burke, in contrast, the terror associated with youth is the abuse of power that can easily become despotic because it has not been chastened by an understanding of the needs of society.

Burke's examples may appear to exhaust the point he is making. His allegiance to the British nobility, to the hereditary claims of power and wealth extending to the inappropriateness of matrimonial links between the daughters of this group and the affluent social outcasts returning from India, may all simply confirm his well-known deference to the aristocracy and his disparagement of mercantile wealth and the property-less.[41] These narrow and specific commitments cannot be denied. But they also point to a more general claim (more general than his commitment to a particular social order) that involves the centrality that Burke places on social order as being a requisite for individual liberty. It is this idea that unifies and gives coherence to the wide range of disparate and often apparently contradictory positions that he defends. It is the well-ordered realities in the American colonies, the sobriety that limits their

39. Burke, "Impeachment of Warren Hastings," 9:357.
40. J. S. Mill, *Considerations on Representative Government*, chap. 2, p. 175.
41. A familiar theme among those concerned with the relationship between Burke's own background and his ideas is to note the awkwardness of that fit. Jeremy Waldron writes: "Edmund Burke embodied a category of person he himself regarded as most threatening to the established social order—the category of those who had ability but no property." Introduction to *Nonsense Upon Stilts*, ed. Jeremy Waldron (London: Methuen, 1987), 77. The most sophisticated and compelling discussion of this link is Isaac Kramnick, *The Rage of Edmund Burke: Portrait of an Ambivalent Conservative*. Also see Conor Cruise O'Brien's introduction to Burke's *Reflections on the French Revolution* (London: Penguin, 1968).

liberal Enlightenment, the "spirit of religion" that confines the "spirit of freedom," that leads Burke to support the colonists in their "revolutionary" desire for independence. This same idea, this time combined with the absence of those well-ordered realities, motivates his refusal to countenance the revolutionary schemes in France. It is also what leads him to describe the landed nobility and "grand families" of Britain as the "great oaks" of society and also underlies his proud condescension toward the duke of Bedford when the latter, with inflamed enthusiasm for the French revolutionaries, overlooked the service of men like Burke for the legitimate exercise of his power. Burke's conception of social order is difficult to elaborate because it is the point at which a myriad of effects converge to create that elusive and yet very tangible sense of individual and collective wholeness. A people's beliefs, which themselves are related to circumstances, the institutions that have molded their habits and expectations, the spaces both physical and social that have channeled their attachments, the obligations and responsibilities that have defined their sense of choices, the prejudices that give coherence to their experiences and anticipations: for Burke these are the felt constituents of social order.

There are two clear senses in which this conception, however imprecise its boundaries may appear, challenges (in a sense by extending) the familiar Lockean sense of social order. First, at both an individual and a collective level, Burke's conception features an experience and a corresponding identity that are profoundly and thoroughly in the middle of things. Their significance is defined by the texture of inescapable constraints, circumstances, and relations. Strip society and individuals of these, and for Burke there is an emptiness that can generate the revolutionary hubris of a wholesale transformation of society. It is the mosaic of circumstances and the prejudices that cling to them that give situations their distinctive hue. As Burke puts it in *Reflections*:

> I cannot stand forward, and give praise or blame to anything which relates to human actions, and human concerns, on a simple view of the object, as it stands stripped of every relation, in all the nakedness and solitude of metaphysical abstraction. Circumstances (which with some gentlemen pass for nothing) give in reality to every political principle its distinguishing colors and discriminating effect. The circumstances are what render every civil and political scheme beneficial or noxious to mankind.[42]

42. Burke, *Reflections*, 6.

There is nothing in Burke's view that corresponds to the giddy exhilaration of Lockean individuals being there at the beginning, covenanting to form "a people" and "a Commonwealth." There are no abstract principles and natural human interests that carry over from the state of nature and prescribe individual obligations, institutions, and norms of justice in political society. For Burke, like his contemporary Hume, obligations and the norms of justice spring from the local and the conventional. But this departure from Locke is so only because it makes explicit what is in fact implicit in Locke. Locke's rational individuals, acting in conformity with the laws of nature, in fact deploy a reason that is saturated with the content of conventional hierarchies and expectations. What Burke makes explicit and raises to the level of prudential political credo, Locke tucks into the pedagogy to which a child must submit before being acknowledged as reasonable.[43]

Second, Burke's conception of social order is deeply psychological. The force of this point is easily shadowed by a term such as *traditionalist* that is often used to characterize the historical emphasis of his thought. The term *traditionalist* misses what for Burke is of decisive importance in traditions, namely that they constitute preconceived channels in which human actions are at home, even when those actions are directed toward changing the contours of those channels. When people act in ways that presume to deny their own reliance on such channels, or when they encourage the wholesale dismantling of those channels, they risk their own survival or, at a minimum, they risk becoming what David Bromwich calls "monstrous."[44] They distort the dimensions of social and individual equipoise. The naturalist perspective that sees human beings as satisfying desires all too easily overlooks the extent to which some of those desires are refracted borrowings—refracted, that is, through a constellation of familial and social dispositions. Even when those dispositions stem from errors, or what the Enlightenment called prejudice, they structure our needs and hence the requirements of our health. In a letter written in 1789, Burke tells his correspondent:

43. For a reading of Locke that emphasizes the significance of conventions through a detailed focus on the content of education, see my *Anxiety of Freedom*, esp. chaps. 3–4. See also Anne Stoler's insightful article, "Sexual Affronts and Racial Identities and the Cultural Politics of Exclusion in Southeast Asia," *Comparative Studies in Society and History* 34, no. 3 (July 1992): 514–51.

44. Bromwich, *A Choice of Inheritance*, 48. In emphasizing the psychological component of Burke's thought, I am indebted to Bromwich's broad-ranging and wonderfully subtle work. Alfred Cobban, in his classic *Edmund Burke and the Revolt against the Eighteenth Century* (London: George Allen & Unwin, 1929), points to a similar reading, as does Harold Laski in *Political Thought in England from Locke to Bentham*.

You have theories enough concerning the rights of men; it may not be amiss to add a small degree of attention to their nature and disposition. *It is with man in the concrete; it is with common human life, and human actions,* you are to be concerned. . . . Never wholly separate in your mind the merits of any political question from the men who are concerned in it.[45]

The counterpoising of theories concerning the rights of men with Burke's alternative focus on human beings in the concrete underscores the significance he attaches to specific and jagged dispositions—dispositions that are lost in the abstractions that concern themselves only with the rights of men. It is also for this reason that Burke's work is replete with attention to human feelings, habits, sensibilities, and prejudices. It is because of this attention that Burke, who in one sense is an outstanding critic of Rousseau, in another sense illuminates an essential preoccupation of Rousseau's social thought.[46]

The psychological component in Burke's notion of social order is really continuous with the historical emphasis. Precisely because we are always in the middle of things, we have a reliance on what precedes us, both chronologically and spatially. No doubt, as the Enlightenment insisted, history is the record of our prejudices. But, and this is a distinctly Burkean contribution to the Enlightenment, these prejudices also give us a sense of continuity, and hence a sense of ourselves. They protect us from constantly having to question our practices and protect us in those instances where practices are by will, necessity, or accident transformed.[47] All of this is true even when the prejudices and the practices have been impugned. Finally, it is the psychological disposition of his thinking that underlies his violently antirevolutionary impulse and his gradualist preference. The process of adaptation is always gradual.

45. Burke, "Letter to Charles-Jean-François Depont," in *Further Reflections,* 13, emphasis added. Later in the same letter he says:

There is by the essential fundamental constitution of things, a radical infirmity in all human contrivance; and the weakness is often attached to the very perfection of our political mechanism, that some defect in it— something that stops short of its principles, something that controls, that mitigates, that moderates it—becomes a necessary corrective to the evils that the theoretic perfection would produce. (p. 15)

46. Burke's most extensive remarks on Rousseau are in "A Letter to a Member of the National Assembly," in *Further Reflections.* For some interesting remarks on the relationship between Rousseau and Burke, see Harold Laski, *Studies in Law and Politics* (New York: Greenwood Press, 1968), 13–47.

47. Bromwich, *A Choice of Inheritance,* 43–91. See also Louis Hartz, *The Necessity of Choice* (New Brunswick, N.J.: Transaction Publishers, 1990), 89–99.

Even when circumstances change, as he acknowledges they always do, individuals and institutions for Burke retain traces of an investment in the past. And only gradual change can accommodate the needs and instincts that correspond to those traces. Burke summarizes this dialectic of history and the psychological reliance it generates:

> History consists, for the greater part, of the miseries brought upon the world by pride, ambition, avarice, revenge, lust, sedition, hypocrisy, ungoverned zeal, and all the train of disorderly appetites which shake the public with the same. . . . These vices are the *causes* of those storms. Religion, morals, laws, prerogatives, privileges, liberties, rights of men, are the *pretexts*. The pretexts are always found in some specious appearance of a real good. You would not secure men from tyranny and sedition by rooting out of the mind the principles to which these fraudulent pretexts apply? If you did, you would root out everything that is valuable in the human breast.[48]

Burke justifies a reliance on history while pointing to the dark record of history. The causes of miseries are constituents of our nature, and for that reason they cannot be selectively erased through the redemptive pretexts of laws, religion, or rights. Only history—and by that Burke clearly means social order in an extensive form—can ameliorate and guide the effects of our passions. The role of the reformer is constantly to decipher and guide the social conditions through which these passions can be contained and expressed.

This line of thinking invites an obvious objection that is leveled at many thinkers who appear to magnify the role of history and in the process become apologists for it. Stated simply, the objection is that a reliance on history or a view of the normative force of history gives us no critical leverage from which to adjudicate between historically possible alternatives, and therefore approaches the existing social arrangements with a presumption of their legitimacy. At an extreme, it justifies everything that is settled and concrete, and in doing so denies the very reasons for which we might appeal to a thinker's counsel. Burke does not engage or anticipate this line of objection, but clearly for him all social arrangements draw on features of the past. But they do not, for that reason, necessarily result in orderly arrangements that secure the psychological health of individuals and the comity of society. Nothing in Burke's conception of history denies the possibility of our individu-

48. Burke, *Reflections*, 137–38.

ally and collectively misinterpreting or incorrectly deciphering the range of stable alternatives. We always retain that possibility; indeed, there are events such as those in France and India where the vast mass of a people are set on establishing the detrimental effects of that possibility. The Jacobins in France overlook the entrenchment of the past when they abolish property and expand the franchise. For Burke, the Terror is the price that was paid for that oversight. Similarly, the company officials, in exercising political power in India, overlook the historical limitations and obligations that have been attached to that power. The massive infusion of money for buying parliamentary seats is the price that the British pay for that oversight.[49]

The link between history or society and the passions also informs Burke's view of freedom, in which he once again brings to the fore something that is deep and fundamental in Locke by challenging a familiar surface characterization of Locke.[50] Like Locke, for Burke the desire for liberty, as he calls it, is a constituent of our nature. But for Burke, this desire is itself an inheritance. It is not, as Locke so often has been interpreted to mean, a given datum of our biological status. Of course, with Locke, too, the exercise of this freedom turns on the capacity for reason, which itself is related to our ability to understand the limits that natural law puts on our freedom. Burke accepts all of this but gives it a distinct meaning. The reason that undergirds Locke's conception of freedom is for Burke thoroughly social, including the social understood as something ineradicably historical. As he puts it:

> I certainly think that all men who desire [liberty], deserve it. It is not the reward of our merit, or the acquisition of our industry. It is our inheritance. It is the birthright of our species. We cannot forfeit our right to it, but by what forfeits our title to the privileges of our kind. I mean the abuse, or oblivion, of our rational faculties and a ferocious indocility which makes us prompt to wrong and violence, destroys our social nature, and transforms us into something little better than the description of wild beasts. To men so degraded, a state of strong constraint

---

49. Of course, situations of terror and disorder in time become the basis of new orders that are not characterized by either terror or disorder. "Every past revolutionary situation," as Louis Hartz says, "gives to subsequent periods certain ideal principles which, if they are to be stabilized, must be bureaucratized and emasculated of their revolutionary meaning. A revolution, if successful, must eliminate from its ideals that quality that inspired the original upheaval." Hartz, *The Necessity of Choice*, 189. See also Hartz, *The Founding of New Societies*, esp. 20–44.

50. Burke always claimed to be a "follower of Locke."

is a sort of necessary substitute for freedom; since, bad as it is, it may deliver them in some measure from the worst of all slavery—that is, the despotism of their own blind and brutal passions.[51]

Every idea in this passage is vintage Locke. The emphasis on the link between freedom and reason, the negative association between freedom and the despotism of uncontrolled passions, and even the link between freedom and moderation (in contrast to "ferocious indocility")—all of these are borrowings from Locke. And yet Burke's meaning is substantially different. Where Burke speaks of inheritance and birthright, he should be understood as implicitly, though emphatically, privileging them over human nature.[52] Both inheritance and birthright carry with them important historical and social attachments. It is not simply our birth as a biological event; our birthright is the middle term linking the past and the future. It is something that can be lost, destroyed, or even stolen, as in the biblical story of Jacob and Esau. Freedom inheres in us because our birth links us to the conditions that make it possible. Domestic choices, economic opportunities, communal experiences, and political responsibilities—these and other existing constraints and possibilities are what constitute the conditions for freedom. Burke elaborates his meaning to his French correspondent: "It is not solitary, unconnected, individual, selfish liberty, as if every man was to regulate the whole of his conduct by his will. The liberty I mean is *social* liberty . . . This kind of liberty is, indeed, but another name for justice; ascertained by wise laws and secured by well-constructed institutions."[53]

Burke is quite specific about the conditions requisite for freedom.

51. Burke, "Letter to Depont," in *Further Reflections*, 7.
52. See Sheldon Wolin, "Contract and Birthright," *Political Theory* 14, no. 2 (May 1986): 179–195.
53. Burke, "Letter to Depont," 7–8. This is clearly also Burke's interpretation of British history. He says

> From the Magna Charta to the Declaration of Right, it has been the uniform policy of our constitution to claim and assert our liberties as an *entailed inheritance* derived to us from our forefathers, and to be transmitted to our posterity; as an estate especially belonging to the people of this kingdom, without any reference whatever to any other more general or prior right. By this means our constitution preserves a unity in so great a diversity of its parts. We have an inheritable crown; an inheritable peerage; and a House of Commons and a people inheriting privileges, franchises, and liberties, from a long line of ancestors. (Burke, *Reflections*, 31)

At least in the societies that he considers in detail (Britain, France, America, Ireland, and India), these conditions always include a hierarchy of social classes, with corresponding titles and norms of courtesy. His views on history make it easy to see why he believed in natural aristocracies that had a prescriptive claim on political authority. But focusing on the hierarchy of classes leads us to miss Burke's more general underlying thought. The sources of our attachments, including the attachments we have to the obligations we feel, are local. For Burke hierarchy is an implied feature of that recognition: "We begin our public affections in our families. No cold relation is a zealous citizen. We pass on to our neighborhoods, and our habitual provincial connections . . . so many little images of the great country in which the heart found something which it could fill."[54] Burke always views the leveling out of these distinctions with the greatest suspicion—such "experiments" invariably provoke the thought that they are motivated by an easy instrumentality that the concrete situation cannot sustain and that they will ultimately exact a heavy toll.[55] Indeed, more often than not Burke uses the term "Jacobinism" (and the term "Indianism") to designate an ideology and a set of practices that are reckless in their disregard for the extant order of the communities in which they operate. They function in the manner of money, one of whose disturbing effects Burke suggests stems from the ease and uniformity with which it "circulates."[56]

54. Burke, *Reflections*, 167.
55. Burke wrote:

I can never be convinced, that the scheme of placing the highest powers of the state in churchwardens and constables, and other such officers, guided by the prudence of litigious attornies . . . and set in action by shameless women of the lowest condition, by keepers of hotels, taverns, and brothels, by pert apprentices, by clerks, shop-boys, hair-dressers, fidlers, and dancers on the stage . . . can never be put into any shape that must not be both disgraceful and destructive. (Burke, "Letter to a Member of the National Assembly," in *Further Reflections*, 30)

He makes the same point with less objectionable language and details in *Reflections:*

After I had read over the list of the persons and descriptions selected into the *Tiers Etat*, nothing which they afterward did could appear astonishing. Among them, indeed I saw some of known rank; some of shining talents; but of any practical experience in the state, not one man was to be found. The best were only men of theory. (Burke, *Reflections*, 38)

56. Burke, "Thoughts on French Affairs," 213. Bromwich rightly suggests that by the 1790s, for Burke the terms *money, speculation, philosophy*, and *atheism* are "rough

Two facets of social order are especially important to Burke, both because of the extent and manner in which they contribute to the social order and, by implication, because of the role they play in securing the conditions of freedom. Moreover both, I want to suggest, are critical to understanding Burke's sympathy and apprehensions regarding the effect of British colonial practices on India and on Britain. And finally, both underscore the sense in which Burke anticipates and gives credence to at least some familiar features of modern nationalist ideology and practice. Of course in his prescience regarding aspects of the nation and nationalism, Burke is largely unacknowledged by nationalists and by contemporary theorists of the nation.[57] The first facet of social order is place, which I have considered in the preceding chapter, and the second, history. Because place and history are aspects through which the continuity of the past, the present, and the future are experienced, they are vested for Burke with a special moral gravity. In his view, both relate to the conditions that are requisite for the psychological and moral integrity of individuals and communities. People have psychological reliance on the places to which they belong and the positions they occupy in a social system. But these reliances can be overlooked both by a failure of reflection (which for Burke is something wholly distinct from speculation) on the conditions that sustain us and by an overinvestment in expedited and convulsive change. The consequences of such failure are, according to Burke, invariably dire and extreme. We risk dispossessing ourselves, as in the case of the duke of Bedford, and we risk dispossessing entire communities, as in France, India, and Britain: "when the subject of our demolition and construction is not breaking timber but sentient human beings, by the sudden alteration of whose state, conditions, and habits, multitudes may be rendered miserable."[58]

This psychological account, which stems from the Burkean insistence on acknowledging our being in the middle of things, implies a posture not only toward place but also toward history. To have a sense

---

synonyms." See Bromwich, "The Context of Burke's *Reflections*," *Social Research* 58, no. 2 (1991): 331. I think Burke would have added the terms *East India Company* and *empire* to this list.

57. No doubt the reasons for this indifference are complicated. But they must include the fact that with few exceptions modern nationalism has been spurred by revolutionary ideologies and has resulted in revolutionary, or at least hugely convulsive, practices. In whatever ways Burke understood and celebrated the attachments and forms of community that subsequent nationalists have tried to secure, he would have hardly countenanced the means and the actions that have typically followed from their aspirations.

58. Burke, *Reflections*, 144.

of ourselves on this account requires being self-conscious of our status as inheritors and as transmitters of an inheritance. At a social level, it involves imbuing institutions with a status appropriate to something that has, at least in part, made us who we are and on which we have a collective reliance:

> One of the first and most leading principles on which the commonwealth and the laws are consecrated, is lest the temporary possessors and life-renters in it, unmindful of what they have received from their ancestors or of what is due to their posterity, should act as if they were the entire masters; that they should not think it amongst their rights to cut off the entail or commit waste on the inheritance, by destroying at their pleasure the whole original fabric of their society; hazarding to leave to those who come after them a ruin instead of an habitation—and teaching these successors as little to respect their contrivances, as they had themselves respected the institutions of their forefathers. By this unprincipled facility of changing the state as often, and as much, and in as many ways as there are floating fancies or fashions, the whole chain and continuity of the commonwealth would be broken. No one generation could link with the other. Men would become little better than the flies of a summer.[59]

To act as though we were the "entire masters" of the institutions that circumscribe our existence is to act doubly against our nature. It is to deny that our institutions are an inheritance and to sever the transmission of an inheritance to future generations. That would amount to giving life a seasonal duration. It is what Burke associates with every kind of absolutism. If Burke in this passage sounds paternalistic, he means to endorse an attitude that is at least parental. The unprincipled facility of changing states has its analogue in parents who do not support their progeny.[60] Both break the chain of continuity that secures healthy human existence. In this, Burke's defense of history is meant as a defense of the conditions that make life whole. The recognition of our temporality is what facilitates respecting the institutions of our forebears and a concomitant concern for future generations.

Burke seems to be suggesting that only through the acceptance of

59. Ibid., 91–92.
60. "Parents, in the order of Providence, are made for their children, and not their children for them." Quoted in Sir Philip Magnus, *Edmund Burke* (London: J. Murray, 1939), 268.

society as an ongoing, and hence historical, partnership can basic human sentiments—such as those that parents naturally feel toward their children—be secure. The same instinct that stops us from consuming at the expense of our children must give us pause in totally transforming the extant order of society. Nothing Burke says here or elsewhere is an indictment against any and every kind of change. It is a plea against only that species of change that has uprooting as its initial motive. For Burke, the impulse to start all over again, or to construct new foundations, is much the same as the attitude that assumes that no one will follow after me. The British may have believed in the illusion of their permanence in India.[61] At any rate, they were insistent on denying the fact that India had a history of its own. They were especially insistent on denying that India's past included the integuments of society and social order. What India had was a long record of despotism with no society to limit or support it. As Bryan Turner has suggested, the overwhelming thrust of Orientalist writings was to suggest that the Orient was "all state and no society."[62] This was a view of India with which Burke was intimately familiar. The core of Hastings's defense was a variant on it. In assuming despotic authority, Hastings claimed he was merely conforming to local customs and expectations. His use of power had not been inappropriate because it followed a norm of arbitrary power.[63] Burke's is a frontal challenge to Hastings's reading of India:

> I must do justice to the East. I assert that their morality is equal to ours, in whatever regards the duties of governors, fathers, and superiors; and I challenge the world to show in any modern European book more true morality and wisdom than is to be found in the writings of Asiatic men in high trust, and who have been counsellors to princes. If this be the true morality of Asia, as I affirm and can prove that it is, the pleas founded on Mr. Hastings's geographical morality is annihilated.[64]

61. This is a claim Francis Hutchins defends in his book, *The Illusion of Permanence: British Imperialism in India.*

62. Bryan Turner, "Orientalism and the Problem of Civil Society in Islam," in *Orientalism, Islam, and Islamists,* ed. Asaf Hussain et al. (Brattleboro, Vt.: Amana Books, 1984), 39.

63. "I had an arbitrary power to exercise: I exercise it. Slaves I found the people: slaves they are,—they are so by their constitution"; "The whole history of Asia is nothing more than precedents to prove the invariable exercise of arbitrary power." Warren Hastings, quoted in Burke, "Impeachment of Warren Hastings," 9:448, 451.

64. Ibid., 476.

Hastings's plea is interrogated in the twelve hundred–odd pages of text that constitute Burke's response. In rhetorically moving prose and with endless details, the House of Commons, and later the House of Lords, are told of Hindu and Muslim public and private law, religion, social structure, commercial practices, of caste mobility and professional change, of the basis of political power and the limits placed on it, of social groups, the patriotism of men, the chivalry of warriors, the virtue of women and the other empires that, unlike the British, settled and mixed their blood and inheritance with that of the natives.[65] Burke is dismissive of Hastings's "geographical morality."[66] Hastings is a British governor-general, exercising the authority granted to him by the company and indirectly by the king. He is bound by those norms, and by the constraints that are attached to those norms.[67] The relativism Hastings invokes in his defense is only a "screen" through which he betrays his own history and that of the Indians by refusing to acknowledge that one is his and the other not. It is this sort of self-betrayal, in which Hastings transposes the substance of his historical inheritance with its form, that compounds Burke's worry when he imagines the delinquents of India becoming the Commons of Great Britain. The prospect of an ancient commonwealth set on committing waste on its inheritance must have filled Burke with horror. For Hastings, geography is merely one of many instrumental ruses and not what, in Burke's view, it was for the rajah of Tanjore and the people of the Carnatic—a weighty index of who they were, a dwelling cemented by the changing though never wholly voluntary alloy of history and sentiments.

The defense of India as having a history, a history with society, with laws, and with classes, is one of the most common postures that Burke assumes. Toward the end of the trial, Burke reiterates this defense:

> On one side, your Lordships have the prisoner declaring that
> the people have no laws, no rights, no usage, no distinctions of

65. See Burke, *Works*, vols. 8–12 passim.

66. "Let your Lordships know that these gentlemen have formed a plan of *geographical morality*, by which the duties of men, in public and in private situations, are not to be governed by their relation to the great Governor of the Universe, or by their relation to mankind, but by climates, degrees of longitude, parallel, not of life, but of latitudes: as if when you crossed the equinocial, all the virtues die, as they say some insects die when they cross the line." Burke, "Impeachment of Warren Hastings," 9:447–48.

67. "My Lords, we contend that Mr. Hastings, as a British governor, ought to govern on British principles, not by British forms,—God forbid!—for if ever there was a case in which the letter kills and the spirit gives life, it would be an attempt to

rank, no sense of honour, no property—in short, they are nothing but a herd of slaves, to be governed by the arbitrary will of
a master. On the other side, we assert, that the direct contrary
of this is true. And to prove our assertion . . . we have referred
you to the Mahometan law, which is binding upon all, from the
crowned head to the meanest subject—a law interwoven with
the wisest, the most learned, and most enlightened jurispru-
dence that perhaps ever existed in the world.[68]

This is Burke's summary statement on behalf of a history that has been
experienced by Indians. Yet the statement is oddly reminiscent of numerous passages from *Reflections* and his other writings on the French
Revolution. The categories that are significant are all the same—laws,
rights, usage, distinctions of rank, honor, and property. There is no contradiction here. The categories Burke points to are the categories that
are relevant to the claim he is making here and in the French context. It
is the historical evidence for these categories, and not any and every
history, that validates the point he is making in both these contexts. Society and social order are not identical with history, even though they
do require having a history. Correspondingly, the sympathy that Burke
feels for India is not merely a sympathy for an oppressed people; it is
instead, as I have mentioned, a sympathy for a people who constitute a
threatened community, and one that he also believed was oppressed. He
makes this clear in his speech on the Fox India Bill, when he says,
"[T]his multitude of men [Indians] does not consist of an abject and
barbarous populace; much less of gangs of savages like the Guaranies
and the Chiquitos, who wander on the waste borders of the Amazons,
or the Plate."[69] Burke's defense of Indian history vindicates a social order
in which freedom would not be "solitary, unconnected, individual,
selfish liberty, as if every man was to regulate the whole of his conduct
by his own will." It vindicates what subsequent nationalists might have
called the conditions appropriate for the right of self-determination.

---

introduce British forms and the substance of despotic principles together into any
country." Ibid., 447.
    68. Ibid., 11:219.
    69. Burke, "Fox's India Bill Speech," 5:389. Also note the following: "In a state
of *rude* nature there is no such thing as a people. A number of men in themselves
have no collective capacity. The idea of a people is the idea of a corporation. It is
wholly artificial; and made, like all other legal fictions, by common agreement. What
the particular nature of that agreement was, is collected from the form into which the
particular society has been cast." Burke, "Appeal from the New to the Old Whigs," in
Writings and Speeches (Taylor), 4:169–70.

Conclusion

In his famous essay "What Is a Nation?" Ernest Renan disqualified religion, language, race, material interests, military necessity, and even geography as appropriate answers to his question.[70] Instead, he argued, "a nation is a spiritual principle, the outcome of the profound complications of history." What Renan meant was itself complicated. But more than anything else, the spiritual principle involved a specific outlook toward a shared history. In the case of the French nation, it meant, among other things, that "every French citizen has to have forgotten the massacre of St. Bartholomew, or the massacres that took place in the Midi in the thirteenth century."[71] Here the sharing of a history took the specific form of sharing in a collective amnesia. Renan acknowledged that in other contexts the sense of a common history could have different expressions. It is not simply the fact of a shared history that Renan pointed to, but rather "an attitude," "a feeling," "a sentiment" that attended this history. The existence of a nation was contingent on this spiritual development.[72]

The argument I have been making in this chapter shows Burke to have anticipated much of what Renan said a century later. And yet the term *nation* and its cognates are scarce throughout this chapter. This is because it would be wrong to view Burke's thought as though it were concerned with theorizing the nation or understanding its underlying basis. Such a view would be wrong with respect to his motives and would, in all likelihood, misplace the emphases of his thought. This is not to say that the interpretation I have offered is without its own tilt. In trying to understand the basis of Burke's sympathy toward India and his reservations regarding the British in India, I have presented Burke as emphatically antiabsolutist and concerned with the conditions of social order, psychological integrity, and freedom. His references to a providential order, his known (even if concealed) Catholicism, and even his deep deference toward the nobility have all been either ignored or slighted in what I have said. And yet, I think, Burke's understanding of the basis of the nation should be mentioned, and in conclusion even featured.

70. Renan, "What Is a Nation?" trans. Martin Thom, in *Nation and Narration*, ed. Homi Bhabha (London: Routledge, 1990), 8–22.

71. Ibid., 11.

72. See Tzvetan Todorov, *On Human Diversity: Nationalism, Racism, and Exoticism in French Thought* (Cambridge: Harvard University Press, 1993), 219–63, for a learned and insightful discussion of Renan and other French theorists.

Alexander d'Entreves in his book *The Notion of the State*, makes the point that "ideas of nation and nationality are entirely absent from the definition of the state" in the writings of Machiavelli, Hobbes, and Bodin.[73] He could have added Locke to that list. The reason he offers for this omission is straightforward. All these theorists broadly start with individuals with defined needs and interests and ask, in light of these needs and interests and given some other constraints, what set of political arrangements would conduce to their survival and well-being. Given this line of inquiry, it is difficult to see where considerations of territoriality and history as bases of individual and group identity could be accommodated. Either they are altogether extraneous to the enterprise or—and with Locke at least this is more evident—they are being presupposed and are hence almost irrecoverably implicit. What follows from this is that considerations of individual identity that turn on the affections of territoriality and the processes of history are similarly displaced. In the conclusion, I will link the absence of considerations of territoriality, history, and the psychological implications that follow from them to the British liberal endorsement of the empire. In the present context, I want to state, in the form of a caption so as to indicate that it needs qualifications, that liberals have theorized the state while either ignoring or presuming on the coherence of the nation.

The contrast with Burke is obvious, and it is one of which he is aware. In his "Speech on the State of Representation of the Commons in Parliament," he states:

> Our Constitution is a prescriptive Constitution; it is a Constitution, whose sole authority is that it has existed time out of mind. . . . Prescription is the most solid of all titles, not only to property, but, which is to secure that property to Government. They harmonize with each other, and give mutual aid to one another. It is accompanied with another ground of authority in the constitution of the human mind, presumption. It is a presumption in favor of any settled scheme of government against any untried project, that a nation has long existed and flourished under it. It is a better presumption even of the *choice* of a nation, far better than any sudden or temporary arrangement by actual election. Because a nation is not an idea only of local extent, and individual momentary aggregation, but it is an idea of continuity, which extends in time as well as in numbers, and

73. Alexander d'Entreves, *The Notion of the State: An Introduction to Political Theory* (Oxford: Clarendon Press, 1967), 170.

in space. And this is a choice not of one day, or one set of people, not a tumultuary or giddy choice; it is a deliberate election of ages and of generations.[74]

A nation is more than the choice that people express in consenting to their government. It is more than the aggregate of individuals contracting to form a state. It does not make possible the giddy exhilaration that may accompany changing government. It is something that stands as a foundation to all of this, and it can serve as this foundation because it represents a continuity in time and in space of a certain social order that has a sanction in the human mind.

Despite the weighty ballast of the nation, Burke knew and understood that it was not assured a guarantee of permanence. Indeed, as is amply evident in the world today, nations that come to view themselves as empires are especially vulnerable to overlooking the conditions that secure not just their empires but their nationhood. Perhaps this oversight is most dangerous when the empires extend to include societies that have the ingredients of nationhood. The simple reason for Burke's sympathy for India and his deep worries regarding the British colonial extension in it was because he recognized in India the ingredients of nationhood and sensed in Britain a disregard for the conditions of its own nationhood.

74. Burke, "Speech on the State of Representation of Commons in Parliament," in *Writings and Speeches* (Taylor), 7:94–95.

———◄ C O N C L U S I O N ►———

Experience and Unfamiliarity

Men may be found of other mold than these,
Who are their own upholders, to themselves
Encouragement, and energy and will,
Expressing liveliest thoughts in lively words
As native passion dictates. Others, too,
These are among the walks of homely life
Still higher, men for contemplation framed,
Shy, and unpractis'd in the strife of phrase,
Meek men, whose very souls perhaps would sink
Beneath them, summon'd to such intercourse:
Theirs is the language of the heavens, the power,
The thought, the image, and the silent joy;
Words are but under-agents in their soul[.]
WILLIAM WORDSWORTH, *The Prelude*,
book 13 (1805 version), lines 261–73

Knowledge as perception, concept, comprehension, refers back to an act of grasping. The metaphor should be taken literally. . . . The immanence of the known to the act of knowing is already the embodiment of seizure.
EMMANUEL LEVINAS, *"Ethics as First Philosophy"*

How did thinkers who were committed to ideas of equality and liberty, and on occasion even fraternity, see in a plurality of extant life forms little more than an occasion to assert a rational paternalism to which their ideas had already committed them? To paraphrase the great romantic humanist of the late twentieth century, E. P. Thompson, how did ideas of equality, liberty, and fraternity lead to empire, liberticide, and fratricide?[1] Similarly how did a commitment to toleration lead to such patronizing and unsympathetic characterizations of the ways in which strangers lived their lives? Moreover, where did thinkers whose deepest convictions made them suspicious of the power of government acquire the confidence to sanction the most extravagant forms of gov-

---

1. E. P. Thompson, *The Romantics: England in a Revolutionary Age* (New York: New Press, 1997), 65.

190

ernment and public action? How did philosophers and historians like J. S. Mill and John Seeley, who were committed to the idea of national self-determination, see in an ancient civilization like India none of the integuments of a nation or of "a people"? These questions all bear importantly on the liberal conception of experience under conditions of unfamiliarity.

What was the response of liberal theorists as they cast their gaze on an unfamiliar world? In a word, it was to see those experiences, those life forms, as provisional. The empire as liberals conceived of it, and the terms in which they supported it, was premised on the idea—perhaps it is even correct to call it, as Conrad's Marlow does, the unselfish idea[2]— that in the face of this provisionality it was right, indeed even obligatory, to seek to complete that which was incomplete, static, backward, or otherwise regnant, and to guide it to a higher plateau of stability, freedom, and purposefulness—to hitch it to a more meaningful teleology. The principal means of doing so were political. It was, in part, from the perspective of a liberal political vision that the judgment of provisionality itself stemmed. That judgment of other peoples' experiences as provisional—and the interventions in their lives that it permits—is the conceptual and normative core of the liberal justification of the empire. Without such a prior judgment and the motivations that follow from it, one would have encountered notions such as the right of conquest or the immanence of external threat in the writings of liberals as they reflected on the empire. As it is, among nineteenth-century British liberals such arguments are almost entirely absent or, when invoked, are of secondary status. The will to power that liberals do express for the empire is always as a beneficent compensation for someone else's powerlessness relative to a more elevated order. As its corollary, the rights that liberals do assert are supported by a higher order of things: a superior knowledge, a more credible science, a more consistent morality, and a more just and free politics. These relative valuations all follow from, and undergird, the claim of the provisionality of other peoples' experiences.

2. The full and well-known remark of Marlow in Joseph Conrad's *Heart of Darkness* (New York: Penguin Books, 1967) is the following:

> The conquest of the earth, which mostly means the taking it away from those who have a different complexion or slightly flatter noses than ourselves, is not a pretty thing when you look at it too much. What redeems it is the idea only. An idea at the back of it; not sentimental pretence but an idea; and an unselfish belief in the idea—something you can set up, and bow down before, and offer sacrifice to. (p. 74)

But what is the perspective from which experience appears irredeemably provisional and incomplete? It is one in which experience is always viewed and assessed from a future point. It is on account of this futural perspective that one can know, or claim to know, the experience's future history, its process of gestation into another stage of life.

I have argued in this book that in their conception of experience, British liberals in the nineteenth century denied both the possible fullness and the risks and challenges of conversing with other realms of experience. It is from this understanding of its impoverished conception of experience and communication, and not in its ideals of liberty, equality, and community, that one should explain and even judge the long history of liberalism's support of the British Empire. And it is because Edmund Burke had a deeper understanding of the ways in which people can, and do, give meaning to their lives including to the aspirations of freedom, equality, and community—that is, because he had a deeper understanding of experience—I believe that he saw more clearly than any of his liberal brethren the full stakes of having an empire, both for Britain and for her imperial subjects. This deeper understanding brings in its wake an alternative conception of how different realms of experience can and should relate to each other. It is one that I have called conversational because it does not presume on the transparency of the unfamiliar nor on a teleology of which it must be a part. In eschewing both the presumption of transparency and the foreknowledge of other people's destiny, Burke refuses to wield the form of knowledge and through it the power that was central to the empire.

DISCONTINUITY AND CONTRADICTION

The nineteenth century, not unlike the present quarter of this century, was an epoch of liberal triumph in Britain. A period of substantial peace extended from Waterloo to the outbreak of the First World War. This long pacific interval saw the growth of industrialization and the rise of the working class, which now at least had many of the legal rights that liberals had championed in theory for over a century. The same period witnessed a significant enlargement of the franchise and the crystallization of the party system, and through these the consolidation of a more representative parliamentarianism became definitive of the rules of domestic politics. Following the Reform Bill of 1867, aristocracy was reluctantly, but irresistibly, losing the battle to retain its throttle on the national agenda. By the third quarter of the century there was relief from many of the political, and to a lesser extent social, discriminations that had burdened Jews and Catholics for centuries. More generally, religious toleration had developed institutional and political norms around it so that religion could no longer define the boundaries of citizenship. In the economic realm the long-standing disputes over free trade had been largely settled, so that those who still opposed it were always on the defensive. The second Reform Bill, the activities of the trade unions, the Fenian revolt, the Hyde Park riots, the campaigns of John Bright: these and similar events—notwithstanding the judgment of "anarchy" that Matthew Arnold would fix on them—all in their own way contributed to the deepening of a liberal "culture" in Britain. In Europe the principle that the boundaries of states should correspond to that of their major nationalities had finally found concrete expression in the cases of Italy, Greece, Hungary, and Bulgaria.

It is testimony to the triumph of liberalism that it was the principal object of opposition of the various other constellations of ideas that emerged and gathered strength in this period. The conservatism of de Maistre, Hegel, Coleridge, and Carlyle; the socialism of St. Simon, Marx, and Engels; the Christianity of Wilberforce, Hannah More, and Cardinal Newman; the positivism and organic emphasis of Comte—all had liberalism as the central target of their various critiques. If judged as a postponed response to the debates that had racked Britain in the 1790s—as to whether the principles of the French Revolution required for their instantiation a similar convulsive turn in Britain—the answer a century later, if assessed in terms of what came to be, appeared decisively in favor of those who had advocated liberal reform over revolution.[3]

This was also of course the period that marked expansion and the apogee of the British Empire. Cecil Rhodes's lament—"these stars . . . these vast worlds which we can never reach. I would annex the planets if I could"—was itself an indication of the imperial congestion that he,

3. As evidence of the triumph of liberalism it is worth recalling that even Fabianism, that distinctly British contribution to the history of socialism, owed much more to the ideas of John Stuart Mill than to Marx. In its faith that parliamentary means would be adequate to transform state power, and in its view that the growth of taxable income would be sufficient to support additional social expenditure, Fabians, notwithstanding some of their rhetoric, gave expression to a serene confidence in the postulates of Victorian liberalism.

For a discussion of the debates regarding the French Revolution in the 1790s in England, especially with regard to how they affected Wordsworth, Coleridge, John Thelwall, and to a lesser extent Blake, see Thompson, *The Romantics: England in a Revolutionary Age*.

and others like him, had succeeded in creating on earth.[4] By 1920, with the exception of the Soviet Union, there was not a major landmass on which, in some form or other, British dominance was not either a fact or a proximate reality. If at that time, to the prescient observer, the nationalist opponents of the empire appeared to be gaining in stamina and the empire itself seemed out of breath and hence fated to decline, to most others, especially while looking at a map of the globe, the patches of imperial red might easily have sustained the fiction of the empire's foreseeable permanence.[5]

It is tempting to see the triumph of liberalism and the concurrent extension of the empire as either discontinuous facts that do not relate to each other or as plainly contradicting each other, and therefore casting doubt on the authenticity of the former. The thesis of discontinuity misunderstands the role of liberalism generally, and especially in this period. From its very inception in the seventeenth century, liberalism had been much more than a mere political doctrine with a local reach. By the early nineteenth century and with added vigor through the course of it, it was a robust mindset with a confidence in its global vision. This liberalism did not mysteriously get transformed into some demonic urge to rule the world the instant the British ventured beyond their shores. In men like Cromer, Curzon, and Churchill and many others of lesser note, liberalism and the empire were tightly braided threads such that their separation would have resulted in the fraying of a well-woven mental and political tapestry. As Lord Curzon said, writing in 1898, imperialism was increasingly the "faith of a nation" and not merely the creed of a political party.[6]

Moreover, among liberal political theorists the empire was understood squarely from within the unified terms of their political and philosophic thoughts such that the claim of discontinuity can be defended

4. Quoted in S. Gertrude Millin, *Rhodes* (London, 1933), 138. The quoted remarks are preceded by the sentence "expansion is everything." For a good overview of the empire from the last quarter of the nineteenth century until the First World War, see Eric Hobsbawm, *The Age of Empire* (New York: Pantheon Books, 1987).

5. Indeed, as late as 1931 Winston Churchill could disparage and dismiss a meeting between Gandhi and the viceroy of India, Lord Irwin, as "alarming and also nauseating to see Mr. Gandhi, a seditious Middle Temple lawyer, now posing as a fakir of a type well known in the East, striding half-naked up the steps of the Viceregal palace . . . to parley on equal terms with the representative of the King-Emperor." Quoted in Martin Gilbert, *Churchill: A Life* (New York: Henry Holt and Company, 1991), 499–500.

6. Quoted in Nicolson, *Curzon: The Last Phase, 1919–1925*, 13.

only by ascribing a deep self-delusion in these thinkers. Among this period's major thinkers only James Fitzjames Stephen gives one the sense that his liberalism and his views on the empire were lodged on two separate axes, thus lending credence to the thought that the two should perhaps be understood as stemming from discontinuous philosophic armatures.[7] But the more typical liberalism of this age as expressed in the writings of Bentham, the Mills, Macaulay, and Sir Henry Maine—all of whom were self-consciously inspired by Locke's thought—has a global vision. Of course that did not necessarily imply the quest for a global empire; but neither are liberalism's reflections on such an empire adventitious to its internal workings.

The thesis that the growth of the empire fundamentally impugns and therefore stands in contradiction to the concurrent deepening of liberalism is also misdirected, though in a complex sense. If indeed one takes liberalism to have a fundamental, that is unconditional, commitment to certain practices characteristically associated with it—such as representative democracy, the political equality of citizens, the political protection of certain individual rights such as expression and association, the eschewing of distinctions based on race with regard to political opportunity, and a credible mechanism through which the sovereignty of the people could be registered and acknowledged, including in the crucial instance when the people call for a change of their political governors—then there is no question that the entrenchment and extension of liberal norms in Britain was plainly in contrast with most imperial practices and policies throughout the nineteenth century. In India, for example, especially following the mutiny of 1857, there was in fact an unmistakable tilt toward the hardening of authoritarian policies and a racializing of political and social attitudes.[8] This was a tilt to which thinkers like J. S. Mill added their prestige and that they justified in their theoretical writings. For example, in *Considerations on Representa-*

7. In any case, the whole question of Stephen's being a liberal in the first place is far from clear. The best and most comprehensive study of Stephen's liberalism and his views on the empire remains, I think, Leslie Stephen, *The Life of Sir James Fitzjames Stephen* (New York: Putnam, 1895). See also the introductory essay by Richard Posner to *Liberty, Equality, Fraternity*, 7–19.

8. See Metcalf, *The New Cambridge History of India: Ideologies of the Raj*, chap. 5. Also for a number of colorful and illustrative examples of the change following the mutiny, see Philip Woodruff, *The Men Who Ruled India* (London: Jonathan Cape, 1953), pt. 1. With respect to the racializing of the norms of political governance in the latter half of the nineteenth century, especially with regard to Africa, see Arendt, *The Origins of Totalitarianism*, chap. 7.

tive Government Mill had made clear that in colonies that were not of Britain's "blood and language" any move toward greater representation was not to be countenanced.[9]

Perhaps the most vivid example of what amounted to a retrenchment of liberal policies and might therefore be taken as evidence of a fundamental contradiction between liberalism and the empire, were the attitudes that surfaced in the late 1870s and the 1880s in the course of the deliberations regarding the Ilbert Bill. The bill sought to give Indian magistrates in the countryside the power to try British subjects of European descent. Despite Queen Victoria's 1858 proclamation that stated that "our subjects of whatever race or creed [will] be freely admitted to offices in our service, the duties of which they may be qualified by their education, ability, and integrity duly to discharge," the issue raised by the bill embittered and polarized liberal opinion in Britain, along with spurring nationalist resentment. Its final and ambivalent passage in 1883 led James Fitzjames Stephen to point out what, for him, was the irreconcilable gulf between liberalism and the British Empire in India. In a letter to *The Times* on 1 March 1883, in language, tone and outlook strongly reminiscent of his *Liberty, Equality, Fraternity,* Stephen stated:

> It is essentially an absolute government, founded, not on consent, but conquest. It does not represent the native principles of life or of the government, and it can never do so until it represents heathenism and barbarism. It represents a belligerent civilization, and no anomaly can be more striking or so dangerous, as its administration by men, who being at the head of a Government founded on conquest, implying at every point the superiority of the conquering race, of their ideas, their institutions, their opinions and their principles, and having no justification for its existence except that superiority, shrink from the open, uncompromising, straightforward assertion of it, seek to apologize for their own position, and refuse, from whatever cause, to uphold and support it.[10]

In his fierce opposition to the bill, and with John Stuart Mill pointedly in mind, Stephen was reiterating what he had said in *Liberty, Equality, Fraternity* and in his "Minute on the Administration of Justice in India," namely that a Millian liberal justification of the empire was a

9. J. S. Mill, *Considerations on Representative Government,* 402.
10. Letter of Sir James Fitzjames Stephen to *The Times,* 1 March 1883, quoted in Eric Stokes, *English Utilitarians in India,* 288.

mockery and a disservice to liberalism. It was a mockery because it overlooked what had become, indeed had all along been, the modus vivendi of imperial governance, which was an assertion of superior British might. It was a disservice to liberalism because the only way liberals like Mill could justify this oversight was by imputing to liberalism a fundamental commitment to being paternalistic. Paternalism, according the Stephen, was the way the British coded the fact of their superior strength and the belief in their own superiority so as not to have to make a "straightforward assertion of it." J. S. Mill, who should have known better, had in his later writings fallen victim to this deceit of softness and had deserted "the proper principles of rigidity and ferocity in which he was brought up."[11]

For Stephen, liberalism and the empire were thus plainly in contradiction with each other. There was no way to square the practices of the latter with the principles of the former. It was power, ferocity, and conquest, and not liberty, that undergirded liberalism in Stephen's view.[12] When the British educated Indians or allowed them into the coveted civil services or permitted them to be magistrates, they were expressing their power and the largesse that it made possible, conditional on it suiting their imperial interests, and not some abstract interest in liberty. What they were not doing, and what Millian liberals, like C. P. Ilbert, only misleadingly claimed to be doing, was extending the domain of liberty by suggesting that Indians were now sufficiently mature to exercise such forms of liberty. For Stephen such temporizing bespoke a bad faith and a weakness that sooner or later would encourage and expose the British to counterdemands in the face of which they would have to show the superiority and ferocity that all along anchored their power.

It is easy, and at one level appropriate, to credit Stephen with prophetic accuracy. As a general matter, from the 1880s onward British policies did become more ferocious and lost much of the liberality of their spirit. The increasingly peremptory arrests of nationalists, the haughtiness and impatience with reform of men like Hunter, Lyall, and Lord Curzon, the escalated rhetoric of imperial permanence, the racism of social activists like Lord Baden-Powell, and the Rowlatt Acts of 1918, which were the legislative ground for the brutal massacre at Jallianwala

---

11. Stephen, *The Life of Sir James Fitzjames Stephen*, 308.

12. In *Liberty, Equality, Fraternity*, Stephen had in fact claimed "that power preceded liberty—that liberty from the very nature of things is dependent on power; and that it is only under the protection of a powerful, well-organized government that any liberty can exist at all" (p. 183).

Bagh (1919), all testify to the accuracy of Stephen's anticipations.[13] It is clear that as Indian nationalists like Nehru countered these measures on liberal grounds, and others, like Gandhi, in broader ethical terms, the British response, more often than not, was one that Stephen could rightly have claimed to have predicted.

But the conceptual coherence of Stephen's view of liberalism is far less compelling. By making the power of government, rather than the liberty of individuals, the fundamental philosophical and political concern of liberalism, Stephen's view is at several removes from the way liberals self-consciously conceptualized their thought and its purposes. Stephen starts from not just a skepticism but a denial regarding what made liberalism distinctive. He belongs to that long line of liberals, often designated as realists, who have always thought of Hobbes, rather than Locke, as the true progenitor and the enduring mentor of liberalism.

The problem with this view is that it cannot make sense of what has been an integral and characteristic feature of British liberalism from the very outset—its deference to gradualism, and its internal conceptual space, which relies on a teleology of progress, and hence the genuine (and not, as Stephen would claim, duplicitous) commitment and appeal to political paternalism. The metaphor of kinship has been central to the political and developmental project of liberalism from Locke onward. It governs the way Locke, Macaulay, and Mill conceive of education, which in turn is central and integral to the political agenda of liberty. In Locke, and only in a slightly less explicit way in Mill, this link is directly elaborated. Freedom requires a knowledge of the laws of nature and the bounds that they demarcate for human actions because this knowledge turns on having reason (in order to know the laws); therefore being free requires having reason. But this reason, as Locke makes explicit in the chapter "Of Paternal Power" in the *Second Treatise* and elaborates in all its behavioral and conventional details in *Thoughts Concerning Education*, requires parental interdiction.[14] Reason may in a Lockean view be a natural capacity, but the specific form in which it services a liberal program requires an elaborate pedagogic scheme. In Locke there is an explicit connection between the education of children by parents and the consensual liberal politics articulated in the latter half of the

13. See Anil Seal, "Imperialism and Nationalism in India," in *Locality, Province, and Nation: Essays on Indian Politics*, ed. G. Gallagher and Anil Seal (Cambridge: Cambridge University Press, 1973), 48–73.

14. See chapter 2 of the present work and chaps. 3 and 4 of my *The Anxiety of Freedom*.

Second Treatise. The categorical distinction that Locke makes pace Filmer, between the power of fathers and that of political governors, such that the latter derives solely from the consent of those who are governed, nevertheless rests on fathers performing an essential preliminary role in the education of their children. Indeed, precisely for that reason the distinction between the power of fathers and monarchs is never quite as stable or absolute as the rhetoric of the *First Treatise* would lead us to believe.[15]

By the nineteenth century, the centrality of education, still conceived and expressed in terms of metaphors of kinship, gets projected on a global canvas through the notion of the scales, or grades, of civilizational progress. The emphasis on history, the progressive purposes immanent in it, and the role of imperial superintendence for realizing those purposes can all be seen as elaborations on the Lockean idea of the need to be educated into reason, and into liberty only thereafter. With this comes the significance of patience, and the role of time, which is such a conspicuous feature of liberalism, particularly in the context of the empire. In this framework the practice of ruling an empire, like that of parenting, can be conceived only as a longitudinal process and not as a succession of lateral encounters. When Macaulay and Mill invoked the need to educate Indians, both as a justification for the presence of the British in India and as an obligation that the British were under on account of that presence, both were drawing on conceptual resources integral to the legacy of British liberalism from its Lockean inception. Those were the very resources that had at one time in Britain itself justified the exclusion of the propertyless, the uneducated, and women, among other groups, from political enfranchisement; and yet, at a later time and under altered conditions, those very conceptual resources had served as the grounds for the political inclusion of these groups.

If one ignores this developmentalism as an integral feature of liberalism, one cannot make s sense of any of the history with which it is associated either in the West or elsewhere. Indeed, it is the developmentalism that links the abstract foundations of liberalism with history and places liberal ideas in time. The specific form of this link has of course varied. In Locke, it is tethered to a conventionalism whose content is saturated with a reliance on the extant attributes of class distinctions in Britain. By the nineteenth century, in the context of the empire,

15. Locke all but explicitly concedes this at the end of the chapter "On Paternal Power" when he says, "Thus the natural *fathers of families,* by an insensible change, became the *political monarchs* of them too": *Second Treatise of Government,* sec. 76.

the link emphasizes the replacement of indigenous beliefs and sensibilities with those that were specifically British. The project of liberalism at that point, in Macaulay's memorably unveiled language, was "to form a . . . class of persons, Indians in blood and color, but English in taste, in opinions, in morals, and in intellect."[16]

The point that I am urging is not that one cannot provoke a contradiction between liberalism and the empire, the way Stephen articulates it. Clearly one can. Liberals have often presented liberalism as having a fundamental, and in that sense unconditional, commitment to the political and institutional arrangements with which it is associated. But liberals have done this without adequately making clear the personal and social—the pedagogic—regimes on which these arrangements rest. This naturally leads to the view that the empire was a flagrant violation of liberal principles and that it must therefore have had its raison d'être in something like conquest, commercial avarice, or a Hobbesian quest for glory. And since these motives have indeed been explicitly expressed so often, it only lends credence to the thesis of contradiction.

I would argue instead that this thesis, by sequestering the abstract foundations of liberalism from its institutional commitments, and both of them from the crucial pedagogic programs that have concretely bridged them, has suppressed a more important and still relevant set of questions. These are questions about how and why other peoples' experiences, especially those that are plainly beyond the ken of the West's familiar associations, become assimilated within a self-confident embrace that knew them already to be provisional. The thesis of contradiction does not allow us to ask these questions because it does not accept that ideas of liberty and equality were really involved in the first place. Moreover, it does not take seriously the crucial ways in which liberals in the nineteenth century engaged with the unfamiliar so that the unfamiliar always appeared to be an incomplete formation of life in need of external political tutelage. Instead liberalism appears as just the convenient ruse and gloss of the empire for those who emphasize its contradictory involvement with the empire.

Throughout this book I have resisted the interpretation that focuses on contradictions because it does not allow us to take seriously such ideas and, moreover, because it does not help us critically reclaim these ideas under conditions where their triumph is either taken for granted

16. Thomas B. Macaulay, "Minute on Indian Education" (1835), in *Thomas Babington Macaulay: Selected Writings*, ed. John Clive (Chicago: University of Chicago Press, 1972), 249.

or their relevance altogether denied. In short, it does not give us guidance where guidance is needed. This is also why from the outset of this book I have placed the question of the liberal endorsement of the empire as secondary to that of the liberal response to the experiences of the unfamiliar. If we are to take liberal ideas seriously and attempt to rejuvenate an edifying vision of human existence to which they give expression, and if we are to do this under contemporary conditions where these ideas are in danger of being reduced to rhetorical placards of summary abuse or self-certain validity, then we must see how those ideas touched and molded reality—even if only in thought. This is especially important when the internal integrity of that reality did not and does not reflect back the familiar associations and the intellectual lineage from which the liberal tradition itself emerged and acquired confidence.

EXPERIENCE

There is a paradox that attends reflection on experience. The concept and the term are often taken as markers of precisely that which exceeds, or remains below, the threshold of what concepts and language can capture. The feelings, the allegedly ineffable modalities to which experience refers, are in this sense always betrayed by the very gesture that is employed to translate them into conceptual or communicable form. Experience, in this view, is so densely tactile that it defies all representations. On the other hand, there is the view, which has gained wide-ranging following after the so-called linguistic turn, in which anything that is meaningful must, on account of that, be available to linguistic mediation. The gravitational field of language is deemed to be inescapable, and therefore experience is and can be no more than what a particular discursive system makes possible. Whatever it signifies, experience cannot be prior to, nor can it exceed, the expressive capacities of that system.[17]

In an absolute version of this binary, one can obviously only speak of the latter, that is the linguistic alternative, because the former definitionally stands beyond the reach of language and communicable expression. Nevertheless, the view of experience as remaining below or ex-

17. As an example of this position see Joan W. Scott, "The Evidence of Experience," *Critical Inquiry* 17, no. 1 (summer 1991): 57–79. One could of course enumerate numerous other examples within this general orientation ranging from Wittgenstein to Derrida ("There is nothing outside the text"), not to mention interpretations of Idealist tradition, such as Hegel's, that emphasize the aim of thought to be to find a language that allows us to synthesize other languages.

ceeding the threshold of expression is an important heuristic for language itself, because at a minimum it points toward an asymptotic limit to which language must aspire in trying to understand experience. The inexpressible may be a limit beyond the immediate reach of a language, but it is precisely in the face of such a limit that language strains to extend itself. In this effort of extension, that is, in the attempt to decipher the tonalities of an experience that does not come coded in a familiar set of notes, language and imagination get allied in an uncertain and uncharted, but potentially rewarding, journey. It is the imagination that indexically gestures, as it were, to an experiential reality beyond what is already plain or familiar, and it is toward this as yet hazy presence that language, and through it the understanding, strains. I will return to this obviously quasi-Kantian formulation, which echoes the "Schematism of the Pure Concepts of Understanding" from the *Critique of Pure Reason*, to consider the link between the sentiments and the imagination as they pertain to experience.[18] But before that, it is worth briefly recalling a few moments in Western thought that point to a denigrating genealogy with which the very idea of experience has been associated.

For Plato and more generally for the ancient Greeks *empeiria*, which is etymologically linked with *experience*, was associated with that form of uncertain and empirical knowledge that compared unfavorably with rational and deductive knowledge.[19] This disparagement of experience operated on metaphysical, epistemological, and moral axes.[20] At

18. Kant, *Critique of Pure Reason*, trans. N. K. Smith (New York: St. Martin's Press, 1963), B176 ff. In the *Critique of Pure Reason* Kant defines the imagination as "the faculty of representing in *intuition* an object that is not itself present" (B151), and in his *Anthropology* he states that the "[i]magination (*facultas imaginandi*) is a faculty of perception in the absence of an object." *Anthropology from a Pragmatic Point of View*, trans. Mary Gregor (The Hague: Nijhoff, 1974), no. 28.

19. See F. E. Peters, *Greek Philosophical Terms: A Historical Lexicon* (New York: New York University Press, 1967). For a more extensive review of the etymological antecedents of *experience*, see Nancy, *The Experience of Freedom*, 20.

20. In a trenchant critique of Plato's view of experience, which is itself part of his pragmatist defense of experience, Dewey points to all three of these aspects:

> There is the contrast of empirical knowledge (strictly speaking, of belief and opinion rather than knowledge) with science. There is the restricted and dependent nature of practice in contrast with the free character of rational thought. And there is the metaphysical basis for these two defects of experience: the fact that sense and bodily action are confined to the realm of phenomena while reason in its inherent nature is akin to ultimate reality. The threefold contrast thus implies a metaphysical depreciation of experience, an epistemological one, and coloring both of the others and

the dawn of the modern scientific era Francis Bacon famously con-
demned experience by displacing and restricting its very possibility to
the well-regulated experiment:

> There remains but mere experience, which when it offers itself
> is called chance; when it is sought after, experiment. But this
> kind of experience is nothing but a loose faggot, and mere
> groping in the dark, as men at night try all means of discovering
> the right road. . . . On the contrary the real order of experience
> begins by setting up a light, and then shows the road by it, com-
> mencing with a regulated and digested, not a misplaced and
> vague course of experiment, and thence deducing axioms, and
> from axioms new experiments.[21]

The scorn and the disjointedness that Bacon casts on everyday experience—loose faggots with no internal or unifying order and hence
no certainty—is itself an inaugurating moment of a broader doubt in
which sensory impressions are suspect, unless governed by a strict regu-
lating method. The quotidian, which Bacon refers to as "mere experience," an event of "chance"—disordered, unreliable, and subject to the
vagaries of ungoverned perception—contrasts with the continuous and
repeatable chain of axioms leading to well-regulated experiments. In
this it anticipates a founding moment of philosophic modernity. It is
after all the deception of the senses that Descartes also associates with
demonic power and against which he proposes the laborious vigilance
(*laboriosa vigilia*) of "method." Descartes's worry is not with the *deus ab-
sconditus* (hidden God) but rather the *deus mutablissimus* (most fickle
God), who as a *genius malignus* (malicious spirit) puts into question
man's certainty in relation to the world.[22] Giorgio Agamben has rightly
characterized the profound change, and the motives behind it, in which

---

giving them their human value, a moral one: the difference in worth between an activity that is limited to the body and physical things, originating in need and serving temporal utilities, and that which soars to ideal
and eternal values. ("An Empirical Survey of Empiricisms," in *John Dewey:
The Later Works, 1925–1953*, vol. 2, *1935–1937*, ed. Jo An Boydston [Car-
bondale: Southern Illinois University Press, 1987], 74)

21. Bacon, *Novum Organum*, ed. Thomas Fowler (Oxford, 1878), 60.
22. There is a sense in which this preoccupation with certainty and mastery
almost entails a militaristic vigilance. Michel Serres in a wonderfully imaginative
discussion of experimentation and knowledge in the classical age makes the following illuminating comment: "Like many other philosophers, Descartes pursued his
military calling in metaphysics." Serres, "Knowledge in the Classical Age: La Fon-
taine and Descartes," in *Hermes: Literature, Science, Philosophy*, 27.

the idea of the experiment and method result with respect to an extant (in this instance Agamben is referring to Montaigne) and intuitive conception of experience:

> The scientific verification of experience which is enacted in the experiment—permitting sensory impressions to be deduced with exactitude of quantitative determinations and, therefore, the prediction of future impressions—responds to this loss of certainty by displacing experience as far as possible outside the individual: on to instruments and numbers.[23]

The broader impulse that informs this displacement of experience on to "instruments and numbers"—that is, its confinement to experiments—is the modern separation of a humanist conception of experience, grounded in the vagaries of common sense and lived traditions, from science and, more broadly, from knowledge. This older conception of experience was, as Bacon scornfully points out, open to the chanceful and therefore necessarily had an irredeemable element of contingency to it. The experiment attempts to foreclose on precisely this open contingency through the *labor* of reproducing experience under *laboratory* conditions. What is novel is not the separation of experience from knowledge per se, but rather that increasingly experience depends for its validity on its being a pathway to the epistemological certainty that now becomes the salient aspiration of the knowledge that validates and hence judges experience.

An important implication of this change is that the knowledge of past experience has no presumptive link with the present and the future; rather, that link is conditional on an experimentation in which the past may in fact be shown to have been false.[24] And all that would be required to establish such falsity would be an account in which the extant condition, or the evolving trajectory, of that past was not consistent with contemporary instruments and numbers—in effect, with contemporary knowledge. Perhaps the most striking example of this is in the work

---

23. Agamben, *Infancy and History: Essays on the Destruction of Experience*, 17.

24. In this context it is worth recalling that the language of "experimentation" is often explicitly invoked in imperial discourse, and seldom very far below the surface. As an explicit example where the entire political edifice of empire is qualified through the idea of an experiment, there is Sir Henry Maine's famous comment: "Nevertheless, the paradoxical position must be accepted in the extraordinary experiment, the British Government of India, the virtually despotic government of a dependency by a free people." "The Effects of Observation of India on Modern European Thought" (Cambridge: The Rede Lecture, 1875).

of J. S. Mill. Mill is justly famous for the emphasis he places on the development of character and the expansive latitude that he seeks for its expressions. It is with these expressions that he associates the cultivation of the higher-quality pleasures and the rich flowering of human individuality. But this very emphasis on character development, or what he more broadly associates with "experiments of living," is itself confined within the certainty of a rigid and crude typology in which such development can occur in some societies through the initiative of individuals and in others only through imperial guidance.[25] This gives further credence to the literal sense in which Mill thinks of "experiments of living" as referring to an experiment in the Baconian sense: as that which regulates things by leaving other aspects out. Of course, what are left out here are entire civilizations and ways of being in the world. As with both the Mills, the experiences of the past are deemed most exemplary precisely when they show that past to have been invalid, thus opening up room for new knowledge and new constructions. This is a knowledge and a practice that by the late eighteenth century, and more confidently in the nineteenth century, gets designated as the science of history.[26]

Bacon and Descartes's preference for the experiment over experience is plainly part of a broader constructivist move that becomes a salient feature of modern thought. The radically disjunctural stroke with which Hobbes inaugurates modern political thought is in delimiting a sharp contrast between human "artifice" or the creativity "of man," and that of Nature—his term for the decidedly secondary powers of God. The superiority of human creativity lies in its being able to "imitate," that is create, that "rational and most excellent work of nature, *man*" and through this construct "the great Leviathan called a Commonwealth."[27] It is this constructivist move that in Hobbes's own reckoning is the generative foundation of his new science of politics.

25. The expression "experiments of living" occurs in *On Liberty*, 70.

26. See Michel de Certeau, "The Historiographical Operation," in *The Writing of History*, trans. Tom Conley (New York: Columbia University Press, 1988), 56–113; and Dipesh Chakrabarty, "Radical Histories and the Question of Enlightenment Rationalism: Some Recent Critiques of *Subaltern Studies*," *Economic and Political Weekly* 30, no. 14 (April 1995): 751–59.

27. Thomas Hobbes, introduction to *Leviathan*, ed. Edwin Curley (Cambridge: Hackett, 1994), 3. One even finds Locke, for whom this featuring of human creativity lacks the radicalness that it has for Hobbes, speaking of the "necessity" to "design" the persons who are to have political power. In the same vein, when Locke defines political power he emphasizes the quality of "*making* Laws with Penalties of Death" (emphasis added). See Locke, *Second Treatise*, chap. 1, secs. 1 and 3.

In Bacon, Hobbes, Vico, Kant, and of course Nietzsche, the idea of construction underscores the thought that the internal ego or *res cogitans* has a controlling grip on the external world and, through it, on the worldly.[28] The genealogy of this idea is of course complex. It is neither necessary to my present purpose nor within my competence to offer the details of such a genealogy. What is clear and relevant, however, since it constitutes the broad framework within which I have located liberalism, is a particular progression that one can see from Bacon, Descartes, Hobbes, on to Kant, through to Nietzsche and into certain expressions of contemporary analytical philosophy and postmodern thought.

For Kant the idea of construction, the root notion of his critical enterprise, works as a bridge: the mind fills an ontological gap between the conceptual and the sensible by producing conceptual generalities of the sensible or phenomenal domain. The mind's ability to master or "synthesize" the apparently intractable realm of the external, the "other," the manifold of sensible impressions, lay in its being able to externalize itself in a way that bore the unmistakable marks of inward origins. In Nietzsche this idea gets radicalized to the point that the mind's facility to produce such rule-governed generalities, i.e., science—Kant's "revolution in [our] style of thinking"—becomes the very basis for obliterating any distinction between *poiesis* and science. Recalling the specific utility that both Bacon and Descartes associate with the new science, Nietzsche identifies the common source of both *poiesis* and science, indeed of all human activities, in a drive for mastery—"every drive is tyrannical: and it is as *such* that it tries to philosophize."[29] Ultimately for Nietzsche these drives—that is, these forms of self-exhibition—get deposited upon a world that at any given time is no more than a mere conglomeration of other perspectival and projected fictions. The world is itself nothing: neither does it serve as the soil in which these fictions, interpretations, constructions are anchored; nor does it constitute a model, or an original, that they attempt to mirror.

28. For accounts of modern thought that feature this idea of construction and indeed see the very distinctiveness of modernity in this idea, see Blumenberg, *The Legitimacy of the Modern Age*; Amos Funkenstein, *Theology and the Scientific Imagination from the Middle Ages to the Seventeenth Century* (Princeton: Princeton University Press, 1966), esp. 299–327; and Lachterman, *The Ethics of Geometry*, which focuses on the centrality of mathematical construction. For an account that focuses less on philosophical sources but more on the broader issue of human making and its implications, see Elaine Scarry, *The Body in Pain: The Making and Unmaking of the World* (Oxford: Oxford University Press, 1985), esp. chap. 4.

29. Friedrich Nietzsche, *Beyond Good and Evil*, trans. R. J. Hollingdale (London: Penguin Classics, 1988), no. 6, p. 19.

In this sense Nietzsche represents the apotheosis of Richard Rorty's claim—made with respect to the seventeenth century—that the "Mind" was itself a recent and modern "invention."[30]

Freed of these moorings, the project of modernity shows itself in its infinite constructive amplitude—an amplitude that is perhaps most vividly exemplified in the postmodern turn of thought. In it one sees a kind of Hegelian Spirit, released by Nietzsche from any constraining links with the "Objective Mind," and thus open to a creative recursivity in which *representation* is always already a *representation*.[31]

The links between Nietzsche and postmodern thought are of course obvious and self-consciously cultivated in the latter. What is less frequently noted is that conceptually Nietzsche can claim a certain paternity—one that is largely disclaimed on the receiving end—to an important strand of contemporary analytical philosophy too. There is at least a conceptual family resemblance between Nietzsche's perspectival fictions and the way, for instance, Nelson Goodman articulates both the latitude of construction and the terms with reference to which he demarcates it. In Ways of World Making, Goodman states, "With the reconception of the nature and significance of reduction or construction or derivation or systemization we give up our futile search for the aboriginal world, and come to recognize that systems and other versions are as productive as reproductive."[32] Goodman's severing of any link between "the aboriginal world" and the world-as-it-is-for-someone, i.e., from some perspective, and his erasing of any distinction between these two—now only nominal—worlds, clearly recalls, despite the gulf of contrasting traditions, Nietzsche's account of "How the 'True World' Became a Fable" from the *Twilight of the Idols*. That Nietzsche is nowhere mentioned in Goodman's text is simply evidence that even in philosophy, families are endogenously and not genealogically imagined, and that perhaps the latitude of construction can also be taken to license a liberality of ancestral amnesia.

The broader point that these very synoptic remarks on a multi-pronged thrust of modern thought are meant to illustrate is the following. The modern constructivist impulse was rooted originally in the

30. Richard Rorty, *Philosophy and the Mirror of Nature* (Princeton: Princeton University Press, 1979), chap. 1.

31. For a very thoughtful account of this Hegelian-Nietzschean genealogy of postmodern thought, see Judith Butler, *Subjects of Desire: Hegelian Reflections in Twentieth Century France* (New York: Columbia University Press, 1987).

32. Nelson Goodman, *Ways of World Making* (Indianapolis: Hackett, 1978), 100–101.

Baconian effort to displace the openness of experience on to the "regulated" experiment and in the Cartesian suspicion of the sensory, redeemed in the vigilance of "method." This impulse gets more complexly elaborated in Kant's critical enterprise, only to be imploded and extended by Nietzsche and his heirs. The final exfoliation of this trajectory is an echo of what was there from the outset, namely a desire to master and possess nature, where nature was understood in the broadest sense as that which was external to the mind. But in its post-Nietzschean extensions, and notwithstanding the differences in style (i.e., between "representation" or "reference," "texts" or "worlds") this desire, this impulse, gets elaborated in ways that bear the unmistakable signature of a self-involution in which there appears to be no residue of nature or of the foreign to be mastered or even understood.[33]

Does the effort that originates in a quest for the mastery of that which is external culminate in a sealed internal freedom, where the distinction between solipsistic self-indulgence and engaging with the Other, perhaps even the unfamiliar Other, becomes a matter of mere taste or the exigent impulse of power? Does the capacity to construct, when valorized as the distinguishing feature of man, issue in the arrogance of self-divinization, or in the searching seriousness with which, for instance, Foucault, toward the end of his life, jettisons "inner experiences" to reclaim ethics as the central province of philosophy? Is not Adorno's lament regarding the "dying out of experience" on account of "the atemporal technified process of the production of material goods"[34] itself to be more broadly located in what he says about "experience [being] the union of tradition with an open yearning for what is foreign?"[35]—a

33. This self-involution in which nature and the foreign get erased echoes a theme that has been there from the outset of modernity. In a letter dating from 1640 Descartes brings together the themes of history, science, and autarchic self-sufficiency:

By "history" I understand all that has already been invented and contained in books. By "science" I understand skill at resolving all questions and in inventing by one's own industry everything in that science that can be invented by human ingenuity. Whoever has this science does not desire much else foreign to it and indeed is quite properly called autarches—self-sufficient. (René Descartes, quoted in Lachterman, *The Ethics of Geometry*, 139)

34. Theodor W. Adorno, *Notes to Literature*, ed. Rolf Tiedemann, trans. Shierry Nicholsen (New York: Columbia University Press, 1992), 2:101.

35. Ibid., 1:55.

question with additional weight, because what is foreign or external cannot any longer be marked as such, since it has lost its contextual density on account of an internal freedom that renders everything transparent—and that too before the encounter with it? Is not Walter Benjamin's comment on the "increasing atrophy of experience" to be understood as he suggests through "the replacement" of "narration by information, [and] of information by sensation"—where sensation now stands for an expressive insular interiority?[36] And is not the "crisis of experience" for which Agamben appears to be writing the epitaph— "The question of experience can be approached nowadays only with an acknowledgement that it is no longer accessible to us"[37]—to be seen as the culmination of a process in which experience becomes provisional on the telos attached to a particular experiment, and in which any "present" can be understood only from the futural orientation and anticipations that that teleology and those experiments make possible?

The full ambit of these questions goes beyond that of this book. They are meant instead merely to draw the outlines of an orientation in modern Western thought within which I locate liberalism.[38] It is not that this orientation exhausts or fully saturates the content of liberalism—clearly it does not. Rather, it is that with respect to the particular view that liberalism manifests of experience, and that I am arguing is determinative in understanding its imperial association, liberalism is a derivative discourse of this broader orientation. In a summary form, being part of that orientation is to share in a *project*, which *projects* itself by anticipation onto an unbounded future. As an implication of this, every "present," whether individual or collective, is judged and acquires its meaning by reference to the *projection* of which it is understood to be a part. The primacy of the *projection* subsumes both judgment and understanding. Whatever is the freedom of thought or the internal freedom that the *projection* stems from gets carried over into its conception of what is involved in understanding that which is, only nominally, still external. In this sense of the term, understanding is tied to the *project* from the outset. It therefore, in a strict sense, lacks the potential to sur-

36. Walter Benjamin, "On Some Motifs in Baudelaire," in *Illuminations*, 159.
37. Agamben, *Infancy and History*, 13.
38. The qualification "Western" is meant to be restrictive. Clearly one can see a similar trajectory in moments in non-Western thought too. Ashis Nandy from a psychoanalytic perspective points to such a tilt in reformist Indian thought from the early nineteenth century. See Ashis Nandy, *The Intimate Enemy* (Delhi: Oxford University Press, 1983).

prise.[39] Similarly, the *projection* subsumes the "present" as a specific, and not as a singular, halting moment, in which the "present is not a transition, but one in which time stands still and has come to a stop,"[40] where, as it were, the "'state of emergency' in which we live is not the exception but the rule."[41] In this *project* the experiences of those who are, or remain, unfamiliar—that is, of those whose "present," whose life forms, are not deemed to be already aligned along the anticipated axis of the *projection*—must necessarily be viewed as provisional; provisionality being the term through which an uncertain and unfamiliar encounter gets mapped onto a plain of temporal and categorical familiarity. For those in that condition there is no *Jetzt-Zeit*, no time of the present, no singular experience in which the Day of Judgment is the normal condition of history—only an infinite future. Within this project man was made for the infinite.

THE SOOTHSAYING OF THE EMPIRE

The question that naturally arises is, how is such knowledge of the future possible? What in effect supports the *project* and its unbounded *projection?* At the broadest level—that is, leaving aside specific epistemological questions through which the future gets constructed—the answer to this question for nineteenth-century liberals, at least implicitly, drew on the answer that Kant gave in the course of querying whether the progress of humanity was continual: "But how is an *a priori* history possible? Answer: When the soothsayer himself causes and contrives the events that he proclaims in advance."[42]

The empire is nothing without this soothsaying, this knowledge in advance of the encounter, and the effort to make events comport with

39. Hence the kind of latitude that Merleau-Ponty courageously wanted to maintain for the "understanding," even in the face of the horrors of Stalinism, is lost or at least weakened: "[T]rue liberty takes others as they are, tries to understand even those doctrines which are its negation, and never allows itself to judge before understanding. We must fulfill our freedom of thought in the freedom of understanding." Maurice Merleau-Ponty, *Humanism and Terror*, trans. John O'Neill (Boston: Beacon Press, 1960), xxiv–xxv.

40. Walter Benjamin, "Theses on the Philosophy of History," in *Illuminations*, 262.

41. Ibid., 257.

42. Kant, *Der Streit der Fakultaeten*, 2:2, quoted in Blumenberg, *The Legitimacy of the Modern Age*, 34. Clearly something like this Kantian response also underlies the Marxist confidence in the potentialities of proletarian and revolutionary action.

the self-certainty of this foreknowledge. From the perspective of this knowledge the experiences of the unfamiliar must necessarily appear incomplete or partial. For it to be otherwise would put into question the certainty on the basis of which that knowledge claims to know those experiences' future development.[43]

What follows from this is central to understanding the liberal engagement in the empire. It is that the extant experience of those in the empire must be seen as in some crucial sense lacking a coherence. By coherence I mean simply a condition in which people's lives and experiences are undergirded by what Wittgenstein calls "a passionate commitment to a system of reference."[44] This system, this habitus, need not be simply a matter of belief or of practices—even though it is likely to involve aspects of both. The coherence of experience therefore does not turn on the beliefs being *true* in themselves, or the practices being *fitting* in some extrasystemic sense. Rather the beliefs and practices cohere because they are part of a passionate commitment to that system of reference—that is, they represent an interpretation that has, for whatever reasons, taken *hold*. This what Wordsworth in *The Prelude* called the "feeling of conviction."[45] In all likelihood such interpretations gather the loyalties of conscience, a sense of belonging, a belief in certain ideas, and a habituated familiarity with certain ongoing practices. But whether it be beliefs, practices, loyalties of place, or matters of conscience, what is important from the standpoint of experience is that all these frame

43. In this sense the nineteenth-century view stands in contrast to the views of a contemporary liberal, Stuart Hampshire:

> [T]he idea of experience is the idea of guilty knowledge, of the expectation of unavoidable squalor and imperfection, of necessary disappointments and mixed results, of half success and half failure. A person of experience has come to expect that his usual choice will be the lesser of two or more evils. (Hampshire, *Innocence and Experience* [Cambridge: Harvard University Press, 1989], 170)

A similar view, expressed in the language and from the perspective of a "modernist reconstruction of the Christian-romantic tradition," underlies Roberto Unger's thought. In *Passion: An Essay on Personality* (New York: Free Press, 1984), Unger writes, "[The] gesture of self-exposure lacks a predetermined outcome. It may fail completely: the heightened vulnerability may be met by rejection or, having been accepted, lead nevertheless to disappointment" (98). Elsewhere in the same work he writes, "[F]or an ethic of love, our ability to imagine one another is both crucial and precarious" (147).

44. Wittgenstein, *Culture and Value*, 64e.

45. Wordsworth, *Prelude* (1805), bk. 10, lines 899, 973–74.

a picture of life with its possibilities of freedom, its boundaries, its vision of a future and therefore make possible a way of living—a life form.[46]

For my purposes it is largely immaterial whether one refers to this "system of reference" and the experiences that are internal to it as life forms, pictures, or language games, to use Wittgensteinian terms, or as "worlds" in the manner of Michael Oakeshott's view of experience.[47] Similarly it does not matter to the argument I am making whether these worlds of experience are well bounded and in that sense whole; whether they are insular and perhaps even resistant to change; or whether they are expressly porous in their self-understanding. The idea of a system of reference and the coherence that it gives to the experiences internal to it does not necessarily turn on these considerations. Similarly, it does not rest on those experiences being informed by a singular, i.e., nonhybrid, ethos. Instead, what I mean to indicate is the mere possibility that experiences can be, in the sense suggested by the idea of coherence, meaningful and hence not provisional.[48]

THE POLITICS OF CERTAINTY AND
THE ETHICS OF OPEN CONVERSATIONS

For the *project* of nineteenth-century liberalism and the confident certainty it places in its futural *projections*, other peoples' experience must

46. "What has to be accepted, the given, is—so one could say—forms of life": Wittgenstein, *Philosophical Investigations*, II, xi, p. 226.

47. Here I am referring to the central insight of Oakeshott's under-studied book *Experience and Its Modes:*

> My view is, in the first place, that experience (by which I mean the single and indivisible whole within which experiencing and what is experienced have their place) is always a world. Not only must we say that with every experience there comes a world of experience; we must say that every experience is a world. What is given in experience is a world, and what is achieved is this given world made more of a world. What is given in experience is single and significant, a One and not a Many. (*Experience and Its Modes* [Cambridge: Cambridge University Press, 1966; originally published in 1933], 322)

48. The reason for this negative formulation—for my saying that I am only indicating a "possibility" and not the actual fact of such experiences—is that I have not in this book attempted to present the experiences of Indians as facts that cohere as parts of a system of reference. Rather, my purpose has been to show how those experiences, whatever the actual conditions, were a priori deemed to be provisional

be viewed as lacking coherence—as being a singular, halting moment in time, an original *place* of man's pleasures and sorrows, or to paraphrase Wordsworth the *Place* where there is a consciousness of presence.[49] If the only way to establish this lack of coherence was to deny that other people lacked even a history, then we have the testimony of the greatest nineteenth-century British liberal, J. S. Mill, being prepared to go to this absurd length to accommodate his progressive projections of the future: "The progressive principle, . . . is antagonistic to the sway of Custom. The greater part of the world has, properly speaking, no history, because the despotism of Custom is complete. This is the case over the whole East."[50] The conflation of custom with the absence of history is significant. It suggests a picture of automatons so completely corseted by customs that with respect to experiences—in effect to life—this stage of human development must refer to something prior to human history. (Ironically this prompts the question, could it in that sense be "paradisiacal" or perhaps a form of innocence before man gets bound to a progressive eschatology?) The further conflation of this condition with despotism is also revealing. It points to the fact that this condition, by being already political, has its redress in an alternative form of political intervention, or what Mill elsewhere calls "a choice of despotisms"[51]—a choice that clearly must be exercised by someone other than the automatons.

By the nineteenth century the confidence and the certainty that

---

from a liberal perspective. Wittgenstein wrote: "All testing, all confirmation and disconfirmation of a hypothesis takes place already within a system. And this system is not a more or less arbitrary and doubtful point of departure for all our arguments . . . [it is] *the element in which the arguments have their life*." Ludwig Wittgenstein, *On Certainty*, 105 (emphasis added).

49. Wordsworth, *Prelude*, bk. 10, lines 973–74.

> One great Society alone on earth,
> The noble Living and the Noble Dead:
> Thy consolation shall be there, and Time
> And Nature shall before thee spread in store
> Imperishable thoughts, the Place itself
> Be conscious of thy presence, and the dull
> Sirocco air of its degeneracy
> Turn as thou mov'st into a healthful breeze
> To cherish and invigorate thy frame. (970–78)

50. Mill, *On Liberty*, 87.

51. Mill, "Government of Dependencies," in *Considerations on Representative Government*, 410.

Descartes and Hobbes had associated with geometrical truths become the hallmark of liberal politics. It is not that liberalism is able to cash out the extravagant hopes reposed in the method of geometry as a means of putting order on the vagaries of the sensible world—though clearly that ambition, now more closely allied with algebra and not geometry, is still alive. Rather it is that the quest for certainty and the corresponding abhorrence for that which made doubt a fact about being in the world becomes the North Star of liberal thinking. In this form of thinking the political comes to represent an attitude toward the world in which the world has been evacuated of ambiguity and uncertainty and therefore does not require of us a posture in which we humbly acknowledge doubt—especially doubt regarding what is appropriate for those with whom we are unfamiliar. The almost pathological extent to which Bentham made precision the guiding ambition of his science of legislation; the confidence with which James Mill could extol the virtue of "A Code" for India even if it required an "absolute government";[52] the certainty with which J. S. Mill knew that "there is nothing for [backward people] but implicit obedience to an Akbar or a Charlemagne"[53]—by the nineteenth century these political impulses become verities of liberalism when faced with the unfamiliar. They are the intellectual precursors of Francis Fukuyama's confident projections regarding the "end of history" and the attitude that typically views regimes like those in Cuba and Iran as being in some provisional interregnum.

What distinguishes Burke, and explains his markedly contrasting assessment of the empire, is that he can and does view the unfamiliar from a perspective that does not a priori presume its provisionality. Instead, Burke thinks in terms of concepts through which the coherence of other peoples' lives can, in principle, become evident as a concrete and experienced reality and not as an abstract possibility that can stand out clearly only when projected onto the temporal canvas of the future. Burke acknowledges the present as present, as a singular moment that refers to a laterally located space among others. From an experiential standpoint this space does not acquire its density on account of being hitched to a more meaningful and rational teleology. I have argued that what makes it possible for Burke to have this perspective is an engage-

52. "As I believe that India stands more in need of a code than any other country in the world, I believe also that there is no country on which that great benefit can more easily be conferred. A Code is almost the only blessing—perhaps it is the only blessing—which absolute governments are better fitted to confer on a nation than popular governments." James Mill, *History of British India*, 1:328.

53. Mill, *On Liberty*, 16.

ment with the very things that, in his view, structure the content and parameters of human experiences at a phenomenological and psychological level—sentiments, memories, and a sense of belonging and place—the temporal frame of which is always the present.

Burke reflects the romantic reaction to the abstract intellectualism that had developed by the late eighteenth century.[54] As with Wordsworth, this reaction in Burke does not represent a simple valorization of nature, human simplicity, piety, a respect for established structures of authority, or even a reverence for the past. Instead, these familiar features of Burke's thought are anchored in a profound, even if simple, psychological insight: Human beings are not born blank slates; instead, they inherit a mass of predispositions from an unfathomable past bounded by the variations of time and place. It is the emplacement within these points of reference that gives to individuals, and to communities, a sense of their integrity and a self-understanding from which alone life can be, and is, richly experienced—indeed, from which alone moral action is possible. The fact that the human mind—especially under politically revolutionary conditions and with the informing legacy of philosophic constructivism—can engender the illusion of a blank slate, of as it were "standing back," and in that sense can dispossess itself is all the more reason for Burke to be wary of its dire effects.

On this basis Burke can see and imagine a form of life in India that is not of necessity in need of imperial superintendence. And when this form of life appears to Burke to violate his own deepest convictions, or when it appears obscure and inscrutable, he can, and does, countenance the possibility of not associating with it, or humbly acknowledging opacity as a condition against which he has no simple and a priori trump—certainly not of power or tutelage.[55] In short, Burke can acknowledge what Wittgenstein refers to as the condition of not "find-[ing] our feet" in a strange country or among strange traditions, and he accepts that condition as a bittersweet feature of what it means to be human under conditions of pluralism.[56]

54. Alfred Cobban, *Edmund Burke and the Revolt against the Eighteenth Century*; see also Basil Willey, *The Eighteenth Century* (New York: Columbia University Press, 1953), 240–52; Bromwich, *A Choice of Inheritance*, 43–79; Bromwich, *Politics by Other Means*, 133–64; Charles Larmore, *The Romantic Legacy*, 41–49.

55. "[I]f we are not able to contrive some method of governing India well which will not of necessity become the means of governing Great Britain ill, a ground is laid for their eternal separation, but none for sacrificing the people of that country to our constitution." Burke, "Fox's India Bill Speech," 5:383.

56. "It is, however, important as regards this observation [of transparency] that one human being can be a complete enigma to another. We learn this when we come

In the face of this pluralism Burke articulates the conditions, really the attitude, for what amounts to a conversation across boundaries of strangeness. I have described this attitude as a posture of imaginative humility, for it accepts that there is no shortcut around the messiness of communication, no immanent truth on which words can fix, no easy glossaries of translation; instead, just the richness or paucity of the vocabularies we use to describe ourselves and those we are trying to understand. The space defined by Burke's voluminous narratives on the empire is therefore never precise in the sense of being tethered to a reality whose contours and destiny are understood as already programmed, decoded, and known in advance. Despite the eloquence and rhetorical force of his words and the stakes he attaches to the debates in which he is involved, there is always something provisional in his narratives. He expects to be surprised and to be puzzled. But precisely because of the contingent nature of this conversation, he is more deeply committed to the ethical choices that arise from such an encounter and more circumspect about political alternatives that are not undergirded by the familiarity of tradition or the effort of understanding without the presumption of foreknowledge.

Burke's phenomenological perspective comes from eighteenth-century aesthetics and the emphasis it placed on the imagination as a way of morally engaging with the world and with others, and not from the more familiar epistemological tradition. After all, even in Kant's aesthetic reflections, i.e., in the *Critique of Judgement*, the intellect is "at the service of imagination."[57] In that aesthetic tradition, the visual and the perceived are alloyed with the art of conversation and to a form of deliberation in which the boundaries of what can be articulated are never firmly established prior to the conversation. And one in which, moreover, the conversation continually modifies those boundaries, that is to say modifies the interlocutors. The conversation is indeed a medium of communication in which new and unfamiliar information gets transmitted and understanding is engendered. But beyond that, and more importantly, it is a space in which there is a constant and unsuppressible negotiation of the boundaries of the selves who are party to, and literally participate in, the conversation. In this form of communication there

into a strange country with entirely strange traditions; . . . We do not *understand* the people. (And not because of not knowing what they are saying to themselves) We cannot find our feet with them." Wittgenstein, *Philosophical Investigations*, II, xi, p. 223.

57. Immanuel Kant, *Critique of Judgement*, trans. J. H. Bernard (New York: Hafner, 1951), general remark to no. 22.

can be no prior assimilation of the participants into the language of membership or kinship, and hence no prior designation of subordinates or children. In the end, Burke prefigures what Richard Rorty associates with his capacious version of the pragmatist tradition: "[I]t is the doctrine that there are no constraints on inquiry save conversational ones— no wholesale constraints derived from the nature of the objects, or of the mind, or of language, but only those retail constraints provided by the remarks of our fellow inquirers."[58] In such a conversation power is denied space, and in this sense the empire becomes an impossibility.

58. Rorty, *Consequences of Pragmatism*, 165.

Scotland, joined with Britain, 37
Scott, Joan W., 201n. 17
Scriptures. *See* Bible
Seal, Anil, 198n. 13
Second Discourse (Rousseau), 143–44
Second Treatise of Government (Locke):
    on education, 62–63, 198–99; ex-
    clusions in, 56, 59; on liberal uni-
    versalism, 47, 52; on property,
    123–24; status of, 16
Seeley, John R.: on empire, 5, 30n. 51,
    154, 155; on India and national-
    ism, 149, 191; on politics and
    history, 106; role of, 155n. 4
sentiments: cosmopolitanism of, 22–23,
    139; denial of, 20–21; imagination's
    link to, 38, 202; language of,
    40–41; social order and, 184–85;
    of understanding, 36–45, 170. *See
    also* experience
Serres, Michel, 109n. 75, 111, 203n. 22
Seven Years' War, 5, 154
Shakespeare, William, 146–47n. 61
Simmel, Georg, 24, 31
Sirkin, Gerald, 15n. 23
Sirkin, Natalie, 15n. 23
skepticism, as thought but not lived,
    39–40
Skorupski, John, 88–89n. 22
slaves, definition of, 51n. 11
Smith, Adam: cosmopolitanism of, 40;
    on empire, 4, 12n. 16; on free mar-
    ket, 38–39; on sympathy, 37, 39;
    on vigilance against freedom, 17
Smith, Anthony, 130n. 30
social class: Burke's allegiances to,
    174–75; comparisons with,
    136–37; developmentalism and,
    199–200; education in, 60–61; ex-
    clusion based on, 56; norms and,
    63–64; as requisite for freedom,
    181; territoriality as root for, 133.
    See also working class
social contract: as basis for society, 128,
    148–49; boundaries and, 130–32;
    consent grounded in, 54–55; func-
    tion of, 132, 144–46; individual as
    subject of, 53–54; viability of, 75.
    See also consent

socialism, opposition to, 193
social order: boundaries of, 131–32,
    164; chance's role in, 143–44; con-
    text of, 142–43; experience and
    identity in, 175–76; foundation of,
    160–62; nature as constraint on,
    143; place and history in, 182–86,
    189; vs. progress, 103–4; psycho-
    logical conception of, 176–83; as
    requisite for liberty, 174–75; senti-
    ments and, 184–85; territoriality as
    root for, 133, 182–84; threats to,
    138–39, 140–41, 160–61, 163,
    182–83, 186. *See also* social class;
    societies
social science: development of, 76; on
    space, 161
societies: alternative ways of forming,
    123, 144–45n. 56; boundaries as
    emblematic of, 131–32, 164; breed-
    ing and, 62; chance's role in,
    143–44; exclusions linked to con-
    ventions of, 58–59, 62–63, 75; for-
    mation of, 97–100, 128, 144–52;
    identity of vs. conditions for legiti-
    macy of, 144–49; indifference to
    nature held in common, 125–27;
    nature as constraint on, 143; order
    and permanence in, 103–4; recog-
    nition of different, 120–22, 139,
    146–49; regulation of, 98–99;
    wealth as medium of, 173, 181. *See
    also* civilization; collective identity;
    education; norms; social order
Socrates, 25
Sommer, Doris, 142n. 49
South Orkneys, in British Empire, 5
sovereignty: pluralism and, 159; ten-
    sions in, 80; territoriality as expres-
    sion of, 118, 130, 151; vested in
    people, 53. *See also* territoriality
space: absence of contiguity of, 38;
    continuity vs. discontinuity in,
    109–11; of empire, 4–5, 36–37,
    115–17; identity's relation to, 133–
    44, 160–62, 188; individuals' at-
    tachments to specific, 129, 131,
    160–62, 182; morality vested in,
    182–85; mythology on, 126–27; na-